Another Time,

Another Place

Another Time,

Another Place

by Jack Judge
Illustrations by Mollie-O Judge

BookPartners, Inc.
Newberg, OR

The characters portrayed in this book are real.

Judge, Jack
Another Time—Another Place:
Autobiography—Service, U.S. Air Force—Bird
Farm—Animal Collecting, South America.
Other than from the author's own experiences, further background information on the United States Air Force, Tenth Rescue Squadron has been excerpted from three articles printed in *Collier's Magazine,* dated December 1949, and January 1950. Entitled, *The Story of Bernt Balchen's Arctic Airmen*, the articles were written by Bill Davidson.

Illustrations by Mollie-O Judge
Cover and Text design by Aimee Genter

Dedication

This book is dedicated to "MOM." After all, I was one of her ideas. Besides, a sprightly sprite of ninety-seven, as she reads this she is bound to remember an idea I've missed!

I further dedicate these ramblings to my "Mollie-O." Having put up with my *Artistic Attempts* for over forty-four years she surely deserves sainthood.

Table of Contents

Illustrations

Introduction

It was a painful time. It was a time when a great many American homes proudly hung small banners in their front windows indicating family members serving in the military. Bordered in red, they presented blue stars on a white background. Many families mourned, the stars had changed color from blue to gold—for the dead. A family named Sullivan presented five stars in their window, *they were all gold*. It was a frightening time. It was a proud, glorious time. It was total Victory. *It was our finest hour*. Making that hour possible, 360,812 American military gave up their lives, 265,000 more were permanently crippled and, lest we forget, a further 1,250,000 civilians—helping to supply desperately needed war materials to our fighting men everywhere—were permanently disabled due to industrial accidents. It was yesteryear.

Even back then, Americans formed a complex group: all races, creeds, and cultures. Nonetheless, we stood together as one nation, strong and united. Parades, marching men, martial music; the flag—reverently carried—waving gently in the breeze; a lump in the throat, tears in the eyes. World War II was finally over. We had met the challenge, suffered our losses and, in triumph, overcome the hated enemy. The "Beast of Berlin" was dead. The despoilers from Japan were totally defeated. It was a time to look one another in the eye, grin, shake hands, shed more tears for the dead, and gratefully thank the living for their hard-won victory. Thank God, the shooting had stopped. We were one!

Don't ask me to explain what has happened in the interim. I simply do not understand our current rage to pooh-pooh that which was once held sacred. Neither do I understand why tabloid grunge is read, heeded and quoted. Why the fervid desire to destroy peoples' characters? Why the overwhelming passion to embrace violence in films, novels, news, magazines, television, schools and everyday life? Why the crass devotion to smut? Why, why, why? Enough! This is not about now, it is about then. It is about yesterday, with maybe an adventure or two thrown in. It is about people helping people.

Blood, sweat and tears went into this manuscript, also truth. The episodes happened some time ago. Memory, especially for those long in the tooth, is fleeting. I have studied photos, talked to old buddies who were there, and dredged through a mired brain. In the end, I decided to just scatter the seeds, water thoroughly, and let the developing cucumbers grope their own way along the vine. Observing process and progress, you will perhaps notice that one or two of the more adventurous gherkins fell into a pickle barrel.

Certainly we all spend time reviewing the past. Hopefully most of those memories are pleasant. When I mind-wandered back I was surprised at how much fun I'd had—even though I've never made a dimpled dime from all my enterprises. In fact, if you tote up all the laughs, count me stacking my loot in a Swiss bank account.

Read on. If I've done it right you may enjoy a laugh or two yourself.

This book is not into heavy breathing. The only explicit sex— and she isn't talking—occurred when our cross-eyed Siamese accidentally mistook a leering tom for a scratching post!

Finally, from many other wonderful educational picks, you chose this one, then—having skimmed quickly through its mesmerizing excitement—you now wonder:

"What person, presumably in his right mind, after freezing his tutu, would further travel to a place where he could flaming well melt it, and then subject himself to the trauma of coping with aggravating animal antics, not to mention baby-sitting feathered friends?" You haven't a clue, right? Very well, in the following pages I shall continue to hint of the real me. You're bound to feel much better about you! Perhaps we shall even become friends.

They say the wolf and cougar travel long distances marking out territory but always return to places of great beauty. Bordering on extortion, today's exorbitant gas prices being what they are, I can't afford to travel very far. What to do for vacation? I have plenty of time, so this year I've decided to stroll down to the dock and unlock the boathouse. After that, I'm going to launch my old, beat-up dugout and take an inexpensive but lengthy meander through the marshlands of my memory, back to a great time and some grand places. Maybe I'll see a wolf or a cougar. If I steer and do all the poling, would you care to come along?

P.S. If you are my age, you'll also recall those proud, post-war days. If you are young, I hope you enjoy learning a tad bit about a time when bonafide *heroes* were people who put their lives on the line for the benefit of others.

ROLL CALL

Mollie-O

Prelude

...Cap tried again, this time gunning the engine full on. Metal quivered and groaned, but still didn't budge.

"Sergeant!" he yells at me. "The damn skiis are frozen to the ice. Don't dawdle, jump out and rock the wings to break us loose. Then get your butt back in here in a flaming hurry, I think we're in for a lousy 'whiteout.' It's over a hundred and thirty air-miles from Tanana to Fairbanks and, unless you're into delivering babies at three thousand feet up, we've got to fly this lady to the base hospital just as fast as this crate will go!"

Prologue

Have you heard the classic about the psychology class who sat, pencils sharpened, booklets at hand, nervously awaiting the professor's deviously designed question, the one for his final exam?

Wearing pink slacks, a Kelly-green shirt, yellow bow tie and white loafers sans socks (he was a *bon vivant*), he strolled slowly to the front of the room, told his victims to open their books and in no more than forty minutes, answer the following simple question, which he then wrote on the chalkboard:

"WHY?"

He then casually sauntered from the room dazzling the eyes of his students in the passing. After anguished looks at fellow sufferers, the class began scribbling like mad. Two students wrote briefly, placed their booklets on his desk, and left. Informed later, the class was told student number one had answered:

"WHY NOT?"

"BECAUSE!" had been the gem from student number two.

The harlequin attired dude, hoisted by his own petard, had to pass them both. Unfortunately, such perspicacity would only work once!

In 1959, another of his victims, I sat, pencils sharpened, blue book at the ready, primed and eager for his lousy question. Not true. I have never in my life been primed and eager to answer any test questions. Besides, sweat dripped off my nose and its heat was fogging my glasses. The only true thing I was primed and eager for was a trip to the loo! Oh happy day, there in all its glory is his exciting question.

"WHO ARE YOU? Don't just scribble name, rank and serial number, enlighten me as to the *inner* you. Be thorough. Try to write in English, not gibberish. And, as always, finish in forty minutes!"

Big problem. Even though I was at the ripe old age of thirty, and had had a few interesting adventures along the way, I still didn't really know who I was. Desperately groping through my mind I finally decided the hell with it. I'd write him some stuff from my first squall to the present and let him figure me out. Here's what I wrote. You get to decide if I passed the course.

• • •

Plink...Plink...Plink!

1

The winter of '28, I am told, was a bitterly cold sucker. Drifting, blowing snow covered fields, yards and roads, then laughed at the puny efforts of wheezing stick figures wedded to shovels. The doctor fought the drifts getting to our house where, not able to afford the hospital, money always being scarce, Mom and Dad anxiously anticipated the birth of her second child. Knitting, sewing, scrimping, she had gathered together enough for a layette for one. Pop had been working up blisters with the coal shovel trying to coax heat from the furnace to travel upstairs. Warm air always played the part of stranger to the second floor of the duplex.

Fortunately, the midwife was already standing by when the doctor fought his way through the front door. Soft music from the Victrola, combined with the chill of an arctic wind beating upon the shivering windows, encouraged maternal doings. I was born during the first movement of Tchaikovsky's sixth symphony, the "Pathétique." Twenty minutes later, my brother joined me!

Beaming, the doctor gently shook my mother's shoulder and said, "Mrs. Judge, you've given birth to two beautiful baby boys!"

Expecting but the one, and everything in pink for a girl, she took one look at him and yelled, "I'll never speak to you again!"

How many times do you suppose she's been teased about that outburst?

I have a hunch Dad aged rapidly over the next few years. No doubt the next episode speeded up the process.

The facts do not come from what I remember as I was only a tad bit past the age of one. I think I have them straight though because this doozy has been told and retold over many years. It has to do with a "thunder mug," a small, rounded and enameled portable potty.

We were traveling to my grandparents' summer cottage at Queenston, a small hamlet not far from Niagara Falls. If one chose to venture on the ferry across Lake Ontario, Queenston would be the boat's last port of call. On this occasion, we were motoring via the highway in Dad's old putt-putt, a four-door Star. At that time the big three in automobile manufacturing were General Motors, Ford and Durant. Willie (Billy) Durant had been general manager of General Motors, but he had quite a temper which frequently landed him in trouble. He'd finally struck out on his own, creating Durant Motors. The Star was one of his products. Actually, his cars were every bit as good as Chevrolet and Ford, but Billy was easily bored and did not market them as effectively. Eventually he went bankrupt. Anyway, the old Star's top speed, flat-out, ate up the miles at forty per. Tools for changing flat tires were stored under the back seat. No trunk. Those old scooters were always coming down with cases of the flats. Les Schwab, where were you? That day was no exception and one of the round became square smack in the middle of the city of Oakville. I think you could safely say that today it's a suburb of Toronto. I don't think the inhabitants would cheer though.

Rest areas were nonexistent, restaurants few and far between. My folks couldn't afford one anyway. Adults gritted, sometimes even ground, teeth and endured. The necessities for young children were handled, thankfully, by lowering their britches in the back seat and employing ye old thunder mug.

The picturesque little city of Oakville fronted along the lake and pretty well catered to the hoity-toity and, I believe, much more so to the affluent today. For my money it is still a delightfully charming place.

When my father once more raised the back seat in order to replace the no longer needed tire tools, he accidentally knocked the potty, fortunately empty, out the open door. PLINK...PLINK...PLINK, it rolled clear across the main street. Traffic stopped both ways while Pop, his face the color of an over-ripe tomato, chased it down. The crowd of guffawing onlookers didn't help his mood either as, hurrying to get back to the car, he desperately tried to find a place to hide it behind his back. Much passenger laughing and tooting of horns from automobiles proceeding east and west. Dead silence in one car headed west! Whenever favorite stories surfaced at the dining table and Pop would get teased about that one, he'd always reply, "Yeah, well you've still got a Roman nose." A Roman Nose? "Yeah, it's roamin' all over your face!" We always hooted him down.

PLINK, PLINK, PLINK!

Other than the day I was born, I believe that was the first time I'd become a trial to Pop. It wouldn't be the last!

Once past the pabulum stage, I think my first clear recollection would have to be Christmas. It is such a magical time for children. Not just the solemnity of the Mass. Although that was still confusing to my young mind it also impressed. And while over the years it has been subjected to a few changes, namely from Latin to English, it has remained essentially the same.

Mollie-O and I have attended Mass in Mexico, Hawaii, Ireland, Spain, Portugal and Italy. The religious celebration and presentation of the Host is exactly the same. I like that.

However, as a young child, that wasn't what impressed me about Christmas. It was the way my family celebrated. Presents might have had a hand in it, too! This is not terribly important, but a puzzling incident occurred the Christmas I lay claim to the age of seven.

First, I'll explain the way we celebrated the festivities and then I'll drop the puzzler on you. Commercial hype never started early, certainly not before Halloween like it does today. "You have to buy now" jazz hadn't even come close to being prescribed. The outsides of houses adorned, nay festooned, with a myriad of lights flashing were definitely numbered among the few. Tree lit views through living room windows, yes.

I keep telling you my parents did not have much money, but it is important you remember that. What they did have was always spent on the children first—always. My father was an honest, hardworking man who stayed toiling for twenty-seven years at a job he hated just so his family would not have to do without. The Judge family constantly had good food on the table and we never had to be ashamed of our attire, but woe betide us if we didn't take care of it. I would never have left a winter coat or jacket on the playground as many of my students used to do. If I was ever foolish enough to do so, you can bet I'd have been ordered to march right back and get it. My generation was a product of the Great Depression and no one ever forgot it.

Christmas preparations at the Judges', not the anticipation, only took place Christmas Eve after excited young eyes and their twitchy limbs were abed and fast asleep—maybe. We never could fool them though and as soon as the Sandman zapped those who'd vowed they wouldn't zonk, Mom and Pop sprang into action. The tree, stashed in the garage and nailed to its wooden stand, was retrieved and carefully positioned in the living room. Decorations: glass bulbs, candy canes, lights, special doodads garnered over the years found just the right places on fresh smelling boughs. Icicles (foil of course) were draped on branches and, to complete the glory, our angel growing gracefully older each year, smiled down from the place of honor at the top of the tree.

Presents: hauled out from the secret places we kids were not supposed to know about (we always did!), were wrapped with loving care and arranged, just so, under the tree. Of course, there were stockings: the long, winter-wear kind filled with candy, nuts, tangerines, a wrapped lump of coal and small gifts packaged in tissue paper that rustled when the dewy-eyed eager squeezed them at the first crack of dawn. Not once did smart kids ever catch the ones who snuck in and fastened those stockings to the bed-post. Santa Claus always got blamed for that little caper. Mom and Pop, after such hectic doings got to bed about 2 A.M. The wide-awake hauled them out at six! Frustration! Breakfast had to be eaten first. Take small bites, chew slowly, swallow carefully, eat more—drink your milk. *I hated milk!*

Finally, we trooped to the living room and beheld *the tree*, dazzling; colorfully wrapped gifts adding to the luster. Pop played Santa. Sometimes one of us would be told to do the honors. I wasn't wild about that. I wanted to tear into mine, not hand presents out to others! Most of the goodies were practical and surely needed: socks, combinations (long-johns), shirts, jackets and gloves. But there was always at least one special gift: a red wagon, a tricycle, a pop-gun. The laughter, and even the tears, were so very special.

While I was still quite young, we attended eleven o'clock Mass on Christmas Day. When we were past the age of wriggling, it became midnight Mass on Christmas Eve which I much preferred. Today? I'm back to the day, the children's Mass drives me nuts and midnight is past my bedtime.

Nobody desired lunch, a snack was enough. We knew dinner

would be a feast and when the time arrived, the dining room table was as dazzling as the tree: First, beside each plate, a festive Christmas cracker that exploded when the ends were pulled, delivering a paper hat and a surprise. These always brought on the giggles. Then, with funny hats adorning heads, here came the first course, crab or shrimp cocktail. It was usually shrimp, crab was too expensive but who's complaining! Next: Prime rib, Yorkshire pudding, peas (I got corn, you can stuff peas!), mashed potatoes and gravy, carrots, hot horse-radish—the kind that cleans out the sinuses and brings tears to your eyes—simply lovely; rolls, relish tray and, for dessert, flaming, brandy-soaked plum pudding with hot lemon sauce. Dimes were carefully hidden in the pudding. Happy shouts of "Hey, I got one!" I don't suppose I have to tell you how long Mom scrimped and saved to provide that feast. Many changes have taken place over the years, but that's one dinner that never changes (I might sneak in a bottle of wine now). Mom, at ninety-seven, still insists on doing it all; everything from scratch. We just celebrated this year's, care to join us for the next?

Ready for the puzzler? Bob, my twin, and I took my new red wagon out for a spin. Directly adjacent to our house was a street possessed of a dandy hill. It promised us a fast, scary ride to the bottom. I sat in front, the place of honor, handle between my legs, feet protruding over the front. Bob sat in back, his legs wrapped around my hips.

In an attempt to keep strangers and other unwelcome critters off their lawns, many of our surrounding neighbors installed wire fences. Most of the persuaders looked like this: at each corner of the front yard, a piece of three-quarter inch pipe about two and a half feet long had been hammered into the ground to a depth close to one and a half feet. The fence consisted of clothesline wire wrapped around the remaining one foot of pipe and stretched from corner to corner. The constant hammering had left jagged edges on each of the pieces of pipe.

Down the hill we raced. Who needed brakes! The wagon, lacking power steering and a good helmsman, roamed from one side of the sidewalk to the other. Even we weren't dumb enough to rip down the road! Close to the bottom, our speed seemingly making the wagon's wheels smoke, I felt a slight tug on the sock on my right foot. Heart thumping but safe at the bottom of the hill I thought to take a look at my leg. Half of my sock was missing. The upper half! My leg, not a scratch or bruise on it, had escaped completely unscathed. My missing half-sock lay on the sidewalk some thirty feet away. It was whole except for where it had been cleanly severed from the other half.

How had I lost only half my sock? Why was my leg not lacerated? How did my sock escape over my shoe? Why were both halves, respectively, still whole? Got any ideas?

Mollie-O

WAHOO !

I have never been one who followed the crowd. No brag, just fact. Consequently, while still a boy I spent hours playing by myself with my collection of lead toy soldiers (I was too dumb to hang onto them when I grew up, and they're purely worth a bundle now!) and, like the result of a real battle, I wanted to see them strewn about having been surprised and subjected to artillery fire. I did possess a number of cannons but they only looked good, they didn't actually fire.

Solution? I gathered all the burnt out light bulbs from home and neighbors that I could. Then, in loose sand in the backyard, I buried them thread-side down until but a small portion of glass still lay exposed. Next, I arranged my opposing armies in battle order, loaded my trusty BB gun, and proceeded to blow soldiers all over the backyard when the BB's blew the bulbs apart just like exploding artillery. I had to be fair, so it was one shot in turn for each army. If I missed a shot, *c'est la guerre!*

POW!

Well, I'm here to tell you it worked a treat and my ambulances were soon working overtime. There was one tiny hint of a cloud on the horizon. Occasionally, the languid swish of the cat's tail interfered with a sensational shot. Depending upon which army the lazy bum was snoozing by, and even though I'd always forfeit a shot, that crummy squalling feline never appreciated my sense of fair play and, in retaliation, he would rise and promptly use the nearest army for a catbox.

• • •

I do not remember being taught to read although I definitely know it happened. Ask me to swear and I'll vow I could always do it. That of course is pure cat fat. To the dear lady responsible (I'm sure it was a woman because in my day all teachers of the elementary grades were) thank you and bless you. I truly cannot imagine what my life would have been like without books.

If there be one thing I am most grateful for in my generation it is that we grew up sans TV. Radio, yes, but radio forced the listener to use his imagination and thus he became involved. While his eyes rest, his ears and mind interpret the sounds and expression of words which told of adventure, detective daring do, fairy tales. How many remember, *Let's Pretend?* Was not the time spent listening to radio magical?

I never go anywhere without a book: to the store, vacation, shopping; the doctor, dentist or ophthalmologist. Why, even while I'm explaining to my publisher why I've written a certain way, if he should happen to nod off, the trusty book residing in my lap will tide me over until he returns from his brief spate of happy dreams. Unplug the TV and pick up a book today!

• • •

If you will promise not to latch on to any of my bad habits, I'll tell you of two escapades in my youth. One made me ashamed of myself. The other to this day still tickles my funny bone.

A callow lad, I still did not fall into the clutches of a Fagin.

However, fate and greed did cause me to skulk among those shabby back alleys belonging to the underworld. Hopefully the following confession of a sinner will keep *you* from a life of crime!

Is it not true that all children crave sweets? How many times do you hear the little monsters clamoring in the markets for mother to 'buy them a can of spinach? I've never known a child who even asked for a first helping, let alone seconds! I liked sweets. So did the guys that I ran around with. Candy bars sold for a nickel apiece, sometimes three for a dime. If I hadn't screwed up, my allowance totaled a quarter a week. Chores for that remuneration were: washing, drying dishes; setting and clearing the table; making my bed; taking out the garbage; sweeping front porch and sidewalk in summer, shoveling snow in winter. If I really lucked out, washing windows would be tossed in, along with helping to paint porch and trim in the summer. Don't misunderstand, my life was not a form of *Angela's Ashes*. Rather, it was much more a case of "take out the ashes."

My parents were not stingy with the work, they believed in doling some of it out to everybody, and if the work was not done properly no allowance—no exceptions. Looking back, learning to work didn't hurt me a bit which is surely most fortunate as there's plenty of it hanging around. Responsibility is really a nice fellow, he should not be ignored. I still do chores today, although I don't do dishes and I don't do windows (Are you listening, Mollie-O?).

To continue with sweets. Twenty-five cents did not stretch very far, especially if I was saving to buy a book or putting some aside to spend at the Canadian National Exhibition in September.

On a warm summer day with nothing to do, one of the guys suggested we walk uptown to the drugstore; there were six of us, everyone broke. Accordingly, the caper was planned like this: Once inside the store the other fellas would distract the owner while the weasel of the bunch, *me,* swiped a candy bar. Why me to make the grab? Do you suppose it was intelligence or because Bob and I were the runts of the gang and he said, "No."

The heist went off slicker than a frog sliding off a greased lily pad and we all beat it to the park to share the spoils. My reward? The smallest piece and a guilty conscience. That's not what deterred me from a life of crime though, not by a long shot.

After thoroughly wiping lips and teeth to ensure candy bar had been well and truly buried and no evidence remained, we returned home and nonchalantly began a game of cards on the neighbor's porch. My mother suspected right away we'd been up to mischief. Don't ask me how or why? I know none of the guys had squealed! Bob and I were ordered into the house and thoroughly interrogated:

"What have you boys been up to?"

"Who, us? Nuttin', Ma, honest. We've just been enjoyin' the sights and sounds of nature on this fine day. We're not takin' the fifth. Your boys are pure and innocent!" (It was a long time ago, those may not have been the exact words, but I've nailed it pretty close.)

"Very well then, stay here. I'll just go and have a little talk with the other boys!"

Quaking in our boots, wondering what had made her suspicious in the first place, Bob and I vowed to stick to our plea of innocent. When Mom returned she didn't say anything for a moment, then out of the blue she outflanked me: "Well, one of your friends has told me the whole story and I'm deeply ashamed of you both, so you might as well fess up."

I could see fifteen to life facing me for sure. Promising myself I'd get the rat who'd fingered me, I caved. Confessing the whole sordid story I mea culpa'd and threw myself on the mercy of the court.

"Your father will take care of this when he gets home. Go to your room and stay there."

Dreading Pop's wrath, I hied me to my room and ran all the events over in my mind. What the hell had made her suspicious in the first place?

When Pop hallooed the house, before he could even take his hat off, he was waylaid by the warden. A quiet conversation ensued; a decision was formed and I was told to report downstairs. My mother gave me a dime and ordered me to go with Pop. We walked, in dead silence, back to the drugstore. Once there I had to confess my crime to the puzzled store owner, sincerely apologize, and then pay him double for the candy bar. Even though all the way home I kept blinking back tears from the humiliation, that still did not deter me. And I soon determined that none of the guys had spilled a thing. No, what deterred me from becoming a member of the "dead-end kids" was my mother. She just naturally could look into my very soul. I knew she'd nail me every time. Now how is a guy ever going to win against that kind of clairvoyance? So, I've been going straight ever since.

P.S. None of the other guys was charged with any part of the crime, and not only did my brother get the biggest piece of the chocolate bar, he didn't even get a licking!

Saturday movie matinees were great entertainment for us. While I won't ever change my mind about the value of books and radio, it was nice once in awhile, even if it was a touch hazy for me, to also see the action. During intermission they would have yo-yo contests. Tommy Smothers is not the only one capable of Rocking the Cradle, Skinning the Cat, Walking the Dog, Going Around the World or Putting the Baby to Sleep. Heck, yo-yo's were second nature to us. They also conducted bolo bat contests. Our dimes bought two features plus cartoons and those contests for which one could win a prize. No money. Some lucky kid usually hauled home a trophy that mom would love to deep six, but the winning was important and we also had fun.

I've told you how sweets got me into trouble; how about a bunch of celery? It happened there resided, two stores up from the theatre, a small fruit market. On the way to the movies the six of us would often stop and shop for healthy food. Remember, this was long before cholesterol was known to have an ugly head. Even though we're all older than auld lang syne now, we didn't all come down when the hazel nuts were shaken from the tree. Okay, I can see I'm going to have to be honest. We did buy that nourishing stuff for another reason. One: Often the main feature would be a scary flick. The one I remember best was *The Island of the Dead* with Boris Karloff. Now that was a spooky movie. Seems like there had been a great battle. Stiffs were lacing the landscape. They had to bury them because disease, including plague, had come to call. Lighting was very gloomy in this film. General Boris walked among the dead holding a lantern above his head. I'm not sure if he was counting or looking for a lost buddy. Much later in the dim, poorly lit living room in the castle—one of the survivors keeled over. They all thought she'd died from plague so they put her in a coffin and then placed the box in a cave. Water drip...drip...dripped from the roof onto the coffin. It was *dead quiet*, in the theatre and in the cave. The audience scarcely dared to breathe. The woman in the coffin was not dead, she'd had an epileptic fit. She woke up and just before she screamed, we six in turn, and spacing it out, bit down on a stick of celery: CRUNCH—CRUNCH—CRUNCH...can you picture the scene? You're right, management promptly threw us out!

Another time, another scary movie, dead silence in the theatre. We'd holler out in the deepest or highest voice we could muster, OH MY GOD, I LEFT MY KID IN THE CAN! Good-bye once again.

"Who knows what evil lurks in the minds of" ...rotten little kids.

Certainly by now you've noticed that, except for the chocolate bar heist, I'd check out as an average, well-behaved, unnoticeable young lad. In my day and bailiwick, public school encompassed first through eighth grades. High school covered grades nine through twelve, thirteen if you were chasing a matriculation degree. In fact until entering high school, except for a few minor incidents, I remained mostly unconscious during my grammar school years.

Oh, there was the time I packed a beauty of a snowball and not even aiming (honest) threw it across the street where a high school student just happened to stick his head in front of it. He was wearing glasses at the time. Naturally, when he got back up on his feet, his flaming glasses were broken. Pop paid for a new pair.

Then there was the episode where a bigger kid took a poke at my brother. I chased him all the way up his street and onto his front porch. I was swinging a baseball bat at the time and if I'd caught him I'd have killed him. He scooted through his front door just in time. If anybody was going to belt my brother, it would be me! No charge for Pop on that one.

If memory serves there might have been another very minor event, but it's hardly worth mentioning. I only refer to it because I'm forced to inform you of the inner me.

One summer day, while with my chums, I was returning home from a morning's swim at the local high school. The school provided free swimming lessons for youngsters during the summer. We stopped along the way to help a local farmer, although he was not there at the time, thin his trees of an overabundance of apples. It was our civic duty and, even though the apples were still green, we didn't mind. Munching, inviting cases of the "dire rears" and minding our own bee's wax, we were interrupted by a loud mouth from our class who, from a safe distance across the street, hollered insults at us. I palmed an apple and tried for his head! As usual I missed by a mile and the wee green missile flew behind some bushes. Two seconds later there was a God-awful crash which sounded suspiciously like breaking glass!

Not waiting to find out, we took off up driveways, across backyards and over fences. Passing rapidly through one yard, an old crone threw up her bedroom window, stuck her head out and screeched:

"You naughty boys!"

Mind you, she hadn't the foggiest notion what crime we'd committed. We could have been running from a rabid dog! Thus, the truly innocent are often labeled guilty, though perhaps not in this case. Regardless, nary a member of the group stopped to argue. After six more fences and three more blocks, puffing but still prepared to run, we snuck onto our front porch and acted innocent. All would have ended well if that mouthy little snot hadn't shown up an hour later, walking beside a huge cop!

Pop and I had to pay a visit to the house whose front window had had its face pushed in. My, oh my, it was one of the biggest windows I'd ever seen. Dad took measurements. We walked uptown to the hardware store, bought the glass and each taking one end, walked carefully back to the house which was suffering from a cruel draft, until he puttied it's new window into place. Once again, Pop paid. I don't think I ever saw any more allowance after that!

Possibly I could cite one other time, but it truly wasn't my fault: Winter sports were popular in my town: ice skating, hockey, bobsledding, skiing etc. I loved ice skating and hockey. Sometimes at night, after dinner, our whole family would gather their skates and hike up to where the city had installed lights, enlarged the local rink and hooked up speakers to relay phonograph music to delighted skaters. It was lovely and we had great fun. Adults never put up with young rowdies or fights. In those days the men skaters would have knocked holes in the ice with the punks' heads and then thrown them in. I'm serious. Adults just would not put up with lip from smart alec kids and woe betide the ones who used bad language in public! We've really allowed a great deal of politeness to slip away over the years, haven't we.

I feel sorry for those who've never learned to ice skate. I enjoy roller skating, too, but it cannot compare to a brisk chill, nor the invigoration of flying over the ice while watching your breath steam and dance in the wind. I wish we had outdoor rinks in the valley, here in Oregon. Of course, then it would have to be colder, we'd need snow and heavy winter clothing, and we'd have to leave chains on the car's tires. Forget it. I'll just sit here in front of this nice warm fire and dream of the good old days!

The peccadillo referred to above which turned into an altercation occurred during an afternoon hockey game on the ice of our public school rink. My friends and I, all around the age of eleven or twelve, were minding our own business playing a friendly game between ourselves. Involved as all schools were in winter sports, that rink was a good size. The Toronto Maple Leafs could have even played there. They probably would have lost.

As I passed the puck to a teammate, a skater cut in front and purloined it. He had not been invited to play and was a wise guy to boot. He was also, I'd been told, the school bully. He was small but quite chunky. I'd say, "Battling Nelson" would fit the description. I do not like to fight. Punching hurts, especially when it's you who's being punched. Nor, when fisticuffs end, have I enjoyed having my face rearranged. This guy had quite a reputation and to be honest, I was scared of him. However, that was our puck and I wanted it. He tried a few fancy moves, but I managed to poke the puck away from his stick and quickly bent down and picked it up. Then it began:

"How'd you like a fat lip?"

"Why don't you work up the courage to knock this little dab of snow off my shoulder!"

"Did your mother ever have any kids that lived?"

"How come you got a face like a wet week?"

"Most guys I know have noses, how come yours is a wart!"

"My sister is really ugly but she's a girl, what's your excuse?"

Jabber—jaw, jabber—jaw! I still held the puck and I think it would have died a natural death if he hadn't made a big mistake. He reached out with his stick and hit the back of my hand. I wasn't expecting that, as a result the puck flew straight up in the air and hit me in the eye. Instantly angry, without thought, I threw off my gloves and belted him! And away we went. I had height and reach on him and most fortunately, before I flattened him, it died. He never laid a glove on me and when I laid a healthy one on his nose, he dropped his hands, started to cry and sobbed:

"Go ahead, I can take a beating!"

Did I feel good? No. I felt rotten. Who the hell was the bully here? This guy was all blow and no go and besides, he's bucketing down like Niagara Falls. I was thoroughly ashamed of myself. Atlas, thumping the ninety-seven-pound. weakling. We gathered around consoling and admiring his courage and then, having lost the taste for any more hockey that day, we all went our separate ways.

I know you'll want to know this. I studied my rugged, manly figure in the full-length hall mirror when I got home. Me, Atlas? Ha—ha—ha, the mirror cracked up!

That one turned out to be a freebie for Pop.

It seems like you are mainly hearing confessions of a wayward youth, and so I suppose you won't be satisfied until you learn of— *the day*! The day I got the "slugs" at school. You would recognize that as a licking. Let me say right up front, I was guilty.

Our schools experienced very few discipline problems. Why? Because of rules which, if broken, brought repercussions. A sort of "you commit the crime, you do the time" thing. I have to say it was simpler back then. Kids didn't have to sit down and, surrounded by a large crowd of administrators, psychologists, lawyers and even soothsayers, answer the question: "Dear child, what is your deep-rooted, serious, psychological problem? Are you related to Eve White, Eve Black or Eve any color?"

Most kids weren't basket cases, they just did things for the hell of it. And if caught, figured it was no big deal and were willing to pay the penalty.

In public school we were not allowed to leave the playground at recess or noon unless we'd been summoned home for some family need and then, we would be released only after the school powers that be had been notified.

A school acquaintance, not a friend, sported some money. As it was burning a hole in his pocket, desiring to fill his face with sweets, he asked me to travel downtown with him and he'd stock up. Naturally, I'd receive my fair share. You know I liked sweets. Funny thing, I don't much care for them at all—today. Foolishly, I agreed to accompany him. Without mishap, we sped to the store, loaded up and hurried to get back in order to be on the playground before the bell rang.

Proceeding to head to class at the sound of chimes, we were collared by the duty teacher and ordered to report to the principal's office. We all called him "Hawkeye." Living up to his name, he'd spotted us leaving and returning to school. In the office, he tendered his report to the exalted one. We could muster up no excuse. A decision quickly made, we followed the duty teacher into the inner sanctum whereupon resided the "slugger," the slugger being a fairly thick, three inch wide by eighteen inches long, leather strap.

The sentence? Three on the palm of each hand. A note of caution to the perpetrator, while "slugs" were being administered by either a nun or lay teacher, the culprit shall not yank his hand away on the downstroke. Well, you can see why. Administrator belts self rather than the hand of the dead-end kid. And that tends to irk the punisher which does not bode well for the punishee!

The swinging, striking strap will sting the palm but is in no way lethal. However, through careful planning, the strap swung by the irked will get even as it tends to strike but a part of the palm before wrapping the rest of itself around the back of the hand. Now that baby hurts! Take my advice. If you ever get the "slugs" and shame on you if you do, *don't yank your hand away.*

My acquaintance was a wimp and called for Providence to intercede. Providence had gone out to lunch, so the "candy king" blubbered awhile, took his licking and headed back to his class. Me? I was rugged and faced up to Swat Palm Day. The only reason my eyes smarted was because I was mad, not at the wielder of the wallop, at myself for being so stupid when I knew the rules. After three here and three over there, both hands now fully awake, I slunk back to class hoping Mom wouldn't find out. I don't believe she ever did—that time!

Timber!

I began to work after school. City transportation when I was a shaver was, in the main, via bus, streetcar or bicycle. Most members of the proletariat did not have cars. That was not altogether bad as Toronto had one of the best, if not best, transportation systems on the North American Continent. No subway system as yet but, rain, shine, sleet or snow the Toronto Transportation Commission (TTC to the natives) never let you down.

I worked from four to six after school and all day Saturday delivering baked goods on my bicycle. Depending on caller location, the delivery could range from a few blocks to as far as a couple of miles. Our bikes had one speed, grunt and pump. Brakes worked off the pedals. If the chain came off—no brakes—better look for a soft landing area. I received three dollars a week for my labors and occasionally leftover bread, rolls, sticky buns, sometimes even a pie. I did not mind the work and did need to save for the big splurge in September at the Exhibition. I don't want to interfere with your train of thought trying to follow this, so if you'll bear with me, I'll clue you in on the Canadian National at the end of this section.

In my youthful days, Mom and Pop stores were it. Nobody had even heard of a "mall." Baked goods could be obtained one of three ways: By horse and wagon where everyday deliveries of fresh goods would be brought right to your door. However, these were mass-produced and lacked individuality. Baked goods could also be obtained at grocery stores, again mass-produced. Deli's, although fresh, were limited in selection. You say you want bread, rolls, buns, cakes, doughnuts or pies, all fresh. Head for or pick up the phone and call the bake shop. I would be at your service toot of the flaming sweet!

Your desire was butter, milk, eggs? Another horse and wagon was right outside your door. Those horses knew the route so well, they'd walk from house to house by themselves and even wait for the driver at the end of the block. Disadvantage? Horse puckey on the street. Not to worry, housewives would scoop it up for their gardens.

Spring, summer and fall, farmers would roll by, different horse, different wagon but fresh produce, so fresh the guy in overalls bragged it had picked itself before sunrise: "We got rhubarb here, bound to put a blush on mother's cheeks. Try the asparagus (I always called it asparagrass). We got cabbage, carrots, turnips, cauliflower, peas and corn. You want strawberries, peaches, pears, apples, apricots, grapes, raspberries? We got 'em."

The litany went on and on. I loved it. Of course, there were different items for different seasons, but you've got the idea.

Porkchops for supper? Call the butcher shop and they're on the way. Produce, Deli, Aspirin? All would be delivered right to the front door. At one time or the other, I delivered for them all. Three bucks wasn't much but then again, I wasn't stuck for income tax!

Tamblyn's Drugstores, possibly Toronto's first chain, supplied their own bicycles. Not important except for one teensy little difference. Most carriers into which one loaded his deliveries, fastened to both front wheel and handlebars. On a long trip when the back began to ache, a person could obtain relief by leaning forward and steering with the carrier. Tamblyn's bikes were different. Their carriers were welded to the frame and did not touch wheel or bars. If one forgot that tiny idiosyncrasy, and I frequently did, you could wrap one's self around a telephone pole. More than once, wearing a bottle of Pepto Bismol, I limped back to the store for a new supply. Pay raises—acknowledging my skills—continued to be infrequent!

At long last it was September, time for the big one. I had managed to put away two whole dollars. I know, but the price of books kept going up and allowance was only a fond memory. Never mind, a guy could have a heck of a good time at the Canadian National on two bucks.

Think of your BIG state fair and make our Exhibition BIGGER and you've got it. Toronto's splashy do was the second largest on the North American continent, exceeded only by the one in Dallas, Texas. We had it all: midway rides, car races, daredevil driving, food establishments, latest inventions, a pure food building, stalls where one could buy ice cold milk, a carnival, hurdy-gurdies, jugglers, balloons, marching bands, concerts, speed boat races on the lake and, at night, fireworks!

Mom always packed a huge lunch and after eating together at a lovely table, Pop never failed to find, we took off to explore. My favorite place was the pure food building. Today, think of sampling at Costco, they dole out beaucoup snacks and appetizers, right? Join me in the PFB and we'll pig out on animal crackers, soup, candy bars, gum, pop, Cracker Jacks, fruit, cereal, cookies. The list is endless. *It was all free.* My two clams lasted a long time spent on candy floss, a couple of rides, a package of collectors stamps, a whirly-gig. Bob and I struggled home loaded down with two shopping bags each! Of course, some of that would be flyers on just about anything and anywhere. Two bucks wouldn't take me to Spain, but the picture in the flyer did! I have to tell you, those were the greatest times. The capper: all sandwiches scoffed, blankets picked up, tired kids in tow, Mom and Pop would lead us out to the car and we watched the nightly fireworks display coming from the stadium. Those inside paid, we took in the show for free. Shoot-amighty, just running it back through my mind sets my feet to moving. How about we go to the next one together?

• • •

Did I hear you mention snow? Great gobs of white yuck that often melts on your neck and, in friendly fashion, runs down your spine in an almighty hurry to soak your shorts? And, if by chance, one takes an unexpected nose-dive into a drift, one's nose and other nether parts—freeze! Is that the stuff you're talking about? We had it and other than now, in my dotage, we youngsters loved the vile stuff.

Let me ask you a question. Have you ever been asked to perform an impossible task where logic and common sense tells you it cannot be done, but compassion forces you to try?

I've mentioned my twin brother. He is almost as bright as me. Once again I'll mention the fact that in our house filthy lucre didn't show up in abundance. Therefore, the desired winter sports equipment such as skis, we did not have. That, of course, does not eliminate the desire. Thus, we have-nots would descend a snow packed hill by sliding on our fannies or belly-flopping onto pieces of cardboard. Sometimes an inner tube would be the form of transport but you had to watch out for the valve stem. Now there was a little item bound to get your attention, especially if the rider wasn't careful how he sat. No matter, kids can always figure out ways to have fun and we were no exception. Having slid down "Bust Your Buns" hill for the umpteenth time I looked up to the top and noticed my brother had come into possession of an abandoned toboggan. It was somewhat the worse for wear and wore a quizzical expression because one of the chains on its bow had gone missing giving it the appearance of a raised eye. Any port in a storm, so Bob decided to use it as a substitute for skis. The toboggan's raised eye seemed to question the sense to that, but brother Bob was determined.

Grinning at me, by then standing out of harm's way, he pulled the rope back over the front, stepped on the 'boggan's backside and set sail down the hill. Great fun! And he skied away the afternoon. I became both bored and tired and so, from a safe distance at the bottom of Bust Your Buns, I threw snowballs at the real skiers whenever they came within range. My throwing arm and aim worked to perfection and I never beaned a one!

Getting on toward dusk, I felt a tug on my arm. Bob, looking a little punch-drunk and still holding fast to the rope of his steed said:

"I lostht my toof! Help me look for my toof."

Right on! When he opened his big mouth, I observed that half of one of my bud's permanent front teeth would now definitely be numbered among the missing; he hadn't broken it quite down to the root, but cold on the remaining stub had to be giving him a lot of misery. Half unconscious, he didn't seem to notice Winter's frigid breath. Actually, he really wasn't noticing much of anything. The obvious had happened. On one of those forays down the hill, he'd lost his balance, fallen, and introduced his mouth to the toboggan's quizzical eye. To slip in an atrocious pun, they hadn't seen eye to eye!

What to do? Snow lay round and all about. What are the odds on finding half of a white tooth in an endless blanket of white? To boot, he had almost knocked himself silly and, still wobbly on his pins, had no idea where he was. I sure had no idea where to hunt. With nothing for it, resigned, I took him by one hand, the toboggan in my other and we looked for his "toof" until dark. Then I led him home and broke the good news to Mom!

The dentist cemented a large gold blob on the stub which, when Bob opened his mouth made him look like he was carrying the Statue of Liberty's torch in there. Made no difference, the girls still flocked around him!

Occasionally, Pop was stuck to pony up for Bob, too.

• • •

"How would you kids like to see the Atlantic Ocean?"

The summer of my tenth year, and Pop had just unloaded some awesome news. A chance to view and taste an *ocean!* I was packed and ready before he finished his dinner. Mom and Pop loaded our sturdy 1930 Durant to the gunnels with camping gear, blankets, bedding and pots and pans. I did my part and threw in a pile of books and away we charged for the state of Maine.

Old Orchard Beach, our destination, lay a touch over 700 miles away. No freeways to speed the drive, no MacDonald's, Burger King's, Wendy's or Taco Bell's. No drive-ins period! A few cabins along the way could be rented. Food had to be purchased on a daily basis, no ice-chests. Most travelers tented and cooked over campfires. Order of the day: "Rain, stay away!" Those older style tents leaked like moth-holed umbrellas, always down the back of the neck or onto the camp cots.

I don't remember the fine points of the trip, how long it took to get there or the number of times Dad patched and pumped tires that refused to stay round and full of air. There had to be wear and tear on parents on a trip like that, but kids, cranky from close confinement, would pay no heed. I do remember stopping at a roadside stand in Maine for fried clams and chips. The first I'd ever tasted and so heavenly I know they beat today's Big Mac's all hollow.

Finally, not far from Saco, Maine, the Durant struggled up the road leading to Old Orchard Beach and, with a relieved sigh, stopped before the cabin Dad had rented for one glorious week. Unloading had to take place first and ice for the icebox purchased along with fresh milk and bread. Then beds made up using Mom's linen. Next, travel grime, especially behind the ears, had to be washed away before it was into bathing suits and off we go to walk a sandy shore. First taste of the ocean—pa-phooey! First view of the Briney—wow!

"Do not, repeat, do not wander far nor wade too far out in that ocean, it is possessed of mean currents," came the orders from headquarters.

With that our older sister, lidded jar in hand, set off to collect seashells and check out the scenery, specifically eligible young males. Junior and I set off to explore. Junior, younger by twenty minutes, is my kid brother, Bob. I call him by that misnomer because he just loves it when I do!

Enjoying the warm squiggly sand running between our toes along with the smell and sound of sea, we walked a fair way up the beach. Bob spotted something laying close to the water's edge about sixty yards away and he pointed it out to me. It looked like a big fat white blob.

"I think it's a fat kid takin' a snooze," he chortled. "Let's sneak up and give him a little poke with a stick."

"Ma ordered us to stay out of trouble," I warned.

"I'm not going to spear him, I'll just give him a little jab. If he gets mad we'll split. C'mon, scaredy cat!"

I'd already read the *Last of the Mohicans* twice and as we were both good runners, Natty Bumpo (me) and Uncas, keeping a wary eye out for marauding Injuns, crept up, oh so quietly, on our snoozing victim.

Turned out it was a dead, bloated, baby shark and it stank to high heaven. Even Junior had better sense than to poke his stick into that!

Meanwhile, not having driven all that distance for nothing, Pop, bathing suit attired and laying exposed on the sand, was absorbing some rays of his own.

"Don't stay out too long, dear. Even though it's partly overcast, the sun is still quite strong," cautioned Mom who, not about to let her hide get blistered, wore a sun dress and sat safely under a beach umbrella.

"Cease and desist woman, I know quite well what I'm doing. A little sun, not to mention this nice cool ocean breeze, isn't going to bother me!"

Defeated, while Pop promptly fell asleep, Mom set off to locate her sons in order to make them put their shirts on. And some time later, hungry, anticipating chow, we all trooped back to our cozy cabin. I was ready for some more of those mouth-watering Maine clams. But no matter, whatever the meal it had to be good, Mom's cooking always was. Not long after supper, wearied from travel, soothed by soft breeze and sound of garrulous ocean, we all yawned mightily and hit the sack.

The cabin portrayed two rooms and bath—rustic. Such cabins smell moldy until the old woodstoves warm them up. Personally, I liked the smell and had no trouble with it. Hey, we were having an adventure! Mom and Pop took the double bed in our one bedroom. Sister slept on a cot in the living room and Bob and I, joining her, crawled onto mattresses on the floor. Snores soon had to be resounding throughout both rooms. Pop could bugle like a freight train lost in a tunnel.

Sometime during the small hours, he rose to use the necessary. Returning, instead of slipping quietly back to bed, he passed out and hit the bedroom floor like the demise of a giant redwood! Naturally, the whole cabin bounced on its foundation, that being but eight stumps strategically placed under the plank floor. The horrible thud when Pop hit the deck yanked us all out of our beds. Jumping up, Bob's right heel kissed the pointed spout of a steel kettle inadvertently left sitting on the floor. But the unfriendly kettle bit him and he soon knew the kiss had been rejected especially when, hopping and hollering, he rapidly began to scatter blood all over the floor. Sister immediately added to the bedlam by screaming and pointing at Bob. All the while my father, looking like a frozen flounder, reposed out cold on the floor. A guy with a camera would have captured a real beaut. Trying to figure what the hell was going on, I crawled out of bed and joined the crowd. My mother— saintly person that she is—was allowed to quiet the racket and solve the problems.

Lovingly, she told my sister to shut up and wrap a towel around Bob's heel. She told me to keep out of the way. Then, using muscle she didn't know she had, she lifted and poured Pop back into bed.

WHEN POP HIT THE DECK!

Mollie-O

Thank God he was still breathing, but he looked like death warmed over. Half an hour later, Junior's foot bandaged and no longer bleeding and Pop safe in bed, we all tried once again to settle down for sleep. I don't know about the rest of them, but I slept fine.

Dad appeared okay if a touch befuddled in the morning. I figured it'd be a swell time to ask for an allowance increase. I got one of Mom's "fire in the hold" looks though, and prudence shut my mouth!

Turned out, after incautiously challenging Mr. Sun, the sucker had sent Pop a touch of sunstroke for his impertinence. He survived as did we all and—hoo-wee—did that week ever fly by.

Want me to sum up that vacation? Put it down in the Judge archives as a jim-dandy!

• • •

You've noticed I do not talk overlong about school subjects. What's to tell? I got A's on my last six spelling tests? The first time I read a complete sentence without sounding out or asking what a word was? Boring!

Let's face it, if you're married and with children, or whatever, you know the routine. Home from school, your pride and joy bursts through the door heading for the milk and cookies.

"Hi, honey, how did school go? What did you learn today?"

The reply—lengthy—will consist of one of two words, "nuttin'" or "stuff." Take the word of a retired teacher, none of the subjects I taught was labeled *nuttin'* or *stuff*! Pressing the issue, you'll continue, "Surely something of interest occurred."

"Oh, yeah, Frank swallowed a fly and threw up on the teacher's desk. That was really cool."

Same thing happens when the little monster jumps into trouble in the vicinity of hearth and home. Outraged, and with an urge to break his face, you'll clamp on to his closest ear and holler, "Putting Ex-lax in her cereal could have been an accident, but why on earth did you tell your sister that skunk was a kitty cat?"

You get the universal and ubiquitous shoulder shrug along with, "I dunno."

"You did that to your loving little sister and all you can say is 'I dunno!'"

Might as well quit, you're facing a no winner. Settle for reading the report card unless summoned for a parent/teacher conference. Then—be prepared. It would also be charitable—when the school promotes him and sends him along to make life miserable for his next teacher—to spare a moment of silence! There certainly were long periods of silence around our house.

As reported, I remained basically unconscious until high school. But, like most youngsters, I awoke during summer vacations. My family enjoyed two major vacations while I was a youngster. By major, I mean where we all traveled a fair distance from home. You know of Maine. Here is the second.

In the summer of 1940, Pop struck gold. For a very reasonable fee he rented another cabin at a place called Picton, on the Bay of Quinte, in Ontario. Picton lay about 220 miles northeast of Toronto. Lodging was once again rustic as the cabin was situated on a farm. Quarters sat on a small raised parcel of land just up from the bay's shore. It was a lovely spot, exactly the place for rambunctious kids to expend energy without getting into trouble—maybe! The plan had been drawn like this: Pop, in his trustworthy Durant, would drive us up on a Saturday and return to work via bus on Sunday afternoon. The following weekend, again taking the bus, he would join us. A week's repeat and then, on the next weekend, he'd travel back to Picton where, vacation over, he'd collect his brood and auto us all home.

Initially, everything unwrinkled, it slicked out smooth as a ripe grape. Trouble was lying in wait at the bottom of the bunch! Bob and I, for some miraculous good behavior, had been awarded a pup. He was a Bull Terrier and sported a black eye. Skipper, named because of his jaunty appearance, was a terrific little dog, loyal and lots of fun. Anybody ever read about Bodger in the *Incredible Journey*? If not, put it on your list of those I gotta read. The dog, naturally, accompanied us on vacation. Between playing with Skip, swimming, barn corncob fights with the farmer's son, an acquaintance who soon became a pal, picking and also face stuffing raspberries, it had been a super swell week.

There wasn't a schoolbook within a mile!

Pop arrived on the weekend. For true and good reason he had no need nor desire to spend time in spacious amounts of water. Dad was the eldest of four brothers. He was not a good swimmer. Frank, next in line, was sixteen when, at Bobcaygeon in Ontario, he drowned as my father tried desperately to reach him. Although it had been impossible for Pop to save his brother he never forgave himself for not doing so. It is understandable why he feared deep water.

Now, kids have been known to bug their parents. Being no exception, we kept begging him to take us out in the rowboat in order for us to impress him with our diving skills. He did not warm to the idea. Continuing to push, we promised to kick Skipper off his bed forever. No sign of weakening. We pledged to not bug our sister who's boyfriend, an air force sergeant, was coming out to visit. We'd do the dishes without complaining. Any mess from Skippy would be promptly tended to and not only would Bob and I not fight, we wouldn't even argue!

Well, you can see for yourself, we were practically going to pledge our lives away. A slight crack in a certain older person's resolve. Here comes the *pièce de résistance*: we would eat all our vegetables for the next three months including (from me) bloody peas! Adult surrender.

Gangway, here comes Johnny Weissmuller and his pal Cheetah. This is my story so you get one guess which of us was the Olympic swimmer!

Eager for the big dive we scrambled aboard while Pop readied the oars. And out into the bay he rowed. By eye, measure about a hundred and twenty yards before Dad shipped the oars and we began to drift.

"Now, Pop?"

"Not quite yet."

We drifted closer to the shore.

"How about now, Pop?"

"No, not just yet."

Our cabin grew larger by the minute.

"Aw c'mon, Pop," griped Bob. "We'll be back on shore in another wag of Skippy's tail!"

Finally, fifteen feet from shore and taking no chances, Pop gave the green light. I dove first. For some reason I've yet to fathom, because I had no premonition, I chose to make a very shallow dive: hit the water, aim hands upward, break surface. Bob, determined to outdo me, performed his super-dooper, spinnopp dive! (There is no such word as spinnopp, but the class of a teacher friend of mine is attempting to talk Webster's Dictionary into accepting it. As that would be quite an accomplishment and the more it's used the better its chances, I promised to put it in my next book.)

By the time Junior hit the water, I was standing up. Where Pop had let us dive, the water was only three to four feet deep. Bob stayed down quite awhile, long enough for us to become concerned. I was just about to go look for him when, suddenly there he was holding his hands to his face from which blood streamed. Attempting a jackknife dive, he'd smashed his face straight onto the bay's graveled bottom!

Father, turning white, became almost physically sick. Determined to protect his sons from the danger of deep water he had almost caused a catastrophe and he was so upset he verged on tears. Who said being a parent is easy!

All's well that ends well. It was a nasty cut but not too deep and no permanent damage was done. Eventually but a tiny scar remained. I kept hoping it would improve his looks. No flaming luck and the girls still flocked around him. And why not around me? Bet I haven't told you we are fraternal twins. I wasn't exactly ugly, my face wouldn't stop a train or anything like that. Neither would you be looking at another Troy Donahue. Don't laugh, but girls also scared me, they giggled constantly and were so—so *feminine*. I always came down with cases of the tongue ties and they'd take a hike. Bob, on the other hand …! Remind me to tell you of the time, in an effort to elicit sympathy from one of the female set, he came up with some baloney about a strange tropical disease. It worked, too!

Sis's boyfriend showed up. He looked ever so poshy in his uniform. Bob and I were quite taken with him. So was Sis. We had a week of vacation left and Mom thought a drive from the cabin to Picton, thence to Belleville and back would be a nice round trip.

Mom rated good driver status, but a mechanic she wasn't. Somebody else will pump the gas, oil and water can take care of themselves. Pop forgot to warn her. After checking nothing, Mom blithely cranked up the Durant and off we sped, all out at forty-five miles a gallop! The old flivver was about ten years into rolling over highways and byways, some of them a touch hard on her frame, and she was tired.

About ten miles of delightful scenery later our chariot began to make some rude noises.

"Wonder what that could be?" warbled Ma, continuing to put the pedal to the metal.

The belching grew louder, one might even say pushy which is an unfortunate choice of word as, half a mile further on, a rod pushed itself right through the engine block and our joyful jaunt came to an abrupt halt! Poor Pop, seemed like trouble just naturally kept dropping in like a rainstorm through a leaky roof.

Mom called a garage and the owner drove out to the stranded and towed the mortally wounded Durant to her last abode. When Dad bussed in on the weekend our landlord drove him to the garage where the bad news awaited.

"Mister, yore car's gotta have a whole new engine. She run outa oil an' the friction 'tween pistons an' cylinder walls become a argument which turned out plumb nasty. The connectin' rod joined in an' they thrun him out through the block. I'll give yuh twenty-five dollars as she sits or, it'll cost yuh three hundred and fifty ifen I puts a new engine in her!"

So long to the Durant. No way Pop could pony up that kind of dough. He took the twenty-five and called a good friend in Toronto who kindly drove out, picked up the whole crew, including the dog, and transported us home. His car was a 1940, two-door Oldsmobile. I had the position of honor on the floor on the way back. I have to tell you, I liked the smooth ride so much that, as you'll discover later on, my first car turned out to be a 1941 Oldsmobile.

We did not enjoy the benefits of owning or of automobile travel again until moving to California. It still checked out as a great summer though.

• • •

Engaging in those childish pursuits as we did, I often wonder how we survived relatively unscathed. The other day some kids on modern scooters chased me off the sidewalk. I have to admit the new ones are a definite improvement over our old homemade jobs. I've no idea what they cost, but Pop couldn't have afforded them. Nope, needs must. So the enterprising scrounged up an orange crate for a body, a piece of two-by-four, four feet long for a platform, two peices of two-by-two, two feet long for handles, one roller skate, the old-fashioned, one size fits all, metal kind, and a tin can for a headlight. The skate would separate when you unbolted the adjustable bottom which allowed for foot size. If the bolt was completely removed and also the two front shoe-sole grippers, which cranked in and held your foot firmly in place, that half of the skate would be nailed to the front of the two-by-four platform and the back half, could then be nailed to its end. Stand the crate upright, bottom forward, and nail it to the top of the front end of the two-by-four. The crate divider made a dandy shelf, and a two-by-two nailed crossways through the sides formed a lip which kept your cargo from sliding out and decorating the road. The handles were nailed onto the top of the crate in the shape of a "V," pointed end facing forward. Pilfer some paint from the garage, daub a name on your creation, and hammer the headlight tin can onto the front, midway down. Next, christen your handy-dandy and you're ready to roll. I pinched a thimbleful of Pop's rye and dribbled it over "Alka Seltzer's" head; I'd built him for speed you see. There are those who question that spill. Why didn't I drink the rye, they say, and baptize Alka Seltzer in ever available cheap water? I could have even had it blessed.

Let me say this about that: I did try a tiny swallow, and believe me it was the vilest stuff I'd ever let slip down my gullet. In fact, I disliked it so much, I never tried another drop until I ran across a rum and Coke in South America, long after I'd left the service. Sad to say, I've been an imbiber ever since!

Advantages of scootering? While on errands for Mom, I had transportation to the store on something that was fun to ride.

Coasting downhill was not only exhilerating, both feet could ride free of the road. Disadvantages? My left shoe, tired from slapping the pavement to engender propulsion, died long before my right. Also, when driving Alka Seltzer uphill I discovered a need for more gas and my lungs tended to carbonize.

Nobody even thought of helmets in those days, yet we rode them all over the thriving city and never once got clobbered by horse, car or truck. Ocassionaly a guy, grown careless, would fall off and skin a knee or his chin but that was it. I say, guy, because in my youth girls were supposed to settle for tea parties and playing with dolls, which was surely unfair. Justifiably, as we all know, that is no longer the case. Some changes are good mind you, but don't expect me to approve of females playing football or boxing, no flaming way! I certainly have no quarrel with helmets. If kids can be protected from possible injury during play or hazardous activity, who's going to argue with that? My point is that you don't wear what you "don't got."

While on the subject of helmets, at the ripe old age of eleven I had a little episode with a bicycle one day where one of those dome protectors would've come in handy. Not far from our house in Toronto, there lay a park called Sunnybrook Farm. Though it was in the city and quite large, one could compare it with a State Park. Here in Oregon, Silver Creek Falls State Park fits admirably. Heavily forested, with streams, but lacking falls, Sunnybrook provided hiking, biking, and horse riding paths. It also featured spacious picnic areas with tables. A lovely pond flourished close by where picnickers could swim. Although it was a posted no-no, one could also skinny dip. Would we dare do it anyway? Certainly, *but never on weekends!*

One entered the park via a spacious paved road which sloped steeply to the iron-gated entrance. Those gates were open from eight to five every day. I've mentioned our bikes had only one speed. Pump the pedals forward and the rider would progress. Push them in reverse and he'd brake—if the chain stayed on. If chain comes off, look for a sky hook or a soft place to land as you and your bicycle were definitely not going to stop! The wise would attend a bike shop and purchase a threading lock which, when wrenched tight, kept the chain securely on. I didn't have the dough to buy one.

Four of us started down the road toward the park. My bike was a well-worn, scruffy old dog and the rusty chain kept flying off. I believe I'd paid five dollars for it which had taken me only forever to accrue. Sure enough, just as we were picking up speed, always a thrill when the wind blew your hair back and puckered your cheeks, that coniving sucker flew off. Options? Continuing at break-neck speed down the road wasn't one of them. Neither was sliding down it on your face! Happened there were fields to either side and I was riding closest to the one on the left. It looked flat. I could see no rocks so I decided to turn into it hoping the long grass would slow me enough to where I could jump or fall off.

At first I knew I'd made the right move as I entered the field smoothly and uninterruptedly. Then, without warning, the front wheel dropped into a hidden, grass-overgrown ditch. There came a parting of the ways, bike remained behind, I didn't. Turning a complete sumersault in midair, I caught a short glimpse of three amazed faces swiveling in my direction before I landed flat on my back in the meadow. I was certain I'd dropped smack in the middle of a feather pillow because I had no hurt and nothing seemed to be broken! If memory serves, that was my first experience with flying and I must confess I rather liked it. Laughing in relief at such a smooth landing, I jumped up and retrieved the rotten bicycle. I figured I'd have to stash it and walk to the park as I had no tools with which I could reinstall the chain. Guess what? When the front wheel rudely belted the far side of the ditch, the shock snapped the miserable chain back on and, not only that, my beloved transportation hadn't even suffered another ding! Nonchalantly, I climbed aboard and pedaled down the road to where my three stopped, wondering companions waited.

"Hey doofus, how come you did a fool thing like that?" they groused.

"Guys, you won't believe me when I say, for a minute there I could have sworn I saw a jack rabbit all duded up in a diamond necklace. I was trying for a closer look, but the hairy little son-of-a-gun hopped away before I could snag him."

FLYING IN ONE EASY LESSON

Why my old punting partner, is that a look of skepticism I discern playing hop-scotch all over your face? Surely you don't question the veracity of what I've just related? Okay, so maybe I lied about the rabbit, but everything else I've related is absolutely true. Ask my brother if you don't believe me.

A Flair for Busting a Flipper

I entered high school in the fall of 1940. I was twelve years old. I had learned four things, three of them well: How to splatter toy soldiers all over the backyard, that I'd never succeed as a thief, girls were not the same as boys (that's the one that would require lots of further study!), and the sheer joy to be found in books.

Entering high school without a clue as to who I really was, still painfully shy, it didn't take long for a couple of incidents to sort of slip a little light into a dim bulb. What is painfully shy? Reddening, if someone even said "hello." Not a delicate shade of pink, more like the deep red one could often see shining brazenly forth from bulbs, strategically placed over porches of certain houses in town. My face and ears burned so badly I'd constantly feel feverish. I lacked confidence in myself and upon attending my first class, I soon found out there was a good and valid reason for that lack.

My first form (freshman) English teacher was a very smart man. He dressed like Mr. Spiffy, too. He was also a snooty old geezer, at least thirty-five! I knew that parts of speech, parsing of sentences, subject, predicate and grammar were no friends of mine which, whenever the opportunity arose, all too often and to the enjoyment of the class, he would point out to me. Oh, yes, English wouldn't rate as good buddy at all. I had to struggle constantly trying to turn him into a friend.

P.E. might provide some release from stress but, all knees and ears, I resembled a beanpole. Football and I would never qualify as chums. Whenever I tried to play the game and got hit, my body didn't bend, it broke! Nonetheless, I needed physical exercise and perhaps some relaxation as bonus. I joined the Leader's Corps, our high school gymnasts team. We exercised and hopefully perfected skills on the rings, parallel bars, mats, high bars and horse.

On one memorable day, I'd been assigned to workout on the horse. You know the horse? That oblong critter stood about five feet off the floor and, securely fastened to its middle, sported two metal loops which the rider could grip with either or both hands in order to perform stunts. Look upon it as an indoor rodeo where the horse, stationary, did not buck but he did throw!

The day's exercise called for a jump on the springboard—this piece of apparatus was situated on the floor by the stuffed bronc's behind—straddle the animal in the air—it wouldn't do to land on one of the loops—tap your hands on its head in passing, land on the mat, roll and, coming up, stand erect in the classic pose. Compared to the skills being exhibited by today's athletes, it was strictly Mickey Mouse. Naturally, on my attempts I kept landing on the bleeding horse and that smarted a tad! Finally, the instructor yelled at me: "Judge, don't just step on the springboard, JUMP on the flaming thing!"

Determined, I took a long run, tried my best to flatten the innocent board and, in the process, flew clean over the bloody horse! Off balance, I hit the mat hard and while rolling, my left arm ended up under my left knee. When the full weight of my clumsy body came down on that arm, guess what? Yep, I'd busted my left flipper! Turning over onto my back, I took a look at the lovely new bow in my catching arm and nearly passed out!

While I lay on a bench in the locker room listening to my arm telling me how much it hurt, the coach phoned Mom and related more good news. When my worried mother hurried in, the coach kindly drove us to the doctor's office in his own car. (No school car, no school ambulance. In those days there was no school nothin'!)

After examining my throbbing arm the doctor, who was a wise old bird, informed me I had a greenstick fracture and therefore he would have to set it.

"What's a greenstick fracture?" mumbled the apprehensive.

He told me it was a lesser break where the bone, while broken, had not quite severed.

"Will it hurt?"

Here is where the croaker played it cute!

"Yes, it will hurt some, after all it is broken. Now I can put you to sleep if you like, then you won't feel a thing. In a few hours...blah, blah, blah."

All the time he was flapping his jaw, he kept moving his hands gently up and down my arm. Suddenly, without bothering to warn me, he exerted pressure and snapped the crooked straight! I didn't even have time to holler before he was starting to wrap a cast around it. To be honest, it hadn't really hurt that bad and, blessings be, I suffered no nausea which is important as you'll soon find out. So, a visit to the doctor, the addition of a dandy white cast to beautify my frame, and another bill my father didn't need. There was no medical insurance for the proletariat in those days. Unfortunately, as I am right-handed, I still got stuck to write the flaming English assignments for my favorite teacher.

Three weeks after my arm was relieved of its cast, said cast having caused my arm to itch like a lovely, inaccessible, case of poison oak, I broke the shrunken thing again! Practice makes perfect and this time I did it right.

Our juvenile crowd was playing a game called, "Relieve-O." She plays like this: two teams, four or five players to a side, one prison outlined in string, bricks, twigs or what have you. Sometimes trouser belts sufficed but not often. A pair of pants suddenly down around your ankles interferes with running. Object of game? Capture enemy by tapping three times on his back with hand (a shillelagh was not couth). He is then a prisoner and confined in the slammer. If team member can set foot in prison prior to three taps on him, prisoner is freed. Much running all over the flaming universe in this game. When all foe members are in the clink, switch sides and start all over. Game ends when exhaustion or twilight settle in. What did you expect, competition for basketball? Besides, it occupies small minds of the energetic.

Remember those quaint little fences? On the verge of capture, turning to run, my knees came up against the wire our neighbor had strung diagonally across his lawn. His was a corner lot. Trying to retain balance, I put my arms out in an effort to brace my fall. Both arms contacted the ground. Weight is on those arms. Left one swears at stupidity of youth and SNAPS!

By the time my hastily summoned mother arrived, I was once again lying on my back staring at a *real valley* in my left arm. No car. Mom had to call a cab. The cabby, a good Joe, carried me out to his cab and away we tootled for a happy visit to the hospital. The doctor took one look at my arm and growled, "This time, my boy, I'm going to have to put you to sleep!"

That's all I remember until, waking up, I saw my Dad standing by the bed. Before either of us spoke a word, I leaned over the edge and heaved into a bucket somebody had prudently placed there. They'd knocked me out with ether and I'm here to tell you that lousy stuff rates as the vilest I've ever experienced. I couldn't stop tossing and, in between heaves, I died. Don't ever let anyone use that horrible muck on you. Pop dug for his wallet again!

One benefit. That cast was much bigger and harder, and even though it itched like crazy, every time my brother and I fought, he'd bark his knuckles on that molded concrete which discouraged him no end. To this day I cannot turn my left arm all the way over. I envy you who wisely learn the lesson the first time.

While we're on the subject of physical disabilities I expect, because it was such a joyous occasion for me, you'll want to know about the trip to the dentist. We'll just take a short hike back to the sixth grade.

I am a "mackerel snapper," a Catholic. That term of endearment was bestowed upon us because, at one time, church edict decreed that Catholics were not to eat meat on Friday. I guess the other side's natural conclusion then was that we would eat fish on that day. Not necessarily true. Macaroni and cheese, or grilled cheese sandwiches accompanied by big bowls of tomato soup or clam chowder ain't all bad. Still, fish can be mighty tasty, and it's loaded with protein and shy on cholesterol.

"Ah, yes, French bread, hot and fresh from the oven. Coleslaw, tangy but not piquant. Chips. Not those anemic shoestrings, but CHIPS! Halibut, beer-battered, fresh and not frozen, add plenty of malt vinegar to baptize the tasty fish and fries. Now there is a feast that will put hair on your chest!"

When my father spoke those words, he was talking to my eighteen-year-old sister. I'm pretty sure she didn't appreciate his little homily. Take my word for it, even though deep fried, it makes for a truly grand meal and to hell with the cholesterol!

Now that you're familiar with the term mackerel snapper, let's go visit the dentist. I spent the first six educational years in Catholic school. Nurses, except for the occasional traveling ones, did not headquarter in our schools. I have to explain something here. In Canada, public and private schools are treated alike. By that I mean taxpayers could designate where they wanted their taxes to go. This meant all schools received a fair share and there was no double taxation like here in the United States. It also meant the quality of teacher, since they were paid the same, stayed high for all schools. I'm not arguing merits, only presenting facts here.

One day the sixth-grade class was informed they would be sent, individually, to dentists up on the boulevard who were going to perform pro bono teeth inspections for the school. Transportation would be via "shank's mare." When my turn came the guy I was sent to see had an office on Yonge Street about a mile-and-a-half distant from our house.

Not overly concerned, I walked from school and reported to his office. I had no trouble finding it because, suspended over the doorway hung a gigantic model of a decaying tooth. Swaying in the breeze, its neon sign messaged, "We don't allow teeth to decay here!"

That flashing sign was definitely sending me a warning. I heeded it not.

Seated uncomfortably in the hot seat, I ah-ah-ahd dutifully when he pried open my mouth and stuck his head in!

"Kid, you got some first teeth here gotta come out. Won't

take a minute."

Not wanting to drop cigarette ashes in my mouth, probably 'cause I'd jump, he laid it aside and picked up what looked like "the jaws of death." Telling me to "open wide," he proceeded to yank out teeth—four of them! He only stopped once for a short breather and a quick drag on the coffin nail. The last of the four didn't want to come, so he lifted me half out of the chair before it finally surrendered and flew across the room. If his nurse had entered right then it would have killed her!

"There you go kid. Hold this gauze up to your mouth to sop up that little bit of blood. It won't hurt for long. Away you go now."

That little bit of blood didn't stop dripping all the way home. Neither did my mouth stop hurting. After Mom recovered from the swollen faced and bloody sight of her son, she fixed some hot water and salt and had me periodically rinse out what was now a quarry. Two aspirin later, an hour of laying on the couch and I began to think I'd live. I get angry, but I don't find it easy to hate. However, in the case of that dentist I was willing to make an exception. I never went near another one until I joined the Air Force and that was only because I was ordered to.

Today? I have had the great good fortune to have been treated over the last thirty-seven years by two superb dentists. I still have all my teeth, too!

• • •

The old geezer pushing English was a firm believer in elocution. Not only were we to write in English, we also had to speak it. He had a cute way of enforcing vocal reporting. Ours was a larger than the norm high school. Accordingly, so was the dandy auditorium. Course requirements included public speaking, shortened to "Speech." The guy with the muscle took his class to the auditorium for those speaking presentations. Each student was required to stand on the stage and, sans microphone, emote for the masses, thirty more victims huddled dejectedly in the front rows. HE, sneakily ensconced himself in the very back row out of sight and yelled for us to step up on the stage, one at a time, and give with the elocution.

I CAN'T HEAR YOU!

Remember me? shy and insecure. Public speaking terrified me. I knew my silly arm cast exposed me, like a terrific draft in the back of my pants. The ogre railed at us constantly to speak up. For him, back there in the next county, to hear us we'd have to bellow. Shy kids don't bellow, they barely vocalize at all. My turn arrived. Oh, Lord, I prayed I wouldn't throw up! Scared? Petrified? Approaching cardiac arrest? They'll all fit. I started off in what I was sure had to be a *roar*. Immediately there came a blast from never-never land.

"YOU WITH THE BROKEN FLIPPER, I CAN'T HEAR YOU!"

Well, right away I started thinking about his Christmas present. A spitting cobra would be nice. Maybe a sackful of starving wildcats. A porcupine slipped under his pillow? How about a rat carrying fleas loaded with Bubonic plague? Not to fret, four weeks still remained to work it out ere Santa's visit.

I passed his class by the skin of my teeth and hated every minute of it. When I became a teacher, I vowed never, ever would

I humiliate one of my students like that; pray, God, I never did.

A little postscript here: To be honest I actually learned some things from him, not the least of which is the importance of being able, standing on the firing line, to verbally communicate to large groups. I also added immeasurably to that skill in college while absorbing from a wise and compassionate professor. So you see, it takes all sorts and something needed can be learned from each.

• • •

I latched onto a new job the summer of my freshman year. Still operating my bicycle, I delivered for Newton's Delicatessen located on Bayview Avenue. Specialties: fresh cooked roast beef, pork or ham, whole or by the slice; sausage rolls, steak and kidney pies, regular beef and pork pies; pumpernickel breads, hard and soft rolls; fresh sausage: link or patty, to cook yourself; pickles, pickled onions, monstrous dills, relishes. The aromas emanating from that heavenly kitchen would start a sphinx to drooling. A guy could fall facedown among all those goodies and not come up for a week!

My hours read: one to six, Monday through Friday and all day Saturday. I received six dollars a week for my labors. Occasionally, upon receipt of a large delivery, a customer would tender a tip. It wouldn't be large, nor often. The folks of my day had yet to be coerced into all that tipping jazz and a dime still meant a fair amount of money.

The Newton's, husband and wife, were wonderful people. Honest, hard-working, they claimed England as place of birth and Canada as home. I really liked them and, as is so often the case with the industrious, they stood on their own two feet, accepting responsibility for actions and welfare. Don't you think that the examples set, not only by your parents but by those you work with tend to help form a few of your own? I owe the Newton's a lot.

At closing on Saturday night, as Mrs. Newton would be horrified if her pies and sausage rolls weren't fresh, all unsold items of that nature would be divided among the help. The married carried home the choicest items as was only fair, but I never had to go home empty. Sometimes I'd make out like a bandit: half a dozen rolls, several meat pies, six sausage rolls, slices of cold meat (none of that processed gunk we get stuck with today!), and pickles.

Unloading the bike's carrier, I'd holler to Mom, "I've got four pies, half a dozen rolls, cold meat and five sausage rolls. Let's stuff our gizzards!"

Think you've got me don't you! I started out with six of those scrumptious sausage delights didn't I? Aha, but five members made up the Judge family. Fairness is all. If I'd walked into the house with six of those little beauties, there'd have been one extra. A decree would, reluctantly, be whispered, "Jack brought them here to our loving abode, he shall have the sixth one."

Sure, and busy scoffing it down, I'd still have to face four pairs of accusing eyes. Anxious to spare them cruel pain, I ate the extra one on the way home!

Two items tickled my memory about that summer, one was a surprise, the other an accomplishment. The one that dumfounded was the discovery at the ripe old age of thirteen that all mature ladies were not necessarily feminine, demure and delicate.

On a summer afternoon, late in the day, and carefully carrying a large deli delivery, I knocked on an apartment door. The location was over on the posh side of town in a cul-de-sac where flowers and shrubs were lovingly cared for. The area smelled of money. When the door opened, I found myself gawking at a rather disheveled lady still attired in her night clothes who, before a word was spoken, promptly belched in my face!

"Ya wanna come in kid?"

In one flaming hurry, I thrust her order into her arms, mumbled an inane adolescent excuse and got the flitsy-flew outa there. Looking back, I bet I've done her a disservice. There was a war on. For all I knew, she could have been Rosie the Riveter and worked on the graveyard shift. Snap judgments will do you in every time.

Delivering groceries to homes via bicycle is not that exciting. What's to fire up the blood? Pump, pump, knock, knock, "Your order has arrived, ma'am." Pump, pump, knock, knock, "Your Newton's delivery is here, sir." Pump, pump, knock…blah, blah, blah! I was bored out of my socks so I taught myself to whistle like a bleeding canary. I have no idea how many miles of—pump,

pump—it took, but by the end of the summer I'd learned to warble and, if I do say so myself, I do it quite well. Elmo Tanner and his *Heartaches* had nothing on me!

I relax myself a great deal when whistling and do it unconsciously. Fortunately, after sixty years of puckering and blowing, nobody has clobbered me yet. Well, there was the time I inadvertently started to whistle in church, right smack during the sermon, too. Mollie-O's elbow sunk my floating rib and put the kibosh on that! It has also been my great good fortune not to decide on the sailor's life. I have it on reliable authority, those who ply the briny consider whistling a terrible hex and anyone caught doing it is immediately thrown overboard!

• • •

Still a survivor, now in the second form (sophomore) at Northern Vocational High School, I continued to read and at the end of summer almost looked forward to classes.

I have a habit when reaching a not necessarily exciting, but an unbelievable section in a book. I hurry to the loo for a quick visit and then, so as not to be interrupted with mundane matters, I make a large sandwich before diving back into the story. How are you supposed to recognize an unbelievable section? Would you believe I just made myself a Dagwood and, to offer it company, only the tiniest of libations.

If you and I had been classmates and competing for the title of "Nerd" of the year, this next little episode will explain why nary a single vote would have been cast your way. To this day I cannot believe I was so unaware.

A vocational high school, in Toronto, in addition to providing matriculation courses also offered classes in: auto mechanics, art, woodworking, drafting, sheet metal and electricity to mention but a few. I desired to acquire knowledge about radio so I opted for electricity as one of my electives. Today in my golden years I can't help but feel sorry for those students who swear no teacher ever inspired or uplifted them. I am most grateful to the teachers who aided me and I've had a goodly number of my students tell me I'd also done it for them. That, after a career in teaching, has been my greatest reward.

I'd like to tell you a bit about my electricity instructor. What he did is not really earth shaking; in reality, by being observant he was only doing his duty. But you have no idea how that observance changed my life. His name was Mr. Chellacombe. It has been over sixty years since I first met him and heard his name. I shall never forget it.

You must remember, I was in my tenth year of school attendance. Parked in the classroom, and at the movies, I always sat in the front row. Mr. Chellacombe's desk sat on a raised dais at the front of the room. There were many facts and formulas to learn during his course and each day he would write some of them on the chalkboard, following which he'd allow us time to copy them in our notebooks. Thinking there was absolutely nothing unusual about it, I'd rise from my desk, walk around behind his and, pencil and book in hand, copy the notes from the board.

One day he asked me to remain after class and gently inquired if I had a problem with my eyes?

"Heck, no," I replied.

"Why do you walk behind my desk to copy the notes then?"

Are you ready? "Because I can't see the writing clearly, sir."

I was beginning to get a tad bit nervous. You know, like when you've done nothing wrong and yet guilt is taking whacks at your conscience. He sent me up to see the school nurse (public high schools retained them full time) for an eye check. Now I truly was nervous, check that, how about scared and you can throw in petrified, too! Knees shaking, voice quivering (I couldn't shake the notion I'd done something wrong), I tried to read the chart. I got the big "E" and, definitely blurred, the "B" and "C". That's all folks. I was blind as a near-sighted bat! My whole world came crashing down. I wasn't exactly known as the second form's "Handsome Jack." And soon they'd be calling me "four-eyes!" I really didn't need that.

I know what you're dying to ask: How, by all the nitwits in creation, had I reached my second year of high school without someone noticing I couldn't see? A: Eyes were not checked yearly in the schools I attended. Today students are examined every year, starting in kindergarten. B: No TV, thus, it wasn't necessary to *see* in order to *listen* to the radio. C: Attendance at movies occurred at Saturday afternoon matinees and my parents did not attend those with us. D: My friends were just as dumb as the guy who's talking, and never thought to ask why I always sat in the front row! E: I knew I was considered to be stand-offish because I never said "Hi" to friends until they were directly in front of me; the reason for that—obvious, but not to me—I flaming well didn't recognize them from a distance! F: As it turned out I was near-sighted which did not interfere with my ability to read.

No matter how many letters of the alphabet I capitalize, for me to grope through life like a bleeding mole all those years remains absolutely incredible, doesn't it? Dad scheduled an appointment with an optometrist. Dreading the unknown I reluctantly reported for an exam. After performing all his tests the doctor whistled and said, "Young man, until you get your glasses, don't you dare walk across an intersection by yourself!" Oh, boy, now that was good news.

Going to pick up my cheaters on the appointed day, I was still mopey and down in the dumps. I put the blasted things on and, after Doc adjusted them, I tested the ugly buggers by reading his crummy chart. He happied out at the results and, grinning all over his mush as doctors are wont to do when the patient lives, he sent me on my way.

I opened his office door, stepped into the street and beheld a miracle! For the first time in my life: *I could read the billboards from a distance. I could actually distinguish individual leaves on trees. I could read license plates on passing cars. From two blocks away, I could tell boys from girls. Girls are lots better to look at!* I could even …! The first time I was called "four-eyes," I laughed. Now you know why I loved Mr. Chellacombe and why I've never forgotten his name. Poor Pop, he dug deep into his wallet again.

• • •

Actually, my life took a definite turn for the better in my sophomore year. I had learned how to form a sentence or two, and even though my favorite instructor was also teaching the next level he lightened up; on a few days he even forgot to yell at me. Just as well, no way I'd ever be able to save the needed bread to buy him a pregnant spitting cobra!

Now that I could see, I began to pay attention to our football team, and I was finally having fun at school. There was a fellow in my history class who always wore a porkpie hat. He also smoked a pipe. He was an old beaver, at least eighteen, and we all thought he was Mr. Great. Scuttlebutt inferred he was a perennial student and would probably attend high school for the rest of his life. Regardless, he was a lot of fun and affected professorial manner-isms which made us laugh. He rated class leader, by right of age if not wisdom, when we attended our school football games. His was always the first voice one heard roaring out our battle cry:

"Pieces of eight, pieces of eight,
Pieces of nine and ten.
Knock 'em down, then pick 'em up,
And we'll knock 'em down again."

We loved that little gem and when the frenzy of the game increased we'd yell ourselves silly. Surprise, surprise, that year Northern Vocational won the city football championship and in doing so we walloped our hated rival, North Toronto. God is good!

At those games, indeed any of our sporting events, we flaunted our school colors and, using the form of ribbons, wore them pinned bravely to shirts or blouses. NVHS displayed the colors blue and gold.

At one of our games a low-life forayer (don't look at me!) went on a raid that was to have unforeseen consequences. He and his band of merry men snuck over to the enemy's side of the field, ripped their school colors from a member of the fair sex, and set fire to them. That dastardly deed was akin to setting fire to the flag; it doesn't go unchallenged. Before long, tiny little fires were spring-ing up all over the flaming stadium. Well, as you can imagine, feel-ings were hurt, blows were struck, teeth removed. The sporting event turned into a lovely donnybrook! I spent the whole afternoon hollering, "Hey, whoa guy, you wouldn't hit a fella wearing glass-es, would you?"

After that, each school's rooters were ordered to stay on their own side of the field. We were put on the honor system which we proudly obeyed as, *cops at both ends of the stadium enforced it*. I'll bet you never did anything like that at your high school football games!

To think, Northern Vocational rightfully wore the crown, "city champs." What shall we do to celebrate? Victory day plus one, school instruction was proceeding at its normal pace. After all, education is important and students must study. Eagerly trying to embrace an elusive algebra problem, I heard a noise emanating from out in the hall which seemed to be growing louder. Suddenly, the classroom door was flung open and in marched a long conga line lustily chanting, "Pieces of eight, pieces of eight, pieces of …(You've already been subjected to the rest of this so I'll spare you any further suffering!)

Around the room marched a never-ending line interspersed with the beating of drums, tootling of licorice sticks and the blowing of trumpets. The furor mounted. What does a patriot do when called upon? Why, we all reported for duty. The conga line g-r-e-w. Classrooms, neglected, grew oh, so, lonely. By and by the whole student body had formed one humongous line, which soon looked like a dangerous reptile hunting for prey. What next?

Open the outside doors. Let the snake out! Away we went, still chanting, still dancing. Traffic on the main drag, both ways, came to a standstill. Oh, look, there's a pretty tree-lined side street beckoning to the champs, let's parade our way up it. Well for heaven's sake, here we all are coiling happily around North Toronto High School, now there's a surprise! Strike up our wonderful band.

"Hi, guys, care to listen to a *real* battle cry? It goes like this, Pieces …."

Captured the scene? Some of the North Torontonians became a touch irked. Must have been something we said or perhaps we might have been a wee bit off key. Nothing serious happened, a shove here, a push there and one of the North Toronto fellows ended up wearing one of our drums, but it was really just good clean fun. After awhile, things settled down and we dispersed. How many times can one holler that dumb "pieces" thing anyway?

That spontaneous happening took place over sixty years ago. It is as clear in my mind today as 'twas then. Wow, what fun we'd had!

• • •

I'd learned teachers were compassionate and understanding. Surely, they weren't also human? Consider my sheet metal instructor. He was a big fella and stern, sort of an Edward G. Robinson in extra large. His size intimidated, yet he was not mean. I never heard him raise his voice or saw him deck a smart mouth. He didn't have to, one of his glacial stares would give any and all loose-lips lockjaw in a hurry. Call him a gentle giant who smoked cigars and could crush metal in one hand. If you can get a picture of a pachyderm ponderously crossing over the Alps, yo Hannibal astride, he'd be the elephant! I have faithfully drawn and presented to you that accurate description of him only because of what follows.

Currently, schools are constantly in need of money. It was no different in my day. Everyone wants the *best education* for their eager learners. Trouble is when it comes time to open the wallet, folks have neglected to memorize the blamed code needed to unlock that old leather. You won't care what I think, but for my money supporting schools by levying property taxes isn't only the worst way imaginable, it is also extremely unfair. Try an income tax.

From time to time the teaching staff at my alma mater, Northern Vocational, would put on plays or musicals for the community. (There would be no additional recompense for the extra time required to rehearse and then present such programs either. What, ho, seems like nothing really changes!) Admission would be charged and the performances, including matinees for the student body, ran for three days. I suspect the majority of the collected moola went for sports activities and equipment just as it does today.

Anyway, the gala which I remember best was a musical. To my wondering eye-glassed eyes, who do you suppose I spotted on the stage? Dressed in pirate's costume, cavorting like a gazelle chasing butterflies and singing, even though the hit song was "Pieces of Eight," like—I kid you not—Luciano Pavarotti, I beheld—I must confess in complete amazement—our own, Mr. Extra Large! The star of the show, he brought down the house and was called back for three encores! What's more, he was having fun.

Next day, back in class and looming familiarly over us, behold our reserved, straight ahead guy. Can you beat it, *a teacher with all that talent!*

• • •

I stepped into another job the summer of my sophomore year. I'd left Newton's Deli only because of the hours. My new job, working for a fruit market, required my services six full days a week, 8 A.M. to 6 P.M. and for my labors I was paid the munificent sum of eleven dollars a week. I was also kindly allowed to kill myself with work as, not only did I still deliver via bicycle, I helped out in the store.

In the *good old days*, Mom and Pop fruit markets were vastly different from say—a modern Fred Meyer. For one thing, items sold would be only varieties of fruit and vegetables. For another, you, dear customer, would not be allowed to handle the produce. No indeedy. I'll bet you've heard the oldy, "Hey, mistah, no squeeza da tomats, bananas, or da grapes. You wanna squeeza da goods, you squeeza da coconuts!"

Ask proprietors for what you desire, even little old me, and you may receive. I say "may" for a reason.

In 1942, World War II in Europe had heated up. In the Pacific, at Guadalcanal and Midway, Japan would learn the error of her ways. Items taken for granted for years, were now either scarce or going to the military. Importing of course had been severely curtailed; fruit not grown in Canada, such as bananas and oranges brought good prices. If one could obtain them at all, one would trill, "It's a good day for havin' a...dah da dah da dah," all the way home. The neighbors would smile, applaud generously, and cheer your good fortune. You still wouldn't give them any!

The store was owned by an older Italian lady and operated by her son. He had suffered polio as a child leaving him with a permanent limp and the military had rated him 4F. Very early in the mornings, he would drive to the wholesale market and be back at the store ready to unload when I showed up for work. Sometimes he'd luck out and latch onto a crate or two of strawberries or rasp- berries, maybe he'd make the raise on some *oranges*, even *bananas*. Those items were immediately taken to the basement where they underwent a quick transformation. "Transformation?" you ask. Perhaps transfer would be a better choice of word. Take strawberries. A crate would hold twelve pints. These, oh, so care- fully found themselves taking up space on a clean tarp, sort of rolling loose you might say. By hand, the boss and I loosely refilled the empty pint boxes. All berries back in containers, voilà, we now counted thirteen, maybe fourteen boxes. Same procedure for rasp- berries. Got the idea?

Oranges (as stated, rare) rested on top of potato sacks. Bananas (rarer) hung by their stalk from a rafter. A customer enters the store and asks for a pound of potatoes, two onions, celery, one bunch each, radish and green onions and a cabbage. Momma picks and bags everything, totals bill, accepts cash, arrivederci's customer and turns to greet new arrival. This one is a regular and a *good* cus- tomer. Once they make their wants known, Momma, *sotto voce*, asks, "You mebbe like a few oranges?"

Not yes, but hell yes! Momma takes bag, hustles her creaky body to the basement, drops three oranges in the sack, returns, col- lects loot and away goes the happy regular, drinking in the delight- ful aroma of fresh oranges.

I am not allowed to dispense those special goodies!

Door bell jangles. In comes a *terrific* customer, Momma would marry him if he'd only ditch his wife. Oranges and bananas go home with him!

Most items were not sold by the pound, only by quantity, three here, four there and Momma or Sonny, even me, picked the items out. You got a wilted lettuce, a bruised onion, scruffy celery? Tough. War is hell!

I truly slaved that summer. One Saturday—a fortunate raise on bananas day—close to the closing hour, and when I was one breath away from collapse, Momma turned to me and said, "You gooda boy, you worka hard."

So saying, she walked over to the garbage pail, reached a

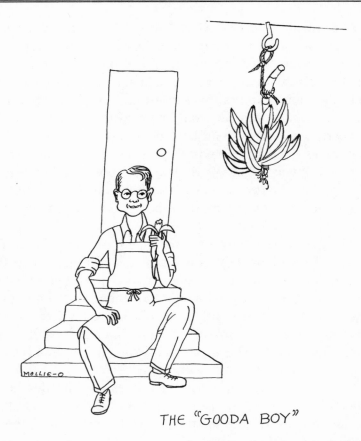

THE "GOODA BOY"

skinny arm in and hauled out a half-rotten banana. Then she handed it to me and urged, "Yes, you gooda boy, you cut offa da badda part an' a-you eata da rest."

Ma was nothing if not frugal! Well, I have to tell you, I became so overcome with her generosity tears just naturally furrowed my cheeks. Overwhelmed by her philanthropy, trying to hold back her own tears, she pushed open the kitchen door and betook her kindly self off to prepare Sonny's dinner.

"Send down your sky hook, Lord, I'm climbing my way to heaven," said I, in an inner but loud voice, and with a slow burn beginning to blister the back of my neck I glanced at the rotten fruit in my hand, tossed it back in the garbage from whence it came, wiped my mitt on my apron, went to the basement and chose the biggest flaming banana left on the stalk. I then plunked myself on the stairs and proceeded to enjoy every sensuous bite; still just a kid, I lacked the guts to go up and toss the peel onto her kitchen floor!

Oh, boy, that was a terrific summer.

• • •

Well just looky here, in the fall of 1942 there I was a new member of the third form. Better yet, Juniors were not perceived as dunderheads. In truth, I no longer was. Why, I even understood logarithms.

There is nothing untoward to relate about my junior year except that I made a decision that could have turned out to be the biggest mistake of my life! Here's how it played out.

At long last I felt comfortable in school. Either study had become easier or I'd become smarter. No fanfare here, I hadn't made the dean's list, other than perhaps that of most wanted, but learning was no longer a headache a day. Once in a long while I even raised my hand voluntarily, eager to *answer* first. I hope you've noticed we're talking real progress here!

Previously I stated I'd a desire to learn about radio: announcing as well as the fundamental workings of such. My courses in electricity, now advanced, did not include the study of radio. Upon reaching the second semester of my junior year, I requested an appointment with my instructor for after school. I then inquired if there would be any lessons on radio during the last half of this year or during the next, my last year of high school?

"There will be no instruction at all," was the answer.

The only way I could get that kind of training would be by correspondence or attendance at a commercial school. Those schools, listed as business establishments, demanded funds to pay for all desired training; if I were going to follow that route, a job had to be the first priority, registration for classes the second. Still think you're a dim bulb in a forest of floodlights? Read on.

With a year-and-a-half to go before graduation, and but the one option open to acquire what I desired as far as my dimwitted brain could see, I quit high school. Ah, yes, first I'd get a *good paying job* and then, radio school, look out! The logic was okay, the plan was flawed. Notwithstanding they were the war years, youths, lacking skills and non-graduated, ex-students—I believe they're called dropouts today—were not offered plum jobs. I ended up toiling as an office boy in the Planning Department of the Toronto City Hall. I'd just turned fifteen.

Good news—bad news. I liked the work. It was interesting but not killing. My title: Junior white collar worker in charge of messages (read that, gopher responsible for fetching and carrying)! Hours? Eight to five Monday through Friday, eight to noon on Saturday. Salary? Playfully called "coin of the realm" it amounted to thirty-two dollars every two weeks. Of that thirty-two: twelve went for room and board—a growing lad still, I ate a lot of the folks' groceries—twelve more went for war bonds. What can I say, I was patriotic. Bob and I were also eight months away from joining the Royal Canadian Air Cadets. Income tax snatched two clams. With the remaining six bucks I paid for transportation to work on the good old TTC, new clothes, entertainment, books and movies. Fortunately, I was still scared of girls and wasn't dating. Naturally that was not to last.

So long to radio school!

The city hall rated *old*: long, dimly-lit corridors, walnut trim by the truckload, hardwood floors, no garish fluorescent lights, thick, half-glass doors. Full of character, albeit somber, she befitted an edifice from which a city, rich in history, was governed. I loved the richness and the history and I could feel those grand old halls relating daring deeds to me as I sped from office to office, fetching and carrying. Do you like history? We'll remain friends if you don't, but the quiet, secluded champagne dinner for four (Mollie-O, you, me, and whoever) is out!

Each department fielded one or more office boys or girls. As a group we became close-knit. None of us were flush so our pleasures necessarily had to be inexpensive and simple: hayrides, barn dances, swimming parties. Simple or no, we had a flaming ball dancing on straw-strewn barn floors when the phonograph excelled while playing the records of Tommy Dorsey, Guy Lombardo or

Glenn Miller. Great times. No booze! Most of us were too young. Besides, we couldn't afford it anyway. Thank God, drugs were not readily available or a problem, pot was something your mother used to cook in! I vowed I wouldn't lecture but, oh, yeah, take the pushers of today and string them up by their thumbs. Be merciful, cut 'em down in a month!

Cigarettes were a different matter. War is stressful. Everybody smoked and, at sixteen, for the dumbest reason imaginable, I reached out and lit up. The damn things were cheap and I grew so tired of either being asked for or offered one, I climbed aboard that "coffin nail express." I rode that killing train for thirty years before I finally worked up the guts to jump off!

The Canadian Air Cadets, a prelude to the actual air force, accepted Bob and me when we reached sixteen; let me explain: we were all caught up in an almighty fervor to knock hell out of Hitler and his lousy Nazis! Canada had already suffered the catastrophe of Dieppe. Our soldiers, sailors and airmen were dying all over the world. Young or no, who wouldn't want to do something about that? We accomplished very little as cadets: parades, sharp uniforms, admiring glances from the female set, the voicing of "up yours mein fuhrer!" That's it; however, that brief experience foretold of things to come.

• • •

June, 1945. Bob, Mom and I entrained for California. I was sorry to leave city, friends and home. I'd miss my old haunts: the St. Lawrence Market, that heavenly haven for, fresh from the farm, bounty. I'd miss the pool hall, and ferry trips to the islands across from Toronto. I'd miss picnics. Yet, at seventeen, I was also terribly excited. Adventure beckoned. So did my future.

If, as has been theorized by shrinks who undoubtedly know, when first we arrive bare-bottomed and squalling our minds are clear and unmarked, like tombstones waiting to meet the guy with the chisel, what momentous experiences over the last sixteen years have been hammered into my *tabula rasa*? One: I'd given up a life of crime. Two: I'd practiced breaking my arm until I got it right.

Three: I could ride a bicycle—no hands! Four: I had discovered that words in books, used in quantity but chosen for quality, could transport the reader all over the world and bring him back unscathed—but not untouched. Chisel that one deep! Five: I could warble when I whistled. Never mind, I'll add that one myself. Six: And, I could also …?

Ah, well, I was heading for "Californy." If I don't chip my *tabula* on the way there's still plenty of room left on it to etch in a line or two.

Pa and Petunia

*R*egistering in degrees Fahrenheit, the thermometer read *forty-eight below zero!* Shivering violently, all I could think of was that silly saying: "Key-key-key-rist it's cold!" cried the Key bird.

"You, you, you, bet it is!" wailed the You bird.

We'd finally fastened the heater's twelve inch diameter canvas tubes to the two Pratt and Whitney engines of our ski-shod United States Air Force C-47, and the roaring, gasoline-fed motor of the Herman Nelson portable heater was blowing a steady stream of very hot air over both frigid engines, so hot you couldn't hold your bare hand in it. That welcome heat would soon warm the sludged engine oil enough to allow the reluctant propellers to move cylinder pistons which, sparked in turn, would fire and cough the motors into life. Even in sub-zero temperatures the oil wouldn't freeze, but it purely wasn't in a flowing mood, either. No movement of oil—no turning of props. No turning of props—no starting of engines. No starting of engines—no flying of plane. No flying of plane and...walking wasn't crowded! The Air Force seldom walked in Alaska!

Hermy, vintage 1949, measuring about five feet long, four feet high and three feet wide, mounted on a trailer frame resting on truck tires, stood some six feet off the ground. Still shaking, like an Eskimo who'd just thrown his last harpoon at a rapidly advancing polar bear—and missed, I'd moved closer to the engine for warmth and had noticed that the heater's gas gauge called for tank refilling. Not daring to turn its motor off, I stuck a funnel into the tank mouth, lifted a full can of gas, stood on tip-toes and proceeded to pour Hermy's life blood into his nearly empty tank. I could not control my shivering and some of the petrol spilled onto the hot engine. SWOOSH, the heater fired and then flamed, like ignition on a space rocket! Panicked, visions of Hermy blowing himself through the hangar doors and taking me with him, I yelled to the two guys perched comfortably atop the warming engines—tending to the hot tubes—to take cover, and in a pure funk I threw the half-empty gas can into a snowbank and dove for the deck.

Prone on the snow covered tarmac, waiting for the sound of Gabriel's horn and the sudden one way trip to wherever I was going, my arms covering my head and an icicle up my nose, two thoughts raced through my mind in those desperate seconds. What was a skinny kid from Toronto, Canada, doing freezing his buns off serving in the U.S. Air Force in, oh-so-cold, Fairbanks, Alaska? And, compounding that question, my rating was radio mechanic not engine jockey, how come I'd let myself get talked into helping out in an operation I knew absolutely nothing about?

The Judge luck held. Good old Hermy, well aware he could blow up anytime, decided to let the surplus gas and old grease coating his frame, burn just long enough for a quick cleansing of his nether parts before he snuffed himself out. As a result of his generosity, you are about to discover why that skinny kid was in the military service in the first place.

HERMY WENT SWOOSH !

• • •

Have you experienced the hustle and bustle, fuss and furor of big city life? If so, haven't you often yearned for blessed country quiet where frogs sing each morning, birds sing all day and train whistles mourn from afar?

My home—as you are aware, being a quaint little hamlet named Toronto in Ontario, Canada—was, in 1945 already blossoming and bulging. Today, though she has a smooth complexion and a sweet face, TO—as the natives call her—has, imitating a fat lady's waddle, become a big spread. The old city hall is still there. Surrounded and dwarfed now by much taller buildings, she looks for all the world like an orphan sitting unhappily in the middle of a gala for the upper crust! Nothing remains the same.

Mom did not care for TO's winters. Come to think of it she

wasn't wild about the summers either. Mother's family lived in the Golden State. Where, in the soothing winters, El Sol shone warm and soft over fragrant orange groves. Mom, desiring to sniff citrus blossoms on a permanent basis added further lyrics to her ode of persuasion and sang, "Farewell cacophony and hello tranquillity." Pop, an adventurer from head to toenails, dug in his heels and trilled back, "Absolutely, once and for all, and for ever-more—NO!"

Once upon a time, some fifty miles east of Los Angeles, there resided another delightful little hamlet. Nestled close to the foothills and named, Yucaipa, an Indian name meaning "Evergreen Valley" it was famed for its orange and walnut groves, apples, chicken and turkey farms, and for being located a rock throw away from Beaumont city where resided "Gorgeous George" the wrestler of television fame in the late 40's. The Judges took up residence in 1946. That was one of Mom's better ideas!

I waved as he flew by. "Whoa, you bloody big goof!" Pop gasped, while Petunia, our sweet-natured Guernsey yearling—on her third circuit and thoroughly enjoying freedom—thundered back into the walnut grove. Dust covered and hanging grimly if haplessly to her fly swatter, my one hundred and thirty-five pound old man reappeared, transformed into a hollering, rapidly diminishing tail on a flying, four-footed kite. Petunia, had unslammered her adventurous self again! Keep the nose blowers handy; you're going to get all choked up as I trot out an explanation. I know I shed many a tear!

Assuredly, sons should listen to their mothers, *most of the time*. At home in Yucaipa, California, on furlough from the U.S. Air Force, I was trying to forget bugle calls, K.P. and passing in review. Having purchased a small amount of acreage, we'd built our home there in 1946. My mother, always looking for a way to save or make a buck, was unloading her current "real winner" idea in my doubtful ears. "Why don't you buy a heifer calf? Father and I will raise her while you're away. When she matures we will have her bred, and later we'll sell her calf and make a few potatoes. There's no way you can lose." Wanta bet?

Off we tootled to a livestock auction yard. What a lucky, happy day. Five bucks purchased an adorable one-week-old Guernsey calf.

It's time to haul out your calculator and start keeping track of costs.

Being learned city folk we knew to plan ahead, right? Wrong! By now, Baby (soon to be named Petunia) had been transported to her new abode—which of course didn't exist. In our haste to purchase, we'd forgotten the need for animal lodgings. Tethering Miss Petunia to a tree, we tossed her some grass and sat down, better late than never, to plan her dwelling. *She didn't eat the grass; she didn't eat anything.* She did bellyache. Are you getting the picture? Correct, the poor wee calf was only a week old, and she had to have milk.

Away to the feed store. After begging for learned advice, we bought a half-gallon feed bottle and a nipple for same, a pail, and for her future, a bale of alfalfa. Total: eight bucks. Away to the lumberyard. Empty the wallet for two-by-fours—too many to count—nails, hinges and one-by-eights; metal roofing; four-by-four posts and a post hole digger; two fifty-foot rolls of four-by-six-inch wire fencing; staples and screws for the hinges. Tote it home in a new truck? Nay, they delivered the whole flaming load to Der Dumbkoff Acres for free. Total: three Jackson's and two Washington's in 1946 bucks.

Just about then Petunia, a tad bit peckish, was loudly verbalizing same to all and sundry. Away to the dairy for some raw milk. In her first week of life she had already tapped her mom for the much needed colostrum which wards off infection and disease. Haste to the kitchen and warm the milk. Fill and stopper the bottle, insert in calf's yawp. Peace and quiet. Thank you Lord.

Furlough time escaping, I had to construct bawler's quarters pronto. At last, tools carefully hung, the pen a flaming work of art, Petunia was happy. Mother was happy. Father was happy. Son was broke! And I'd barely enough leave time left to wean calf from bottle to pail. How does one accomplish this? Easy: take away her bottle, fill pail, place pail before calf and command her to drink. Petunia, mooing plaintively, ignores contents and the milk soured. Next, she kicked the pail of milk all over kind feeder's boots. Good-bye milk, hello loud, unladylike, Guernsey bellowing. What to try now? Another flying trip to the dairy for a grand suggestion, "Stuff Petoonie's head into another pail of hundred proof and hold until, desperate for air, calf will open mouth to breathe, in the process she will also drink." Piece of cake. I hurry home, eager to try terrific suggestion. Petunia, her head in pail, blew, snorted, bucked and bashed the pail which kindly scraped most of the skin off my left shin!

Might reinforcements be needed? I commandeered half of the neighborhood to help hold submerged head of the recalcitrant one in bucket. Seven minutes later: gurgle, gurgle, glug, and hallelujah—swallow! Chalk up one each weaned Petunia.

A limping airman (me) boarded a Greyhound for the new base in Illinois where, soon busy with his studies, the Guernsey's continued progress is relayed via mailed photos. By grab, the little sucker grew bigger and prettier with every letter.

All too soon Petunia approached cowhood. Water, scarce and not to be wasted on our tiny homestead, made growing of pasture costly and unrealistic. Consequently, expensive grain, alfalfa and hay had to be purchased. You won't care, but in 1948 the Air Force didn't pay large in remunerative bread to Pfc.'s; more like a stale crust. Petunia, being a growing heifer, chomped off a lot of that crust! This didn't leave much of the monthly stipend for foolish pursuits like movies, eating off base, cigarettes and other wasteful things I wished to enjoy. However, radio school was hard and my head was thick, so more of my time went to studies anyway.

I'm not going to dwell much on my eleven month schooling, except for *that* weekend when two good buddies and I went to the big city. Enjoying the simple things in life, we went to a lovely little park in St. Louis (the name of which escapes me after fifty years), rented a canoe, rowed happily to the middle of a charming little lake and, not being sensible sailors, promptly overturned the cantankerous beast, ending up, class A uniform clad, in the drink! From there, leaving three watery trails from three sopping drips we boarded and rode a streetcar until spotting a Chinese laundry. Having generously washed the floor of the car for free and disembarking, we invaded the laundry and sat, miserably wrapped in Wa Chang towels, while the chortling owner dried and pressed shirts, socks, skivvies, uniforms and caps.

Neither will I mention highs I experienced attending the trans-

DRIP OF THE WEEK

mitter section of school. I simply could not force understanding of how signals are sent into my thick skull. Where others devoted a normal after class hour of study to electronic machinations, I threw in three. I passed by the skin of my teeth. Sweating and grateful, I headed off to vacuum tubes. I entered the classroom filled with trepidation after what "transmitters" had done to me, but the flaming course was a piece of cake. In fact I did so well the instructor asked me if, after graduation, I would be willing to stay on at Scott Field and *teach* the subject to their future trainees. Don't ask me to explain it!

• • •

Almost a year had passed. I'd graduated a bonafide radio mechanic, and once again on furlough I headed for Yucaipa before proceeding to my next assignment. Petunia—now fully petaled—was positively blooming. She was really a sweet young heifer with a penchant for sliced bread and from our point of view had but one bad habit. Her life on the outside purely beat life on the inside! Accordingly, even though her quarters had been masterfully built, she slipped her shackles, figuratively speaking, with ease and took to roaming thither and yon—through the flower garden, sampling on the way; through the vegetable garden, ditto the sampling; over the front and back lawns leaving definite clues, and thence on into the neighbor's walnut grove, her absolute favorite hoof-kicking and galloping place.

Having hoofed full circle we are now back to the tail of the flaming kite. Unbelievably, my father used to get a touch irked when Petunia went AWOL. Cruel comments about calf pen builders were cast freely upon the wind, even some four letter words. That day's event was but another in a long line of "flaming cow bust-outs," which brings us to the point of diminishing returns. Why the old man thought his one hundred and thirty-five pounds could restrain the cow's five hundred, shall forever remain unclear. Suffice to say, thought it he did, but do it he didn't. By this time I was laughing so hard I could barely move and my staggering feet were a long way from catching up. From tear-filled eyes three tree rows away, it seemed that a pair of legs, separated by a skinny butt, had become one with a large bovine behind! Convulsing still, I wobbled up to *their* tree in time to hear a gentle "moo," while standing nose to nose—the trunk in between—Petunia licked my father's face!

Huffing and puffing like a submarine blowing ballast tanks, still holding on to her tail, my father snarled at me to hold her. Reaching down, he picked up a loose tree branch, wound up and took a mighty swing at L'il Petoonie. Off balance and wheezing, he missed by an acre, spun around and fell flat on his butt! With tears of joy pouring down my face, I let her go and collapsed helplessly against a tree of my own. I'd never laughed so hard in my life.

PA AND PETUNIA

You got it. During that slight interlude the mooing one, deciding to go stoke up on dessert in the vegetable garden, split. Having
followed the flying duo, Mom, prying her laughing self off her own
tree, checked on puffing Pop, then told me to administer CPR and
she would collect Written on the Wind. How to calmly corral the
errant one? Simple: two thick slices of rye waved enticingly under
our bovine's nose would do it every time; until her next self-admin-
istered three-day pass. I'd checked into my new base in Fairbanks,
Alaska by that time. There—pre-Korea—it was calm and peaceful
with nary a cow in sight!

While my nose became an Alaskan icicle and I caught my first
glimpse of moose, caribou, black bear and polar bear, Mom wrote
that they'd had to sell Petunia. Her sojourns were becoming too
costly and their Geritol blood wasn't pumping fast enough to keep

up with the nomadic one's flying feet. Not to worry, the guy who bought her lucked out and also became the recipient of a lovely soft-eyed calf.

Motherhood slowed Petunia's dancing feet and, giving only an occasional plaintive moo for her beloved walnut grove, she decided to stay home and raise her young but sedentary Guernsey.

Not bad huh? Best of all she only cost me about three hundred bucks!

• • •

I can't tell you how pleased I am you decided to take this trip with me. Help yourself to the thermos of coffee and don't be shy about using the pillow, backsides grow numb sitting on flat boards and we've a long way to go. Soon as I pole us around this oxbow bend, I'll lay out my life in the Air Force. Never can tell, you might end up eager to enlist, too!

You're Going to Love the Air Force

S o okay, why did a Canuck enlist in the United States Air Force in the first place?

My cautious father informed the clan that before he'd give in to Mom and move west, my brother and I had to be the Judge vanguard; we were to go first, accept lodgings with Mom's stepmother, find jobs, and start paying our way. Pop was not going to sponge off relatives—ever!

Accordingly, Mother, my bud and I trained into Los Angeles in June, 1945. The war continued. Bob and I had been members of the Royal Canadian Air Cadets but, as yet, were not old enough to enlist in any of the services. Complying with the U.S. law for aliens, we dutifully registered with Selective Service and then started pounding pavement. Work was plentiful. In no time we had been schooled and were pumping gas for the Rockefellers.

To this day my two favorite flower scents remain night-blooming jasmine and orange blossom. Those lovely aromas were a terrific welcome to Sunny California. In those days they truly proved her portrayal as a paradise. Those of you lucky enough to reside there in 1945 (provided you're still alive) know exactly what I'm praising.

In a few months, with cash coming in, Mother returned to Toronto to dispose of household goods, bid farewell to friends, and collect Pop. In early October, our family whole once again, we wallowed in those wonderful, perfuming, ubiquitous blooms.

Walter Smith, Mom's half-sister's husband, careered as a general contractor. He had done much work for the services during the world's big dustup and rated high with them. Consequently, Mary talked to Smitty, Dad turned around twice, and the unemployed became the hired. Early in 1946 Smitty landed a big job in the desert at a place called Yucca Valley. He was to build a caravansary for a religious group. The buildings were to portray a rising from barrenness, thus the private inn would need an abundance of native desert rock to form walls held in place by concrete. If done right, it would last over a hundred years; at least that was the premise. Last time I looked, the edifice still stood wind-blown but proud. Chalk up the first fifty.

Family quarters went with the job. Pumping gas wasn't that much fun and Smitty offered jobs which would pay more money to boot, so Bob and I bid farewell to Standard Oil and signed on as drivers of single-wheel, mobile bathtubs. The foreman called them wheelbarrows!

The work was damn hard but it also added up fun. We became good friends with people from vastly different backgrounds: Barney, a young guy with muscles Samson would have envied. Slim, the foreman, who called the yolk of an egg, a yelk. Phil, an expert plumber. Don, Smitty's son, and Joe, mother's half-brother; the list goes on. Include Riley and his boys, a crew of rock layers and cement finishers, they were a group comprised of older black men and service veterans. And best of all, they were fun to tease. Being obnoxious eighteen-year-olds, we bugged them unmercifully. Bob, Don and I discovered Riley's bunch were afraid of snakes and there are sidewinders and rattlesnakes in the California desert. Foraging in the foothills for colorful rock, truck drivers often ran across the nasty little critters and occasionally they'd bring a carcass back to camp. You see where I'm headed don't you?

Don, Bob and I lived with our families in furnished cottages. Barney commuted from Joshua Tree, which was two miles away. Riley and crew set up housekeeping in an older building on the premises which served as a bunkhouse. Did you know snakes can jump, some as high as six feet? An unfortunate one, a near-sighted sidewinder accidentally right obliqued himself into our campfire! Rattlers can also stand on their tails and pirouette three hundred and sixty degrees, conducting sweeps. No way you could sneak up on 'em. Eager to enlighten, we furnished all that information to Riley's gang—free. That may be the reason for the ropes on their beds that suspended them—two feet off the floor—from the rafters. One day the rock collectors brought in a bull rattler over three feet long which they'd tied to the front bumper of the truck. He was all through rattling. We swapped a rabbit, who'd dodged the wrong way, for the snake carcass. After work, the incorrigible among us snuck down and made hissing, rattling noises under a certain bunkhouse window. Naturally, all that racket created consternation within their home away from home. Were we rotten little snots? Absolutely!

Some of those great guys are gone now, but memory still paints them sharp and clear. In retrospect I don't think we ever really fooled Riley and company; otherwise, how come no one suffered a heart attack when we eased the bunkhouse door open and threw the snake inside?

Walking in the rain yesterday, resurrecting those harmless, boyish pranks, a bolt of lightning bit off a chunk of tree smack dab in front of me. I bet that was good old Riley!

I've mentioned Barney's strength. Topping out at one hundred and twenty-five pounds, very little of it muscle, I made an ideal candidate for the title, "weak as a rained-on bee." My job alternated between mixing concrete and wheeling it to the ever rising walls. A pure piece of cake in the beginning, when the ramp slope was low and gradual. When yon rock wall reached an oxygen-scarce height, unless I got a running start, I'd stall, out of gas and wheezing. More than once, about halfway to Heaven, my forward gear would start to slip into reverse and things got dicey. Not to worry: Barney hustled up behind, grabbed me *and the barrow*, and pushed us both to the top. What stuck in my craw? I think Big Barn did it all with one hand!

Instead of mixing the three of us in with his concrete, Riley and company accepted our bugging ways good-naturedly and construction life continued friendly. The whole crew worked half an hour extra each day which allowed for quitting at three o'clock on Friday, to resume again Monday morning at seven thirty.

What a deal! The Judge family had time to explore and enjoy Southern California—Elsinore, Beaumont, Banning, Palm Springs, San Diego, Oceanside, La Jolla, Hollywood; anywhere and everywhere two-and-a-third days would take us. If you could have seen her beauty then. No freeways. Clean, mostly uncrowded beaches. Orange groves up the dump stump. Gorgeous vining bougainvillaea on white stucco. Gas just eighteen cents a gallon, a mere twenty cents for ethyl. NO SMOG! Happy people. She was young, vibrant, full of promise, and carefree. That's the word, *carefree*! Paradise? Oh, yes.

Those long weekends were some of the best we'd ever known until one day, Bob and I received letters which truly began in a most friendly way—GREETINGS from Uncle Sam!

Though the war was over, we had been drafted and were ordered to report to Los Angeles for our physicals. After our knees had been hammered, checking reflexes, our feet found to be not flat, and we'd coughed dutifully when ordered, we passed the exam. Three days later, further orders arrived. We were to report for induction into the Army on the following Tuesday. Grateful to the draft board, the guys on the job threw a party for us on Friday, presented generous parting gifts, held a profound moment of silence for the unsuspecting, "so-longed" us and took off for the weekend.

On Monday *they canceled the draft.* Bob and I were off the hook! Hoping not to have to return the gifts, we still could hardly wait to see the looks on the construction crew's kissers when we showed up for work.

While work on the caravansary progressed, Smitty looked for other projects in L.A. and elsewhere. Needing someone he could trust he promoted my father to foreman of the desert job. The city of Yucaipa was just beginning to bud: it drew Walter and while there, he bid successfully on some smaller jobs. Yucca Valley was a short commute from there which meant he could keep an eye on progress in the desert. That was a boon for Pop. An indoor career man all his life, he was doing on-the-job training in construction, and if trouble stomped in, Smitty could bail him out in a hurry. A quick study, Dad learned swiftly. The men liked him and building proceeded rapidly and well.

While overseeing the work in Yucaipa, Walter spied some appealing acreage and he bought it. Mom and Mary were quite close and so, kindly, Smitty offered to sell an acre-and-a-third to the Judge bunch. Pop hastened to accept. It would be the first land we'd ever owned. Tickled doesn't express our pleasure. Things were definitely looking up.

Weekends after that were devoted to building our own house. Eager to mature, 1947 outgrew her britches during that work crowding time. Mom was bursting with ideas of the honeydew kind: "honey do this, honey do that." She cruised right along, planting, painting and planning. Pop, Bob and I, palm blistered, kept trying to row for shore!

Desert caravansary and Judge's casa grande were both completed in late November. The relative-by-marriage building contractor had placed an idea on the table, "swapping." Labor from us on his home, expertise from him on ours. Two new, albeit small houses, soaking up sun, laughing at rain, graced both properties.

Mom had already planted night-blooming jasmine. Shovel in hand she was hunting for a spot to plant the umbrella tree while her face looked like she was wrestling with one of her "honey-do" jobs. Sure as hot dogs love mustard, she was working on another *idea* and the three Judge males desperately ran for a place to hide. It was December 17, 1947 and it was her *birthday*. Yuh really should oblige 'em on their birthdays, right?

Bob and I enlisted in the United States Air Force!

"Why did we do a fool thing like that?" Would you believe too many wobbling wheelbarrows of concrete, often slopping over the sides onto careless feet and then hardening, eventually worked all the way up to the brain? You know what happened then!

Paperwork and physicals complete *again*, enlistment oath taken, all aboard the sunset special (there's an omen there) for San Antonio, Texas and Lackland Air Force Base. Yahoo!

In late afternoon on New Year's Day, 1948, I disembarked from the choo-choo at San Antonio and proceeded to enjoy the most miserable day of my entire life! Within a period of twenty minutes it blew dust, rained, hailed, snowed, and the sun returned. Next, a nasty person that we learned was a corporal screamed at us to stand still, turn around, stand over there, move over here, form a straight line you IDIOTS, "an' board dis nice bus," which then shuddered and groaned its way up, to, and through a gate onto Lackland Field, finally stopping before a large, white-sideboard building. Further yelling: "Vacate da bus an' form *two* straight lines. Now, youse human rejects, not tomorrow!" Outside, surprise—more rain, followed by snow! Last, without exception, bystanders and passing trainees jeered, "You'll be sorry!"

Feet of doubt began to jog through my mind looking for a way out.

Personal gear now God knows where, obeying further unnecessary hollering, we marched to and through the building's forebod-

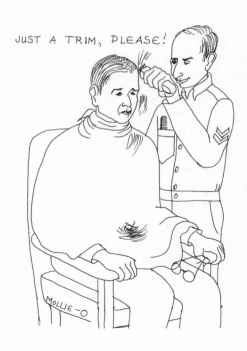

JUST A TRIM, PLEASE!

MOLLIE-O

ing doors. Inside, as a reward for good behavior, our heads were introduced to the GI haircut—cut it close and make it gross! A demanding bellow, "Remove jackets and shirts, march in single file through that DOOR!" On the other side of that *door* lurked two ugly hitmen, gleefully enjoying sadistic highs while repeatedly plunging long needles into unsuspecting shoulders. Turning to belt the one on the right, I got zapped by the louse on the left. Shoved by the line of recruits, I found myself half-naked and shivering outside in freezing, abusive hail.

"Form two lines ya miserable excuses fer hooman bein's," screamed a man I was learning to hate. Off we dragged to another building, another single line. Sheets, blankets, pillowcase; socks, underwear (a charming pea soup green), fatigues, T-shirts, all too big, all ugly; boots, two pair in dire need of polish, gym shorts and sneakers; razor, soap, towels, toothpaste; polish, brushes, polish rags and a laundry bag. Heavily laden and snarled at again—by now we had learned some new cuss words—we staggered off to one more architectural failure. It would be *home for the next three months.*

"Grab a bunk, dump ya geah an' line up in front of ya sack," bellowed a familiar baritone voice. Out we stepped again, mostly on one another's heels.

Naturally, while we'd been wasting time getting scalped, stabbed and clothed, the mess hall had closed for the day. Yo big mouth made the cooks reopen it. The cooks were not happy. Name somebody who was! Supper, for the bewitched, bothered and bewildered, displayed canteen-style before us as: chunks of white bread, baked beans you could carve, gunpowder coffee and— insults. It didn't matter. I hate baked beans and by now my shoulders were so sore I couldn't pick up a fork anyway!

"Now hear dis, tink a me as ya "Mudda" while youse little boys is away from home. Offa ya duffs, scrape ya trays an' line up over heah by dis door."

Picture "Mudda." Shaped like the Graf Zeppelin, he also displayed a face like a Shar-Pei with mumps! Claiming "Mother" status was a bit much!

Hurt, confused, and homesick we staggered back to what we

now knew was our barracks.

"Youse bums brush ya teeth, polish ya boots, make them beds an' hit da sack. I'm goin' ta renew acquaintance wid youse tomorra at 5A.M. Dem lights goes out in fifteen minutes."

In my whole flaming life I'd never despised a gravelly voice more. *Happy New Year*! On that high note my first day in the U.S. Air Force ended.

Dredging up memories today, that first week of basic training still remains one of unremitting horror. A cacophony of screeching, snarling, yelling, screaming, insulting chaos; damned if you did, damned if you didn't. It wasn't that we refused to obey. None of us knew the hell enough of what they wanted to be disobedient. With every expended breath—determined to destroy the last vestige of one's individuality—they hounded us. The silly phrase "separating the men from the boys" made no sense. It doesn't make any better sense now. I wanted to learn. Why else join up? I also respond better to "please," rather than, "do dis, dummy!"

Gradually our nightmare reduced to a scary dream, then an involuntary shudder. Kept on the run every waking hour, at night, we slept like the dead, too tired for dreams. Besides, all things pass except hanging and that's always a long stretch.

Basic training proceeded apace. Surprisingly I began to like it. Marching, ground-pounded from rough to smooth. Big Mouth, da corporal who talked like he was opening a tin can with his teeth, grew on me. I almost looked forward to his loving, nightly, "Youse bums hit da sack an' don't worry, *I'll be back tomorra*." Tears rushed to my eyes over his tender concern.

Our DI, a sergeant, rated tops. He was intelligent, knowledgeable and fair. I liked and respected him. I did not like the sucker who woke us for KP. He had fingers like steel ramrods which he jabbed into a snorer's chest rapidly and repeatedly until desire for further sleep became hateful.

Hey, I even survived a GI Party. What did I know? We had been training hard, it was about time for some ice cream and cake. Wrong! You who have enjoyed one or two of those parties know to what I refer. For the unenlightened, don't rely on me to shatter your illusions.

Inspections! Ah, yes, where a roomful of men stood rigid in front of their bunks beside open footlockers. Those bilious green shorts and undershirts nestled cheek by jowl; socks all neatly rolled; soap stands at attention; razor presents arms. A place for everything, and everything had better be in place!

Our DI and the captain, he of the gimlet eye, strolled past the wary line of men, inhibiting the still bewildered. Stopping, he suddenly thrusts his face forward and two inches from mine, he barks an intelligent question.

"Recruit, how do Texans get so long and lean?"

How the hell would I know? Unsure but pressed for an answer I queried back, "The Alamo string bean diet, sir?"

"No, you ignorant person," he snarls. "They get that way by reaching over and robbing Oklahoma! Next time I ask, you better remember that."

There were many such questions, equally brilliant, but I see no point in putting you off your lunch.

Mess hall food improved although one needed to stay alert to GI rules. After an active endless day, tray in hand and proceeding cafeteria style, anticipating a full platter as one grows ravenous, servers would ask where you hailed from. Let me give you an example: I'm moving through the line and I hold my tray out to the meat server. He inquires, "Where ya from, buddy?" I answer, "California." He is from New York. Anyone from California is either a fruit or a nut, right? He doesn't like members of the Golden State. Nobody does! New York forks onto my plate the smallest piece of gristle he can find: objecting, I inform him he is not very nice. New York is a gorilla. As I have irked him, he immediately offers to move my mouth to another part of my face! Next server: "What lovin' state you from, pal?" Resigned, I reply, "California." "Cool, man, so am I." He is serving peas. I get three giant spoonfuls. *I also hate peas*! See what I mean, you had to stay alert.

That problem demanded a solution. What? Observe what the server is dishing out and how he talks. Example: mouth-watering pork chops. "Weah all is y'all from, boy?" Imitate his dialect and say, " Ah comes from Raleigh, No'th Car'lina." "Well ah be ah goobeh pea, ah'm from Geo'gah." Bingo! Two fat pork chops take up residence on my tray. The mashed potatoes server hails from Maine. I sell him half a pound of Kennebunkport twang. Lovely! Two generous helpings with doubles on gravy. Dumbo, from Florida, is hustling—PEAS! Quickly I volunteer, "I'm a Californian." A tiny half-teaspoon rests beside the chops. Dessert? "What state trew youse out, chowdahead?" "New Joisey, buddy, gimme five," sez I. Well, look at that, a double helping of chocolate cake plus two huge scoops of vanilla ice cream! I just love dialects. I've been practicing them all my life and I still have all my teeth. I wish I could say the same for my hair.

It may have occurred to you to wonder why we recruits were not selective in the food line? Da "youse bums" corporal, our "Mudda" away from home—terribly stressed over our health—desired us to sample each offering. It would never do to write mother that her pride and joy, due to a failure to eat, now walked in the angels' chowline. Unfortunately, portions dispensed were left to the discretion of the servers, you know how democratic they were!

One-third of the way through Basic, Bob and I were ordered to report to the adjutant general's office. Mystified and apprehensive we complied and were informed that being Canadians, we were in the air force under an erroneous enlistment. There was but one choice. File an application for first papers signifying intent to become U.S. citizens, or we would be discharged and sent home. Puzzled, I inquired as to how come we'd once been drafted? "Couldn't happen, the law forbids it," he said. Bet me. We'd both received Army draft calls, experienced physicals, and had had orders to report to prove it. "No way," brayed he of the fixed opinion. We'd just experienced our first encounter with the inflexible bureaucratic military mind. They really are pretty thick, aren't they? Bob and I elected to sign papers of intent and remained in the service. It worked out truly well for him. He served and retired after twenty-six years. They only got four out of me.

I really had a big laugh back in the barracks. Our DI told me he thought I was a member of the CID and had been called to the adjutant to report on our squadron's activities. Strange as it seems, it's not too unusual to plant an intelligence spook among recruits in order to be sure that abuse from the cruel isn't making Air Force life miserable for the innocent. But me, a CID troop! Ha! It must have been my honest face or, could be all that basic training fun was making me look years older than my bunkies!

The series of tedious tests complete, graduation stumbled through the barracks door and we finally rated a day pass to visit San Antonio. Class A uniform, brass polished, shoes shined. Hurry! Go push for a seat on the bus.

These images remain vivid in my mind of that long awaited visit. Booze, beer, and broads weren't a priority. With a couple of buddies, I went to dinner and the movies. The name of the theater escapes me, but, I do remember that the ceiling, softly lit, had been painted depicting moon, planets and stars. Looking up, one had a feeling the film was being shown outdoors under a live sky. The result was quite striking and for me most impressive.

I remember riding back to base with a staggering, falling down, puked all over themselves, bombed to the eyebrows, bus-load of young airmen who had, he-man-style, way over-indulged in beer and booze. I've seen it many, many times since. Always it saddens and disturbs me—it's so damn demeaning!

I also recall polite signs on lawns of the city's leading citizens that read "DOGS AND SOLDIERS—KEEP OFF!" There were many such posters.

Paroled at last! A single stripe now decorates my arm. No more: "Youse bums line up ovah heah, da captain wants ta inspect dis dump youse call home! Now don't worry, aftuh his inspection, I'll be back ta tuck youse in an' kiss youse all goodnight." Oh, bless all the saints and wee folk, even though my prayers for a permanent case of laryngitis never struck that bum, I would never have to listen to his insults again. A further bonus was two full weeks home leave where I would be allowed to pony up five bucks for Petunia, and run smack into a whole bunch of new—you know whose—"ideas."

Bob and I parted company after Basic Training. He hied off to Kansas, there to make life a daily challenge for the Air Force. I willingly contributed to the welfare of Scott Field, near Belleville, Illinois.

My most memorable recollections about Radio School, besides

canoeing, drip-drying, transmitters, plain old nervous sweat, and the numbing lack of concern for America's uniformed servicemen, had to be the fourteen hundred mile bus trip I thoroughly enjoyed just getting there. Flying in the tunnel of a noisy B-29 was living at the Ritz compared to that. Today, people say I don't walk with a straight back, I am lazy and slouch. No way! The considerate and just will blame it on that lousy bus. Manufactured before air conditioning, it was sweltering and lacked the leg room required for a midget. Smelly and crowded, it seemed like it was transporting hundreds of whining children. The bus shock absorbers had long since sprung, and pit stops erected during the Civil War and then dedicated to the moldering remained the norm! Food stops occurred only at condemned restaurants. I could go on, but I've forced that journey to lie dormant. However, cached close to hand is a big fistful of rocks in case some fool ever tries talking me into taking another!

Who Said King Kong Was Hard-Boiled?

I have hinted of a touch of concrete in my head. The following will prove what I say is true. A basket case after transmitters, behold a miracle! The Air Force called it a three-day pass. Lock and load! From Thursday evening until Monday morning, radio training could take a long walk off a short pier.

An opportunity to visit my grandparents in Toronto had just sailed out the orderly room door into view. Agreeing to share expenses five of us plus the owner climbed into his jalopy right after dismissal from duties late Thursday afternoon and burned rubber heading for Chicago. I planned to overnight there and board a train for TO by sunrise on Friday. Some three hundred uneventful road miles later, close to the train station, I unlimbered my pretzeled body from the car, shouted, "Enjoy your weekend" to my friends, and began to scout for lodgings. This was not the posh section of town and the clock had already chimed midnight. Being the bravest of the cowardly I stayed out of shadows and looked over my shoulder—often! As I rounded a corner, a deep voice inquired, "Now then, fella me lad, where might you be going?" Standing in my way was the biggest upward and outward Irish cop I'd ever seen. Nervously, I explained my presence and need.

"Well, now, you just follow me, me young bucko, sure and I'm not Irish if I don't believe I'll be after havin' a solution." And away he lumbered like a buffalo heading for fresh grazing.

Gigantic in size, but seemingly gentle of nature, he walked me two blocks and into a bar. Uneasily, while he spoke to the bartender, I checked out the surroundings. Okay, I'll admit it, *I was scared!* Lodgings in a bar? The bartender nodded to the cop and came out from behind his counter, a long beautifully polished bar complete with brass rail and spittoons. He beckoned me toward some stairs. My guide smiled. "You'll be safe here lad, 'tis a short walk to the station and I'll be keepin' me eyes open. Enjoy your leave, and Godspeed."

My bartender host led me one floor up to a room which was clean, housed a sink, toilet and bed, rented most reasonably— and had no lock on the door!

"Sleep good, kid," smiled the landlord, heading back to his *familiar* bar and leaving me in my *unfamiliar* room.

Tired and still apprehensive I undressed, stuck a chair under the doorknob, hid my wallet under the pillow and slept like a baby!

Count up fifty years. It was that long ago. I have never forgotten the awesome size nor kindness of that Chicago cop. No one will ever convince me that the vast majority of the police do not try to look out for their citizens.

Early Friday, after a great breakfast in that same bar, I walked to the station, caught the early-bird, chugged off to Detroit and then Toronto.

Close to five hundred miles east, in late afternoon, my class A pass having been perfectly valid at the border and just enough time to get to a bank to exchange to Canadian currency, I detrained in TO. My soon to be nightmare began at 2:45 P.M. Eastern Standard Time! How come I recollect the exact time? You always remember when nightmares begin!

Having changed American dough for native and already

knowledgeable of my hometown, I headed for an area in the vicinity of Bay, Bloor and Spadina Streets. Aesthetically decorating those neighborhoods there are or were some stately old homes from a bygone era. The owners occasionally rented rooms with shared bath. Best of all, they allowed for a low-ranked airman's pocketbook.

I live right (temporarily ignore the word—nightmare—written above), glitz and glitter do not impress me, nor do acres of glass. I don't deny I picture a grizzled fossil now; nonetheless, at any flaming age I've always enjoyed and appreciated the older impressive style of architecture. I found a dandy, handsome, graceful colonial. Old world courteous, the landlord welcomed and escorted me to an immense room. It offered scalloped ceiling moldings, velvet drapes, a brass bed adorned with handmade quilts and large picture windows. The bathroom loomed large—about the size of a double garage. You could throw a party in the claw-legged Victorian bathtub. The whole home, including mine host, radiated quiet dignity. Squeaky clean, after a long, soothing soak in that tub, I slipped between the sheets and in two blinks soared among the clouds. I don't remember if the mattress was feather-filled, but after a year and a half of GI cot, it sure felt like down to me. Oh, indeed, I'd truly been kissed by the angels.

After breakfast, which included crumpets and homemade strawberry jam of which I'm overly fond, I climbed aboard the finest streetcar system in the world—servicemen of any nation still rode free—and headed for my grandparents house on Oak Street.

They were then in their late eighties and I was the last member of the California Judges to see them alive. My grandfather had built the house including all wallpapering. He was an expert. My mother—no mean paper-hanger herself—often told that it was he who'd imparted his skill to her. I believe I also picked up building skills from him. Pop and tools did not get along, he shone at baseball instead. A southpaw, he gave his watch, his most cherished possession, awarded for a year's batting title (.428) playing in a semi-pro league for the Toronto Argonauts, to his daughter who'd desired it. Pop was like that.

Gramps had also been proud of Dad's baseball pitching skills and loved to reminisce. Our last, warm, nostalgic reunion concluded too soon and it was time for me to leave. A brief visit to some old haunts, some quick calls to neighborhood pals, a sincere thank you to my landlord, and I boarded the train heading back to Chicago. I planned on then busing back to St. Louis and thence, having plenty of time, on to the base.

Here's where the nightmare tiptoes in sneaky and black!

Sunday had started off a real smiler. Customs folks passed me cheerily through the gate. Again the train, including a good lunch, added up nicely and she arrived on time in Chicago. All businesses, banks etc., of course, were *closed* on Sunday. The "mall" young of today couldn't imagine anything like that!

A quick hop and a step to the bus station and the ticket line. A day later, it was my turn. "One way ticket to St. Louis, please."

"This is Canadian money, bud. We don't accept their dough!"

Ever feel like your airplane wasn't going to make a successful landing, and sure enough she runs right off the end of the runway? I'd foolishly exchanged all my American money for Canadian. I hadn't anything else. There may have been credit cards in those days, but I purely didn't have one! I begged the guy to take a twenty-five percent discount and sell me a ticket. I had to catch that bus! He wouldn't have budged if the buyer had been his mother: "No way, bud. Go try the Salvation Army, make way for the next person in line." To this day I offer a weekly novena for the salvation of his miserable soul.

I raced to the Salvation Army: "We can't and won't help you, airman. Try the Traveler's Aid."

Valuable time gone wasting and my bus due to leave, I panted up to the Traveler's Aid. "Forget it fella, we only help in emergencies."

Every year during fundraising campaigns I contribute big to them both.

Desperate, panic settled in. My bus long gone, I started walking the streets and finally entered a bar similar to that of my original savior. This one sported Canadian, British, French and American flags. Verging on tears of frustration, I explained my predicament to the bartender.

"Them sons-a-bee's," he snorted. "Gimme your dough, I'll take care of it."

Take care of it he did. He exchanged American for Canadian, *straight across the board.* "Them money-dunnin' clowns is more iner'ested in gettin', stead a givin'. To hell wit' 'em. Have a safe trip back to base, kid."

I could have kissed him!

Bestowing fervent thanks I raced back to the bus station, bought a ticket from my favorite S.O.B., and anxiously waited for the next one scheduled for St. Louis. A touch relieved but still not out of the woods, I reached most of my goal by 8:30 A.M. Due at the base by 8:00 A.M. I was late but not that late, however I still remained quite some distance from Scott Field. I further added to my mistakes and grabbed a cab. Eyes glued to the meter—after counting my remaining American cash—my old friend Panic sat upon my shoulder while the last of my loot tick-tocked away. To be sure, my wallet contained sufficient money but only in Canadian. As I had been raised honest, I now compounded my errors and informed the cabby he was ticking me out of legal tender. Fret not though, I had more than enough of the kind used by our northern neighbors. If he would transport me to Belleville, I'd whip into the bank, exchange bucks, pay him off, add a fat tip, and pray for him every Friday.

That kind man—probably an ex-Nazi—immediately pulled over to the curb, took all my American money and ordered me out of his cab. I also pray for his soul on a daily basis. There I was, standing on the sidewalk halfway between St. Louis and Belleville, the clock ticking inexorably and tolling my doom. As you can imagine, I'd given the cabby a big tip from the remaining Canadian change and bills in my wallet. With nothing for it I flagged down the city bus, climbed aboard, and dropped adequate change down the slot. Continuing my good luck, I was the only one to board.

The driver fished the coins out of the box, examined them, turned to me and said, "Now wasn't that a cute trick, airboy. I suppose you think you're pretty damn smart!" Blast, I'd run into another lover of mankind!

You'll have to forgive me but I believe I lost it and used some bad language; nothing really nasty, maybe just a word or two you wouldn't use before the kids! Having run into a gang of unconcerned people, experienced one horribly hairy time, not over yet, I believe I colored a tad bit apoplectic. I really needed one more bozo making a federal case out of two Canadian dimes! This I recollect: I told him that once we made town, to park his lousy bus in front of the Belleville bank and follow me inside where I'd exchange funds, pay him off, and if desired, add a bonus. Meanwhile, as I found his pedigree objectionable, he could shut his fool mouth!

The rest of the ride passed in silence.

At the depot and preparing to disembark, I asked Clyde if he intended to enter the exchequer with me? Totally ignored, I wished him a happy, lucky day, hot-footed into the bank and exchanged Canuck for Yankee bread, then I trotted back out and grabbed a local to the base.

My weary carcass now two-and-a-half hours late, our commanding officer failed to smile cheerfully while acknowledging my salute. Neither did he kill me! He knew my story was too complicated to have been invented. Accordingly, I received confinement to the base for a month. In addition—on the short edge, left end of my pass—they typed...*restricted to a one hundred mile radius.* Sayonara to one bummer of a nightmare!

Coincidentally, it so happened, when inserted in the window of my wallet, that little addendum affixed to that all important pass slid under the flap and disappeared from view.

One of the friends I'd phoned while in Canada happened to be of the female persuasion. Some three months later, having received an offer via the mail to renew friendship, I traveled back to Toronto. Happily, upon reaching the border, I wasn't requested to remove my pass from the concealing wallet although a pretty Canadian customs lady asked if there were any restrictions to it? I threw her my innocent look and she smiled and waved me through. Upon returning to the states, our

American guardians just waved at me. They all say my countenance relates to those of the saints.

That brief vacation also turned out refreshing. Via ferry, we sailed across Lake Ontario and then, back in TO, attended a dance at the Casa Loma. There, I kept circling the wrong way, while numerous foreign elbows thumped my ribs. I'd reserved plenty of Yankee loot and those two relaxing days had furnished lots of laughs. Revitalized, I almost decided to take another shot at transmitters!

Those of you contemplating a career in the service will find military schools are challenging and quite good. Whatever you do, don't buy into tabloid negativism where they'd have you believe everything and everyone in the country caters to the shoddy, the inept and the inferior. We didn't get to the moon by being stupid!

I'm truly grateful to those who instructed while I attended school at Scott Field. They taught me a lot, especially that knowledge doesn't come easy. Life is a four letter word; another one you should use most while living it—is *work*. That slice of pie you've got your eye on doesn't come free!

I was once honored by being asked to give a speech in college. At that time I told the graduation class that it was an appropriate coincidence that the word American ends in "I, Can." That was true then. It is still true now.

• • •

Stepping off the bus onto Hamilton Field near San Francisco, I was whistling cheerfully. I'd just graduated from a tough military radio school and two stripes prettied the sleeves of my uniform. I was heading for Alaska, land of the midnight sun and, in another ten years, our forty-ninth state. Adventure, excitement, danger; like Bojangles, those thoughts tap-danced in my mind.

Happiness was life in the Air Force and I was enjoying that life. Hamilton, a processing field, was a jumping off base for overseas. Militarily speaking, Alaska was out of the country. In future, once my orders were cut, Cpl. Judge's address would utilize an APO number. In addition, his monthly clam allowance might almost merit entree, like meatloaf, status.

Oh, yeah, the world was my oyster except, in those days I hated oysters as much as peas and beans! No, the world was my cheeseburger—big, fat, juicy and *rare!* Nobody frowned about cholesterol. Jack-in-the-Box didn't despise the term E.coli. Today, go order a rare burger. How will it come? Like a cremated discus. It'll put out the eye of a goat at two hundred yards!

For a fact, the big spinner was mine. Every time I bit off a delicious chunk, grease dripped off my chin. Who was it that said nothing lasts?

I spent a little over thirty days on that base. Unhappily my good cheer decided not to pucker up and continue whistling. Boils. I came down with the mother of all cases in my armpits—*both armpits!* Our Air Force uniform still included the Eisenhower jacket. That jacket was a snug fit. Boils hurt. Boils in a snug jacket hurt like hell. Pain so bad I couldn't fully lower my arms. Picture this: I walked like a ninety-seven-pound weakling version of King Kong!

In desperation, I marched over to our base hospital. The croaker's eyes lit up when he glommed onto those disgustingly inflamed ugly lumps. He was an old geezer—at least forty. Happy in his work he crooned, "Oh a-lancing we will go, a-lancing we will go, heigh-ho and merrio, a-lancing we will go." He swabbed, picked up a scimitar (he called it a scalpel), and promptly carved his initials in those swollen suckers. He had a glorious time. I nearly passed out. For his *coup de grace* he made me drop my trousers, got a running start and speared my derriere full of penicillin. Crooning still, he baritoned, "Simply lovely excisions. Betcha that didn't hurt a bit, did it?" IT damn well had! I mumbled, "Nog mush." Privately I dearly hoped that beloved Saint Tremor, kind patron of the ancient and feeble, much renowned for his compassion, would decide to take the old age shuffle out of that pill-pusher's walk and starch his shorts.

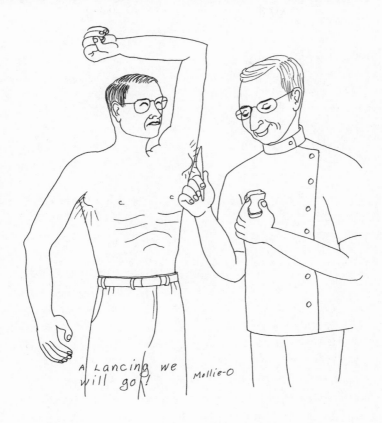

Cackling—like the demented in *One Flew Over the Cuckoo's Nest*—he ordered me to report back in two days for a repeat performance, much to my dismay, and sent me on my way. I wanted to slug him!

Agony gone! I'll be a stunted dwarf if the cure hadn't worked. With both arms hanging comfortably at full length once again, I could even slide my hands into my pockets. Chalk one up for the wannabe medico troubadour from Sherwood Forest. I still wanted to slug him!

Weah's Da Galley Mops?

Passenger friend, if you'll bear with me, I'm going to tie our dugout onto yonder cypress stump for a brief spell. I'm a touch long in the tooth and all this poling's put a stitch in my back. Marsh meandering sometimes circles back on itself. Fry me a fresh catfish if it hasn't happened to us. I'll just rest my aching bones during this next little section, and then I'll float us north along this slough which will lead back to the main channel and on to Alaska.

Mother had another idea...you already know the dope who listened.

"Why don't we raise chickens and rabbits? We have plenty of room. Fresh eggs are better than store bought. Can't you just taste your own fried chicken or rabbit? How about delicious baked chicken, rabbit stew, chicken enchiladas, rabbit and dumplings—yum-yum. Rabbit fur also sells. We'll all eat better, and best of all—*make money*. They won't cost hardly anything to feed and they're easy to take care of. Our dear Petunia would not have been the local pest if she'd only had animal neighbors."

Here I was on a forty-five day furlough from Alaska, my first in twenty-one months, both ears still ringing from the roar of a B-29's four engines, so I bought the hard sell. Besides, I was never one to read the fine print!

Away again to the local lumberyard: four-by-four posts, two-by-fours, chicken wire, metal roofing, staples, one-by-fours for chicken nests, nails, hinges, screws, half inch hardware cloth for bunny hutches, two-by-two's for framing, small hinges for doors. Hippity-hop to the feed store to buy cracked corn, chicken feeders, water dispensers, alfalfa pellets, and water dishes. Thirty chicks: one buck, five does. Oyster shell for chickies, salt blocks for bunnies. Wallet suffering from advanced state of malnutrition! Not to worry. Rabbits breed and multiply (overnight) don't they? This GI was truly fond of eggs: boiled, scrambled, fried or quiched. I also thought Welsh rarebit was an exotic English dish comprised of baked rabbit with onions!

Temporarily housed in large cardboard boxes—grow, grow, growing—the chicks and bunnies stood on one another's shoulders critically observing the construction of their permanent abodes. Came completion day. Their quarters were christened in true military style with a bottle of beer and tastefully named, The Fowl Up and The Bunny Hug Hotel. I hadn't crippled myself hammering and sawing so I relaxed as moving day proceeded smoothly and uneventfully. I could almost taste Der Dumbkoff Farm's, soon-to-be, world-famous fried chicken or rabbit dinners, original recipe or extra crispy.

"Dear, you still have time left on your furlough. What do you say we add pigs? Bacon, ham, pork chops and cracklings. Sound pretty good? Easy to take care of—they'll eat anything—and we'll save a bundle on the grocery bill. Sure wouldn't need much of a pen...a few slats...a little wire."

"Turkeys! You know how fond you are of turkey." She had me there. I was and still am a gallinaceous fowl freak, roasted, burgered, barbecued, stewed, or souped. In truth, I never met a turkey sandwich I didn't like! Nonetheless, while I might work up enough courage to knock the occasional big bird off, there was no way I would deck a pig!

You know the routine: up to the lumberyard for the usual, over to the feed store for sacked meal, away to a turkey farm for young poults. The pigs were easy. Right next door there resided yon farmer known in the big valley, for obvious reasons, as Piggy Smith. In two shakes of one lamb's tail (undoubtedly next on the list) we were bunking and feeding two piglets—Durocs. How'd I let myself get suckered again? Must've been Alaskan permafrost, 'cuz my noggin was still thawing. Anyway, Pop would have to feed 'em!

Construction complete, inhabitants abed, furlough and money distant memories, I flew to Seattle where I had a four hour layover before continuing on to Fairbanks. Storing my gear in a locker at the field, as I was still lugging my Mae West and parachute, I hopped a bus to town. Seattle is a great city but it does bucket down hard and often, bring a heavy duty raincoat! That memorable day 'twas sunny, so I wandered around doing the tourist bit. Walking is exercise. Exercise wears off excess fat. Jack carried no fat, Jack was lean. Jack grew hungry. Two more blocks and Lean Jack accidentally stopped outside a building from whence wafted enticing odors. Jack began to salivate! The door opened and *the* grand aroma grabbed him by the throat and drew him inside.

Glory be if it wasn't a darlin' seafood restaurant! Their special of the day: Clam chowder, Manhattan style. I ordered a large bowl. Would you believe it came royally served in an abalone shell, no spills over the sides, and it purely had CLAMS in it? That chowder was the best I'd ever tasted, then and since. Busing back to the field, I savored the taste over and over. Bless 'em all there are some wonderful chefs in this world; I'm not cook enough to name all those ingredients which had formed such a lasting friendship in that abalone shell but the flavors remembered continue to pleasure my palate. If I were to bestow a title on that dish I'd call it "Perfuma da Clama Upa You Nosa Ambrosia." The downer: I've been back to Seattle many times and never found that bit of Heaven again. Near as I can recollect it was located close to the waterfront but for the life of me I cannot remember its name.

In time for my plane I retrieved my gear and boarded the night flight to Fairbanks. My enlistment originally read three years. The

tragic Korean war interfered and Congress generously extended it
to four. (One senator voted no. The enlisted of the 10th Air Rescue
sent him a bottle of Scotch.)

Having been ordered to serve four years instead of three my
discharge date now read December, 1951. My pocket calendar indi-
cated the middle of February, 1951. But six months of my Alaskan
tour remained. They would indeed be momentous.

I must relate how that particular forty-five-day leave had begun.
A rescue squadron is a busy and quite active place. Being a radio
mechanic I'd been kept hopping, and Alex (as we called electricity)
played devious little games close to the North Pole, usually right
in the middle of a search when communication is vital. Although
I'd seen much of Alaska—Nome, Anchorage, Barter Island,
McGrath, Galena, Talkeetna and Point Barrow to list a few—over
twenty months had passed without a break. It had been frightening and fun, satisfying in terms of accomplishment and education
and gratifying in terms of promotion—yes. Yet, I was tired and
eager for a vacation.

December of 1950, a snowball's throw away, would mark the
third Christmas I'd missed at home. I put in for furlough.
Unfortunately my request was not acknowledged in time for my
leave orders to be cut and that portended no holidays for me. Luck
snowshoed in. I had come up with a tiny invention to overcome the
nagging, constant loss of trailing wire antennas on our Cessna
search craft. As furnished from the factory, equipment was a heavy
lead ball fastened to a cable which fed out from a reel positioned
inside the cockpit by the pilots left side. The reel handle had a tooth
on it which fit in slots on its face. Pulling the handle free of a slot
would allow cable to feed out a tube on the bottom of the plane. The
weight of the ball would trail the wire out until the pilot located the
desired frequency on his radio. In practice it worked fairly well, but
trouble usually occurred upon landing. Busy with runway instructions and stress, pilots constantly forgot the ball dragging through
the air behind them. Envision this: the plane touches down.
Friendly ball *truly attached* to friend plane touches down too—
smack on its head on the runway. Good-bye ball, hello yards of
snarled cable. Give problem to radio mechanic!

Radio mechanic, snarling at snarls and mentally diagramming pilot's pedigree detrimentally, puts on thinking cap. Commandeering a jeep he heads to a hardware store in town. Searching through rows of merchandise he finally locates and purchases six tapered rubber socks (think windsock, only firm), twenty swivels, and twelve, two inch steel couplings having a three-eighths inch inside diameter.

Back in hangar, mechanic cajoled sheet metal buddy to remove tubes from bottoms of four aircraft and mount 'em topside. Further bribing resulted in construction of two struts per plane: one eighteen inches, one six inches. Top of short strut was molded around steel coupling and riveted, locking coupling in. Bottom of long strut was bolted to top of fuselage, small one to top of tail. Cable from reel was then threaded out original slot, now on top of plane, through coupling of large strut and then on through coupling on tail. Next, a swivel was fastened to the cable's end at plane's tail. Swivel's other end is then fastened to metal crosspieces in center of

Trailing Wire Antenna

wide mouth of sock which provide its stability. With cable and sock snug against tail coupling and secure, I painted a mark on the wire where it stops on reel inside cockpit. Pilot and mechanic go for a test flight. Flaming invention works tickety-boo. Even if next pilot—dumb—forgets, odds are fifty percent better sock will still be attached when he taxies up to hangar. Sensibly, I'd also purchased spares including swivels. The new antenna was much easier to crank in and reel out, radio frequencies also located quicker. Our commanding officer, quite pleased, wrote a commendation for my file.

When he discovered I'd applied for leave, even though I was too late, he called me in to his office, cut my travel orders VOCO (verbal orders of the commanding officer) and told me to get my butt in gear. I packed in six minutes flat! Just in time, I managed to hitch a ride on a B-29 leaving immediately for Fairfield Suisun (now Travis) AFB near Vacaville, California. Hoo-boy, that flight was an experience to remember. First, I had to check out a parachute and, as we'd be flying over water, a Mae West. The quartermaster ordered me to retain and to return with both, as the idiot airman that paid for the lost wouldn't be him. Next, there being no crew room for me, I snaked up into the long tunnel of the plane, ending up cocooned but in sight of the waist gunners. Once airborne, I noticed each gunner had focused a lit spotlight on an object outside the plane. Curious, I asked one of them for the skinny.

"These engines are bleeding beasts and catch fire all the time. We keep light on the buggers every foot we fly…just in case!"

"What do I do if things suddenly get warm?"

"Do what we all do, old buddy—*pray!*"

Counted excess baggage and as much use as a fly swatter on an iceberg, I did what any helpless GI would do. I stretched out, made a pillow of my chute, ate a candy bar—maybe two—and listened to the four roaring engines, waiting for one to miss a beat. Alert for that dreaded word "FIRE," I kept swiveling my head from one waist window to the other. B-29's were not insulated but were pressurized, and the monotonous thundering acted as a soporific. Nothing happening, I finally thought, "The hell with it," pounded my parachute for a soft spot, lay my weary head down and tried to sleep.

In that time between half-drowse and total zonk, I began to run some of the events in which I'd participated during the past twenty months through my lazing mind: I had walked on the Bering Sea and the Arctic Ocean; to be exact, I'd trod out onto the Beaufort Sea which became part of the ocean. No longer a member of the Army Air Corps, I'd been promoted to sergeant in a brand new branch of the service called the United States Air Force. I now wore blue rather than khaki. I'd narrowly escaped making a large grab bag of pieces of my bod and scattered parts of an irate Hermy! I'd participated in many a rescue of persons in downed aircraft; I'd invented (perhaps only loosely created) a device which saved the tax payers some bucks. I'd become a foster parent to Devil, the squadron mascot, who, having been indiscreet and most careless, found herself in the family way. (She had then decided to deliver her litter of pups in our Quonset hut.) Flying in a C-54 as a passenger, in company with two famous explorers, I'd almost made it to the North Pole. I had checked out pack, rifle, ammunition, helmet and shelter half. Then, along with the rest of the squadron, bivouacked on cold ground waiting for possible invasion. The Korean war—pardon me, police action—had begun. Not long after "camping out" I'd had the further pleasure of digging a foxhole in solid ice! I had seen the mystical aurora borealis undulate across the sky, so close that I could almost reach out and grab a handful. I'd also flown through the heart of a forest fire where smoke was so thick, in order to locate our bearings we'd had to lose altitude and, by flying the course of the Tanana river, grope our way back to the air base. I'd seen salmon so thick in the river you could almost cross from bank to bank by stepping on their backs. I had also stood in front of the shaft to a gold mine, but nobody had left any nuggets lying around loose! Yep, I'd purely experienced an adventure or two.

Listening, and I guess taking for granted the continuing drone of the B-29's engines, I had to admit that all in all, it had been a momentous time for a beanpole kid from Canada. I could hardly wait to get home to exaggerate, elaborate and maybe just plain lie to the innocent and unsuspecting while relating my war stories.

• • •

Cast us loose shipmate, the main channel and the land of the midnight sun is just a fat, frog jump away!

My Alaskan adventure begins—horribly!

Rumor and then excitement pervaded Hamilton Field. We were shipping out. I was actually looking forward to that day. Final shots had been inflicted and duffel bags hefted to shoulders, then we quick-marched to trucks waiting to transport the Alaskan group to the pier where we'd begin boarding ship. Those of you who have experienced life aboard a troopship may wish to skip this part; God knows, you've already suffered enough!

Eagerly, we staggered up the gangplank of the first of two ships we would board. Personal opinion formed the moment I set foot on deck; this was a dirty old rust bucket manned by a slovenly crew. A shovel would've cringed at the amount of dirt gracing every part of the ship that the eye could see.

A screeching capstan rotated and a groaning anchor lifted free of the muddy bottom. The engines throbbed in sympathy as our scow edged away from the dock. Hard a-port, the Ark rumbled under the Golden Gate Bridge, rocking and rolling her way out to a white-capped sea. I suddenly realized I'm truly going to miss San Francisco—starting twenty minutes ago!

Universal GI lament, "Hurry up and wait." But not this time, we were land free before breakfast and, at that point, ready for a full load of bacon and eggs. Times and seating positions scheduled, we prepared to descend to the galley where hot food awaited. Hold on! Surging afloat through lead-colored waters, what's the first thing one participated in? Boat drill! Yo sausage and eggs would have to wait. While the eager to eat took station opposite assigned lifeboats, how were eggs kept hot? Why, one covered them of course. Sitting snug in pans which rest in very hot water, they were gently caressed by steam. What happens to steamed eggs? Bless my soul, they turn a ghastly shade of green!

Heading below decks I thought, "Funny, this old bucket's rolling is making my stomach a touch queasy. Wonder how my buddies are feeling? Put it out of your mind, boat drill is behind us, let's find that galley and *eat*!" Grabbing a tray I load up. "Damn, I wish this sucker would quit funky monkeying with my stomach. I see we all sit at mess hall type tables, I'm used to that. No insert to hold my tray? Guess I'll have to anchor it with an elbow. Oh, man, these eggs are totally GREEN and this lumpy sausage is dripping grease. Whoops—yo big lurch to starboard—there goes my tray. Whoa, here comes another guy's from the port end of the table. God! Someone else has already tossed in it. Quiet stomach! Oh, Lord, I've got to get the hell out of here, please let me make it topside before...!"

That is exactly how it was. Above, below, between and on deck, both coming and going, the poem rang true, "Hasten Jason bring a basin. Oops, plop, bring a mop!" One guy heaving would promptly make his buddy sick. Puking chain lightninged all over that dancing derelict. Vomit decorated bulkheads, companionways, decks, heads and rails. The stench would have hustled a skunk off to search for a shot of Chanel #5! I made it topside and over to a rail to loo'ard before contributing my share. Another dandy little touch made it a perfect day. The calendar read...*Easter Sunday.*

First a memorable New Year's, now an unforgettable Easter. What comes next on the bleeding list, a constipated Fourth of flaming July?

Nothing improved. By the time Seattle hove into view, I was ready to jump ship. However, service life is to endure so we endured the unendurable. Of a certainty though, disembarking from the dirty old wreck was one glorious relief.

Marching up the gangplank of our new ship could we passengers be a tad apprehensive? Surprise! Manned and run by the Navy, I believe, she was immaculate right along with her crew. The balance of our voyage had to improve, right? Wrong! Truthfully, nausea troubled less so we must have been getting our sea legs. And certainly, the quarters were cleaner and better. Chow rated good and was plentiful; the navy sets a fine table. All in all conditions were on the upswing until a certain party got stuck with KP. Mind, I'm not one to complain, but you'd think out of a whole boatload of victims they might have nailed some other model airman besides me!

Frank, Charlie, and I reported for duty to the cook—a chief boatswain's mate resembling a beached whale—and were assigned tasks in his spotless galley. "Look aroun' youse men, I bettah be able ta eat offa this here deck afta youse is t'rew." Nobody elected to argue with Porky. Frank, as was just, ended up with the plum job. Dispersed throughout the galley were five huge cauldrons, each bolted to the deck. They were used for coffee, soups, stews, hot cereal, you name it. One cleaned them by ascending a step stool, which allowed leaning over and lowering the upper half of one's body far enough inside so as to allow cleaner's hands to touch bottom. Sponge in one hand, the other hanging onto cauldron's top for dear life, one would then, using the soapy water currently awash in the bottom, thoroughly scrub all around the inside.

Ships frolicking upon the sea roll back and forth. Water in the bottom of each kettle, did the same. By the time cauldron three was clean and poor Frank surfaced for air, his face pictured lunch which had been pea soup and he said his dome rang. He likened it to swinging upside down inside Big Ben while the old clanger tolled twelve. None of us could figure the reason for this. Of course, being considerate souls concerned with his welfare, we'd frequently banged on those oversized cooker's sides to alert Frank, in case he fell into those dark depths, that help was at hand and we'd all vowed to rescue him. Naturally none of us volunteered to relieve him. There is this rule in the Air Force: all assigned tasks shall be completed—alive or dead—to the best of each airman's ability.

Listen, you gotta support a buddy. Evil spirits dwell in cauldrons and Frank needed protection. By continuing to beat on his kettles, we scared 'em away, he was saved and never did fall in. He still walks a little funny though.

Duties completed after noon chow, floor hand scrubbed and mopped to chiefy's satisfaction, we asked what to do with the mops?

"Take dem up ta da fantail an' t'row dem ova'boad," he growled.

Puzzled, we set off to do as bid. Charlie looked at me. "Dat big load a pasta ain't serious, is he? You t'ink mebbe he been inta da suds dis early?"

"If you ask me, I think he stuck his head once too often into one of his precious galley ovens," chortles Frank.

"Guys," say I, "'T'row da mops ova'boad,'" he tells us. When was the last time you disobeyed a *request* from a non-com, especially a moose like him?"

"Orders is orders," chuckled Charlie. "Let's go give 'em da ol' heave-ho."

A passing swabbie told us what and where the fantail was. Up on deck, timing the rolls, we lurched our way to the stern. After another questioning glance from each of us, followed by shrugs, Flopsy, Mopsy, and Topsy, hair in wild disarray, soared, sailed and sank!

Away from the garbage scow and KP now a memory, food began to appeal more although I stuck to bacon and toast for breakfast. To this day I can't abide green eggs, colored or cooked!

"*Flopsy, Mopsy and Topsy*"

Life aboard a troopship, for non-combatant passengers not required to continue to hone their skills, is boring. Willie and Al amused themselves by testing each other verbally on Morse Code. We stood their incessant dit-dah-dit-dit chatter as long as friendship decreed, and then offered to send them to practice communicating with a certain mop trio!

Occasionally, attempting to elude boredom, Frank, Mac and I would visit the fantail and wager uncollectible bets as to which of those three swabbers was still closest to the ship.

"Topsy had da longest haih, she's da best swimma," bet Charlie.

"Naw, Mopsy had the thickest hair, she'd move through the water faster," wagered Frank.

"Gentlemen, you lose your money. Flopsy's hair had both length and thickness, she also had competitive desire. I win, pay up," challenged the expert!

I know, but what are you gonna do when they don't provide shuffleboard?

I've walked on one and flown over three oceans. Except for boarding a ferry heading for Vancouver Island, I have been back reluctantly sailing on the briney but once more.

Together with friends, the wife and I *paid* to go salmon fishing. Some terribly long hours into that venture the boat's captain, anxious to please, stopped the motor while he headed below to prepare food for us. The boat immediately began to rock and roll and my stomach began to practice somersaults. I mentally measured the interminable distance to the rail and knew I'd never make it. Food was not what I craved. What I craved was for the skipper to start the motor, turn his lousy boat around and, at speed, head for shore. Deposit me on land I prayed, any land. I'd walk part way if I had to! After an eon he returned bearing coffee and warm Danish which had been heated on a kerosene stove. My Mollie-O ate hers to the last crumb. When I tried mine, it tasted of bloody kerosene. Oh, Gawd!

The Blue Boy

All too soon the navy bugled evening mess call. After chow, we chosen few repeated the noon performance. Frank had but one cauldron to contend with. He'd threatened serious damage to our good looks if even a single straw were to tap his tub, and though competent and ready to go on Ed Sullivan as Jamaican kettle drummers, we tapped not. When Frank gets riled …!

Except for swabbing the bleeding deck, count KP over. When that final task checked in for us to do, Chief Porky looked around and rumbled, "Where was dem mops?" "Where you told us to put them chief, we t'rew dem ova'boad. About now they're between thirty-five and fifty miles back," we chorused. Have you ever watched when a lobster goes from uncooked to boiled? Turns a lovely orangy-red, right? Behold the cook. I thought he was going to have a whale of a stroke.

"Youse dimwitted pinheads! Youse wuz supposed ta tie a rope on 'em an' drag 'em t'rew da water ta clean 'em, an' 'nen pull 'em back on boad. Whadda youse fly boys use fer brains? Youse bums gid ta hell oudda my galley!"

I may not have been quite accurate there, his language might have been a scosh more graphic than that. It was such a long time ago.

Shoulders shaking with suppressed laughter we three slunk quietly out of his galley. At the door, Charlie asked. "Chief, does dis mean weah fiahed?"

That was the only highlight of my voyage upon the sea. Today, every time I visualize those soaring, sinking mops, I see the chief's face and I recollect the peals of hysterical laughter we'd all shared, then I crack up once again.

• • •

Docking at Whittier, our duffel bags still making walking the gangway hazardous, we saluted the Navy and entrained for Anchorage. Riding that ancient old rattler was a ball. I love swaying around curves in rail thumping clunkers. It has become a biggy on the tourist circuit now and I'm glad. Nostalgia belongs right up there with ice cream! Too soon the enjoyable part of our journey ended. Like the little train that could, we chugged confidently into the outskirts of Anchorage—directly into a shock. Big guns suddenly swiveled on their stands on both side of the train and then *aimed* directly at the train and its occupants! Oh, God, what have I done wrong now?

Reassurance came quickly. The Korean War was still a little over a year away and the Army was but engaged in maneuvers. You'll remember the Soviets had declared war on Japan two days *after* the atomic bombing of Hiroshima! In the interim, they slipped 15,000 troops into North Korea above the 38th parallel which in effect sealed off North from South. The Reds were not amenable to the democratic elections proposed by the United Nations to form one country, thus they forced the North to go communist. Diplomacy a tad shaky, the success of the Berlin Air Lift a large boil on the Reds' backsides, the U.S. Military were practicing the boy scout motto. Russia isn't far from Alaska!

The 10th Air Rescue Squadron in Alaska was, arguably, the best rescue service in the whole flaming Air Force, excluding only those in harm's way!

As their rescue operations for civilian and military covered the whole state, including the Aleutians, the Tenth operated out of Ladd Field at Fairbanks, Elmendorf Field at Anchorage, and a small detachment on the island Chain. Anchorage covered the south and west including Juneau. Fairbanks attended the north and west counting Point Barrow, Nome and Barter Island. Flying Grumman amphibians, the detachment which serviced the Aleutians was also on call for rescue efforts at sea. All branches covered the east as far as Whitehorse, Canada.

My orders read Ladd Field. After a few days of indoctrination I boarded my first tenth Rescue C-47 for the flight to Fairbanks. Still snow-covered, Alaska pictured truly beautiful from the air. Better yet, my stomach stayed calm from tarmac up to 18,000 feet. I liked her. Had I also found adventure?

The squadron flew C-47's and C-54's, both used for long range searches, which could include glider snatching off snow, ice or flat terrain. Those two and four engine planes carried cargo, the Trail Crew—who were also parachutists—sleds, dogs and rescue gear. In addition we flew a B-17, and single engine L-5's and Cessnas, both equipped with floats, wheels and skis. Further, we used two egg-beaters (helicopters) and the occasional C-82 flying boxcar. Our C-47's also utilized skis. We're talking World War II vintage, but remember, this was 1949 and for my money the C-47 and C-54 are two of the best airplanes ever built. Ask the pilots of the Berlin Air Lift!

I came to love all those planes—not necessarily their radios. It became my job to keep them working. I clocked many hours repairing, then in flight testing, the sometimes uncommunicative little beasts.

On final approach to my new base, I knew I was going to enjoy Alaska. Even a fresh dusting of pristine snow seemed a sure sign of welcome. I'd come a long way from an unchewable piece of gristle and a triple helping of lousy peas!

The Tenth had located on the far side of Ladd, opposite the control tower. After reporting in to the adjutant in the orderly room, I'd been assigned quarters and then not required to report for duty until the next day. Curious and a little excited, I went exploring around the immediate squadron area. Memory plays tricks on old fogies, and unfortunately, back in 1949, I never did take a bird's eye photo of the whole field. I plan to rectify that on today's journey and I've borrowed one of our old helicopters for the occasion. Climb aboard and buckle up. Bring the jacket, this crate's heater may be on the fritz.

We're now hovering above the Tenth's main hangar facing across two long runways. Beyond those taxiways, you'll notice two large hangars, more buildings and the control tower. Those are F-80 jets sitting on the surrounding tarmac. Occasionally civilian airlines and bush pilots also use these facilities. We figure, so to speak, they live on the other side of the tracks and seldom have much to do with them. Not that we're snooty, mind, it's only that our squadron, a separate entity unto itself, is self sufficient. Of course we do avail ourselves of the services of Ladd's control tower.

As we hover, looking down to our left is the work area hangar. Large sliding doors on both ends allow for ingress and egress of large and small planes needing service and/or repair. On an inside upper level running the full length of the building are located the commanding officer's orderly room, radio and flight officers ready rooms, and the engineering office. Outside, dispersed around the hangar you will observe two C-54's (DC-6's), two C-47's (DC-3's), the other helicopter, four gliders, our B-17, four single-engine Cessnas and one L-5 (single engine, slow flying, canvas body, observation plane used for artillery spotting in World War II).

Do you see that path? It wanders amid trees from the work area to our living quarters, located to our right. Here, you'll view the mess hall, latrine and shower building, squadron orderly room—beside which stands the flag pole—and troop assembly area. I use the terms "airman" and "troops" because the Air Force is still part of the army at this time, wearing khaki, not blue. The enlisted men's quarters fan out in rows. Called Quonset huts, they house six men to a unit. Entrance is obtained via small framed doorways. Positioned in the center of the entranceway resides the most essential appliance of the hut—an oil stove. Line connected to a large elevated drum outside and gravity fed, this old love gives off dandy heat keeping our thin-shelled Quonsets toasty warm unless, of course, the stove goes on strike. Upon that event, if one can crack one's jaw open he'll cuss and then, to keep blood circulating, he'll bail out of the sack. While two men work on the stove the other four will chip the ice off the floor!

Heading away from quarters, now flying parallel with the runways, off in the distance and a touch further to starboard we catch a glimpse of Fairbanks and the officers and non-com's trailer park where those who have brought their families along, bunk. To the left, is the University of Fairbanks.

Ladd Field is much larger than the little we've seen of course but I'm low on petrol so we'll have to head back. Besides, this old darlin' is due for an overhaul, its engine's been sneezing and cutting out lately. As we whirlybird down to mooring, how about I relate the Fairbanks brag. It reads: For those stationed by this icebox city of the far north, every third building, devoted to business, is a *bar*! I'd never been able to get away to town long enough to check them all out!

Tenth Air Rescue Headquarters located at Anchorage, and two-thirds of the squadron operated from there. Our Ladd detachment numbered roughly one hundred airmen, officers and enlisted. I showed you our squadron mess hall, we also enjoyed the services of our own cooks. Rating those guys, to let us say the ones in Basic training, is like comparing dining at the Waldorf to a soiree at Bathless Groggins! The bad news: until I gained enough rank I still got stuck with KP—for a week at a time. The really bad news: I am a night person. Early rising, in my book, is a heinous crime. Having taken a vow to never break that law, I always ended up with *pots and pans*. Last to leave at night, I further had the dubious pleasure of turning off the lights!

Over a cup of coffee in the mess hall, curious, I questioned one of the old-timers as to the origin of the 10th. His narration was something else again: "The Tenth Rescue came into bein' because, after the war most military services left Alaska. Very little rescue equipment remained, but when Russia began thumbing her nose at us, Air Force units were sent back in. By that time, a hundred and twenty-five thousand new Alaskans had no protection against emergencies.

"On March 30, 1946, an agreement wuz reached an' signed between the Army, Coast Guard, Navy and CAA. Two days later, the Air Force activated the squadron. It took a series of disasters before our outfit came into its own. Equipment was limited and we wuz unable to land on the ice. We operated under the orders of each base commander an' the red tape would have strangled a pregnant hippo! Valuable time kept gettin' lost on emergency missions while trying to effect agreement between the 'Wheels' of each base.

"That changed during the winter of 1946 and 1947 although it took a disaster to accomplish it. In December, 1946, a doctor flyin' his plane on a mercy mission disappeared between Seward and Homer. Red tape between Elmendorf Field at Anchorage, an' Ladd Field at Fairbanks wuz so dip-de-doodled, that way too much time went bye-bye before the squadron's ten planes jumped into the air to search for the missing physician. A piece of the plane's fuselage, floating in the Gulf of Alaska, wuz all they ever found.

"Quite soon after, a B-29 weather plane made a dandy navigational error at the North Pole an' planted its feet in the wilderness near Thule, Greenland, three thousand miles from where it shoulda been! The Tenth strangled on tundra grass 'cus all our planes were short range. We wuz desperately tryin' to fit a C-47 with skis when a C-54 flew up from the States, landed on wheels on the ice an' flew the downed crew to safety. Because of that mish-mash, we got gliders, B-17's an' C-54's so's we could operate anywhere in Alaska.

"What finally put the icing on the cake though wuz when another B-29 crashed. On December 24, 1947, a bomber, unfortunately monickered the Clobbered Turkey, wandered way off course an' did clobber onto the ice near Nome, Alaska. A local Air force general took charge of the rescue operation an' what happened next, you won't believe! A doctor an' two paratroopers bailed out over the wreck in a temperature of fifty degrees below zero. While the search planes circled helplessly overhead, they all died before hiking one hundred and fifty yards. Two of the crashed plane's crew, disgusted, decided to walk out. They also froze to death. In Nome, an overloaded rescue plane crashed on takeoff an' a C-47 an' glider were lost on ice-covered Imurak Basin 'cuz the untrained C-47 crew let the plane's fuel lines freeze. Finally, while the trail crew members and their dog teams made their way across the ice, a bunch of small *civilian* planes on skis, landed 'longside the wreck, loaded the survivors aboard an' flew 'em to safety. That one made the Air Force look like a scarlet pimpernel blossom—with hives!

"Right quick after that, the Tenth Rescue Squadron wuz removed from control of the base commanders. It became an independent unit with total authority over its own planes, operations an' personnel. A retired "chicken" colonel by name Bernt Balchen wuz called back into service to take over the outfit. The old boy wuz an' is a natural, bein' one of the world's top three polar experts, an' he surely knows more about arctic flyin' an' rescue than anybody else. If you wanta know more about him check the library; he's been flyin' since 1926 an' what he's done I know you ain't gonna believe!

"Balchen took over command of the Tenth on November 5, 1948. An' he found we had already gone through rigorous practical trainin' in arctic rescue methods. Our outfit had grown from fifty-seven officers an' a hundred and thirty-five enlisted to a hundred and three "brass" and five hundred an' forty-one enlisted. We wuz assigned to Anchorage an' Fairbanks, plus Adak, Cold Bay an' Shemya on the Aleutian Chain. Each of the big detachments, includin' us, had C-54's, hospital gliders an' special Flyin' Fortresses which could carry lifeboats, attached to their bellies, capable of bein' dropped over water on long searches; ski an' wheel-equipped C-47's, single-engine wheel-ski-float planes that could land damn near anywhere in Alaska. We had helicopters, snow jeeps, amphibious weasel trucks, our own mechanics, dog team men, doctors an' the trail crewmen. *We also had over four hundred and fifty rescues to our credit*, ranging from simple to downright hairy!

"All this talkin' is parchin' my throat, kid. Go get us refills on java. Grab us a couple a doughnuts too an' I'll tell you a little about the caliber of men you're lucky enough to be servin' with today."

Hastening to comply, I also dripped a touch of syrup on the cook over the excellence of his coffee. Hey, what could it hurt? Who knew, maybe one day another lucky troop, late riser or no, might get stuck with pots and pans. Around a mouthful of doughnut, the old timer continued his story.

"As I wuz sayin,' you're lucky to be in the Tenth, son, an' here's some of the reasons why: Last April, one of our pilots from down Anchorage way an' a sergeant passenger wuz ditty-boppin along on a routine flight in a eggbeater when they heard a voice on the radio callin' for help. The speaker wuz leadin' a group of F-51 Mustangs practicin' gunnery over Susitna Flats an' one of his planes had gone down. Our guy kicks his helicopter up to full speed an' heads for where he sees the tall plume of smoke. He gets to the wreck quick an' he seen three things right away. The plane's fifty-caliber ammo is uncorkin' like a case of champagne on New Year's Eve. He sees the pilot bang his way outa the cockpit's bubble canopy an' painfully start crawlin' slowly away from the salvos goin' off all around the wreck. Next, our pilot sees that the beach is strewn with huge cakes of ice washed up by the tide. He knows a small ski plane can't land there so he decides to do the job himself. This guy's got guts, an' he sets his chopper down between two junior icebergs not far from the wreck. KA-bam, KA-bam, two rounds blow holes in his eggbeater before he gets her settled down but neither of 'em wuz hit. The two rescue guys hit the deck an' start crawlin' over to the hurt pilot just like they wuz infantry under fire. They reach the injured guy, who had passed out a short way from his plane, an' start draggin' him to safety. He had a broken back so they hadda move slow an' careful. To make matters worse the tide wuz comin' in an' they run as high as thirty feet at that point, among the highest in the world. 'Hurry up,' our pilot moans. 'If we don't get blown away, we're all gonna drown!' Finally, they lift the unconscious pilot into the chopper an' take off straight up, amid a final KA-blooey from the wreck, an' head for the hospital forty miles away. They land right on the front lawn an' an immediate operation saves the pilot's life. From the time the F-51 crashed until the pilot wuz wheeled into the operating room, exactly twenty-six minutes had passed. Before the Tenth Rescue, it probably woulda taken men an' dogs three days to get there!

"Last October, another of our guys set his four-passenger plane down on the Alcan Highway an' picked up two women who had been bad hurt when their car skidded over an embankment. On another mission one of our squadron doctors wuz transported through a blizzard in a helicopter, a twin-engined ski plane, a small single-engine ski plane, a highway patrol car an' a twin-engined plane on wheels, so's he could deliver a woman havin' her baby way the hell off in the boonies at a mountain lodge!

"Our new boss, Colonel Balchen, got a good idea of how well the Tenth performs a few days after he took over. Sittin' in his office an' casually lookin' out the window, he sees a small Air Force plane off in the distance pop some smoke an' then fall apart in mid-air. Two parachutes open beneath the plane about six hundred feet off the ground. Stunned, the old man leaps outa his chair an' rushes off to the Tenth's hangar about a quarter of a mile away. He makes a wrong turn an' don't get to the hangar for sixteen minutes. Huffin' an' puffin' his big bod through hangar doors he hollers to the captain on duty: 'Did you see that plane blow up?'

"'Yes, sir,' says the captain. 'The injured have just been delivered to the receiving door of the base hospital by one of our helicopters.' That chopper had got into the air at 9:52 A.M., exactly four minutes after the explosion. The pilot found the first survivor on a frozen lake at 9:56 A.M. an' dropped him off to a Tenth Rescue ambulance rushin' to the scene. At 10:03 A.M. our guy spotted the other chute on a hill-top clearin'. That guy wuz hurt pretty bad, but the chopper pilot loaded him aboard an' set down at the base hospital before the call for help had even been processed at Squadron Operations!

"Of course, Cheechakos like you don't know, but folks up here figure dyin' is the price a livin'.' A scant two weeks later one of our pilots in a small ski plane wuz flyin' back from a mission when he run into a mess of freezin' rain over Cook Inlet. Gettin' back to Point Possession for an emergency landin' wuz out. Sneakin' a quick look out of the window he seen the ice pilin' up on the leadin' edge of the wings an' the controls wuz startin' to get mushy. If you've never flown in an aircraft that wuz all of a sudden startin' to ice up, you don't know what scared is! By this time his plane wuz truly beginnin' to fly sluggish, just like a pelican with too big a load in its beak, an' the pilot figured he wuz a dead sure goner.

"Well, right about the time his engine wuz about to conk out, he remembers that not too far back, he'd passed a fair-sized ice floe floatin' in the freezin' man-killin' waters below. He circled round real quick an' found the berg smack in fronta him. Takin' a second look, he started to sweat 'cus that baby didn't seem near as big now. Rapidly considerin' the few options open to him, he decided to set his crate on the floe, an' that one wuz extremely risky; yet, a plunge into the Gulf wasn't to be thought of, he wouldn't last ten minutes in those frigid waves. Frantically, he calculated that if the skis hit the water just right the shock might bounce the plane up onto the

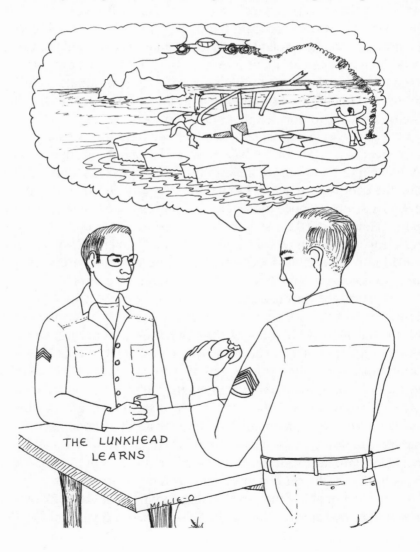

THE LUNKHEAD LEARNS

floe or, failin' that, the ice might tear the undercarriage clean off and allow him to slide onto it. Takin' that desperate chance, he cinched his safety belt even tighter an' aimed the plane's skis for the edge of the floe. At the last possible second as they hit the water, he cut the switch an', still grippin' the wheel tight, said a fervent but quick Hail Mary! He flat lucked out. The skis hit the edge of the floe but didn't tear off; instead, the plane flipped over on its back on the ice, skidded to within five feet of the far side of the iceberg, an' stopped. Sufferin' nary cut, nary bruise an' with nothin' on fire, one thankful guy popped open the cabin door an' crawled shakily out onto his icy savior. Thanks to a combination of superb skill an' super good luck he wuz alive, but floatin' free an' alone out there in the mean tides of Cook Inlet at thirty degrees below zero.

"When he didn't show up at Anchorage on schedule, the search got underway. First, Balchen sent a B-17 to Point Possession to see if he wuz there. He wuzn't an' soon as this report came in, the colonel sent two more B-17's out to hunt. Meantime, that blessed floe had described a complete circle of around twenty-five miles an' wuz back where it had started. Our downed guy wuz sure our Tenth Rescue planes would be searchin' for him by now, an' almost right away he hear's a plane's engines roarin' above the thick cloud bank. Just then, he seen a tiny opening in the clouds. One more time he done the right thing, an' tearin' up his survival clothes he soaked 'em in oil an' set fire to 'em. One a the B-17's spotted the black smoke, dived through the clouds an' come out right over his head. When the B-17 pilot recovered from seeing what wuz layin' on the ice, he radioed base an' a chopper wuz soon on the way. The big four-engine job kept circlin' over the floe an' guided the helicopter in. Soon, one amazed pilot wuz hoverin' his eggbeater to within two feet of that humongous ice-cube, an' one chilled but happy guy scrambled up a rope ladder an' into a lovely warm cabin.

"His troubles wuz not over. Headin' back through that freezin' rain the entire eggbeater includin' the rotors iced up. The pilot hollered, 'I can't see, the windshield is frozen over!' Immediately his sergeant assistant opened the right side door, leaned out, an' stretchin' his arms six inches longer than they wuz, scraped a tiny hole in the ice with a metal washer he'd had in his pocket. Peering through a hole no larger than a quarter an' navigatin' along the tree-tops, our pilot found the field an' then landed sideways on the tarmac 'cuz he could only look out through his ice-free side window!

"Some of those old timers datin' back to the 1898 gold rush compare the Tenth Rescue Squadron to the Royal Canadian Mounted Police. They say we are always there when needed. To them, we are more important than the Governor, the Legislature, the Department of the Interior an' all the rest of the United States government. Over seventy-five percent of our rescues are civilians." (An official report issued on September 1, 1949 reads: The Tenth Air Rescue Squadron has flown 550 missions for a total of 6,123 flying hours; and some 1,197 people owe their lives, or at least the alleviation of their suffering, to the intensive activity of the squadron.)

"Kid, this outfit has saved a village of three hundred Eskimos facin' starvation on a bay in the Bering Sea. A C-47 on skis landed on the sea ice bringin' 'em canned provisions. When a polio outbreak threatened the city of Juneau, a Tenth Rescue C-54 flew a stricken PFC to Seattle where he could get proper care. We stopped an influenza epidemic when a B-17 flew serum to the tiny Bering Sea island of St. George an' dropped the package by parachute. A seriously injured hunter was rescued when one of our C-54's dropped a glider into one a them small forest clearin's an', once the hurt guy wuz aboard, then they snatched it out again. Son, the Tenth Rescue, United States Air Force, does it all. An' also, in that doin', *thirteen of our people have been killed* savin' or trainin' to save others lives." (By the time I rotated back to the States in mid-1951, *that number had risen to twenty-two.*)

"Kid, we got Air Force guys from all over the world tryin' to transfer their bods into this outfit. Now how come they sent us a lunkhead like you?"

He was grinning when he said that, but to tell you the truth, after all I'd just heard, I was beginning to wonder the very same thing myself!

• • •

This next section tends to chill a tad and you might want to slip back into that jacket. Try to ignore the fishy smell. I've painted this canvas with the color blue because, two days later a robbin' hood STOLE MY CLOTHES!

Ladd Field was cold and covered with deep snow. Prior to beddy-bye, settled snug and warm, I did not want to brave the elements, but the necessaries had to be attended to at the latrine/shower building, some three rows over and five down. My teeth chattering like a woodpecker boring holes in an old aspen, I sped swiftly over icy walks to the showers for nightly ablutions. The johns, urinals and sinks took up one half the building, showers the other. Blessedly the joint was heated. If you've seen one you've seen them all. Aesthetic they ain't, efficient they are! They hold hooks for clothes and long benches for sitting to dress; a dividing wall separates showers from johns. Slatted boards for standing on cover the shower floor. The wise used foot clogs as a precaution against picking up athlete's foot. Naturally, I'd forgotten and left mine behind in my footlocker.

I had the place all to myself and it was so quiet and peaceful I heard the stove snoring. Glasses tucked carefully away in my fatigues pocket, clothes neatly hung and boots stashed under the bench, I thoroughly enjoyed a long, piping-hot, scrub. Brr-r, so chilly outside and so cozy warm inside. When I was pleasantly parboiled, I turned the handles off, stepped from the shower room and reached for my towel on the peg. *No towel.* Second look. No clothes, no boots, no flaming nothin'! GIs love to tease. It's got to be a macho thing. Aha and ho-ho! One of my new acquaintances was having a little fun; for sure I'd find my gear hidden in one of the stalls. Having a hunch as to the culprit and planning revenge, I checked out all stalls. NO CLOTHES! Under the sinks—zilch. Back I went to check below the shower bench and found not even fluff off the towel. Fun is fun but this was getting serious—it was *cold* outside. Surely the bum who had heisted my duds would have stashed 'em close by? I can't see much past the end of my nose without my glasses! Cautiously, I stuck my head out the door and quickly examined the snow piled by the doorway. Barren. No one had entered. I couldn't ask for help. The huts were so distant that yelling wouldn't penetrate their snow banked sides. With nothing for it, I took my little bare feet, little bare legs, and little bare arms, and hauled my little bare a—across the snow, praying I wouldn't step on glass, nails, pointed rocks or—unable to see—run into a bear! I ran as fast as my rapidly freezing bod could back to what for the next two years I called home. Gasping on freezing air, I burst through the door and snarled at my bunkmates, "Soon's I thaw out, whichever one of you bums stole my clothes better stand up 'cause I'm sure as hell going to knock you down!"

It's probably just as well both of them convinced me of inno-cence, as either one of them could have killed me. Dressed, teeth no longer doing the St. Vitus dance, I returned and rechecked the showers. Still no clothes. Next stop the orderly room, where I informed the OD of someone's idea of humor. He gathered a crew and using flashlights we searched the compound. Eventually my gear, including glasses, was found reposing in a trash can some dis-

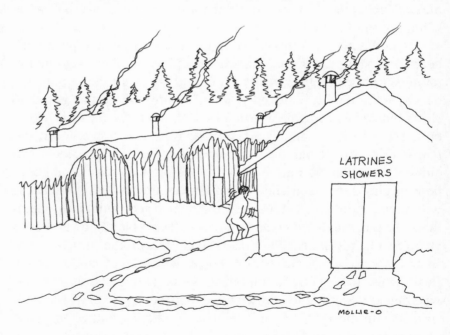

"The Blue Boy"

tance from the latrine. I never did find out who the S.O.B. was. An educated guess? He was a member of the Trail Crew who, enviously observing my robust and manly figure from behind, in pique, grabbed and ditched my duds. Those guys jumped out of airplanes, *they always carried things to extremes!*

Of further interest to the art world, if Gainsborough had used me as a model, his *Blue Boy*, becoming a modern acclaimed masterpiece, would undoubtedly now reside in the Paris Louvre rather than Sunny California's Huntington Library!

• • •

Could a rescue mission start out possibly tragic, be prolonged, and then end up somewhat humorously? Consider the hunt for ninety dozen eggs!

My first major search with the Tenth Rescue began on July 3, 1949. Later, the old hands told me it was just typical. A small plane, flying from Fairbanks on a short hop to Circle Hot Springs and carrying a seventy-nine-year-old Louisiana State University botanist, his seventy-six-year-old wife, ninety dozen eggs, and the pilot vanished into thin air.

At 11:34 P.M. that day, the plane's owner reported by phone to the CAA at Anchorage that one of his charter planes, due in at Circle Hot Springs at 5:02 P.M., was now six-and-a-half hours late. Considering the age of the passengers, he was terribly concerned. "We'll inform the Tenth Rescue," replied the CAA operator. Using our direct line installed for just that reason, she called headquarters at Elmendorf Field. On another direct line, the operations officer immediately called The Tenth Rescue's Detachment B at Fairbanks. Exactly eight minutes after the worried owner at Circle Hot Springs had alerted us of the missing craft, four of our single-engine planes, a C-47 and two C-54s were ready to climb the clouds and start the search.

I was in the C-47. It stays light in Alaska for a very long time in the summer, but nothing was spotted that night.

On our first full day, we hunted along the route followed by the missing pilot. The small planes flew a couple of hundred feet off the ground and the big jobbies worked at six thousand to ten thousand feet scanning big chunks of area. No sign of any fresh wreckage. Next day, our Detachment Boss took personal charge and added two more C-54s, 5 C-47s, four smaller twin-engined jobs and two more single-engine Cessnas. Nothing was reported.

On the third day, the colonel called planes in from Adak, 1700 miles away on the Aleutian Chain and more from Anchorage. Along with every civilian bush pilot in the area, nineteen military planes searched that day. Alaska's radio stations broadcast for any information from homesteaders who might have seen the plane before it disappeared, and even trappers walked in twenty miles to tell their stories. The boss sent the trail crew members to the Steese Highway and they stopped every car to ask puzzled occupants for their possible sightings. Nothing had been seen.

We were dog-tired by the fourth day but just the same the Tenth had every plane in the air, including twelve extra C-47's and four Flying Fortresses. Our light planes landed on roads, rivers and lakes trying to elicit clues from folks living way off in the boonies. False alarms up the dump stump poured in. Any actual plane wreckage spotted was that of old crashes which had occurred in areas too inaccessible for our trail crew guys to go in and cover up the debris.

On July 8th, a few trappers and Indian villagers reported having seen a low-flying plane on July 3rd and, for a change, all the stories jibed. The sighting was in the Fort Yukon area. The trail seemed to be getting hot, but by the sixth day there was still no sign of plane or passengers. The boss who'd slept little for a week and was not about to give up, added another B-17 from Anchorage.

Discussing the frustrating search that evening, one of our B-17 pilots from Adak said, "We've been assuming the pilot knew what he was doing. What if he went to school with Wrong Way Corrigan? Maybe he turned left instead of right on the river." Tracing on a map he added, "Figuring the gas he had in his tanks, that would put him a hundred and forty miles from where we've been looking and he'd have had to fly over Fort Yukon to do it."

Early next morning, given the green light to follow his hunch, our pilot turned out to be dead right. On July 10th, the wreck was spotted neatly crash-landed on the slope of a mountain. Happy as a Kodiak bear with a snout-full of beehive honey, he radioed the good news back to base.

"Is anybody hurt?" asked the colonel.

"Doesn't appear to be. Two of the folks are waving, but one guy seems to be chasing and catching bugs, or else he's just been stung by a bee!" An hour later, the seven-day mission was labeled successful. The boss sent two helicopters to the crash scene where they picked up the survivors and carried them to Fort Yukon. To make sure there were no injuries, the colonel sent a doctor to Fort Yukon to check them over. The doctor radioed back, and his report was brief: "No injuries. A few bruises and mosquito bites. Survivors escaped most "skeeter" attacks at night by sleeping in plane which was sealed up in adhesive tape. However, they all have a touch of indigestion from eating too many eggs!"

Care for a summation, one added by the professor himself? Stepping off the plane at Fairbanks, he exhibited a bottle of Alaska-bred beetles.

"Look," he said, "what I got for the museum at Louisiana State."

Fifty-one years ago this month, there I was participating in that rescue mission from start to happy ending. Do you suppose I've remembered every detail as clearly as though it were only yesterday? Not bloody likely. Rather, it's been much like groping about on a foggy day in London town trying to catch sight of Big Ben! Fortunately, doing the research for more background on my old outfit, The Fabulous Tenth, it all came back.

If there's any coffee left in that thermos, I could stand a swallow or two. I haven't yacked this long since I decided to try to explain the function of fractions to my fourth graders.

Seargeant, Hogtie the Plane!

Things definitely looked up after my streaking episode. I came to love the Tenth Air Rescue. We were needed. We fulfilled that need and I was a part of it. Searching for and finding lost aircraft and the military or civilian injured was, to each of us, privately rewarding. God, we swaggered proud when successful—which occurred most of the time. Hours were long, flying excessive, and often hazardous. There was stress, frustration and anger when nature or misinformation prolonged searches, jubilation when the lost were found—alive; cheering when we brought the injured safely in from the bush.

Once the emergency bell rang, knowing our help was needed, all other activity took a back seat. For me, repair work was put on hold unless one of the search craft's radios had sparked from the living to the dead. I'd better perform a miracle resurrecting that cantankerous wireless then—or else!

Have you met Captain Mustache? Stateside fresh and oh so elegant, he had been placed in charge of the radio/radar sector. As Charlie said, "I tink dis guy brushes his soup straina wid shoe polish." I liked him even though, at times, he'd have trouble communicating with the rank and file (amend that to read, we, the *ignorant* of the rank and file).

One day, some GIs working on a radio in the repair shop adjacent to the officers ready room, gave frustrated voice to lengthy and bad language. The *captain* appeared in our shop doorway and called those guys to attention.

"Gentlemen," he intoned. "The locution emanating from this room is vulgar and reprehensible. I will not have it! In the Air Force we select, examine, reject or use only that which is civilized English language. For your edification this estimable establishment is not a *bawdy* house!"

Sotto voce from the Bostonian, "What body? I don't see no body. He talkin' 'bout me? What'd dis guy do, swallah a dictionary or sumpin'?"

To which I replied, "Not to fret Mac, me old son, he undoubtedly refers to the famous Body by Fisher, your frame doesn't resemble it at all; however, I most emphatically concur with yon learned wheel, your language—atrocious, abominable, harsh and coarse—also offends my delicate sensibilities!"

"Aw, yer both nuts! Besides, ya bum, you wuz doin' most a da sweahrin'."

• • •

Much happens quickly when the alarm rings. It wouldn't do to race out, hop in a plane and go haring off all over the country. If point of origin and destination of missing craft are known, further information will still be needed: type, condition, speed, and range of airplane; health and flying experience of pilot; severity and condition of weather at last known position. Next, distance to possible site of downed plane must be calculated with allowance for head, tail or cross winds. Once variables have been determined, the area to search is plotted and marked out in the form of a grid.

In a grid pattern each square is assigned a number. This pattern is followed religiously while search craft are airborne. Of course a hot tip, a call from the bush where an outsider either saw a plane going down or heard it crash, called for immediate investigation. Not by all searchers though, most stay with the plan; false sightings weren't uncommon and valuable time following erroneous leads, perhaps that which could have saved a life, would be lost. Operating in 1949, in pre-computer days, the above calculations—demanding as much accuracy as could be determined from the given facts—takes time. Air crews fully equipped and ready, now on the run and carrying their dittoed copies of the search area, head for their planes which, in the meantime had been serviced, flight-checked and fueled.

All personnel including the lame and the halt were pressed into service when the buzzer snarled. Here's a, "Grandma, you ain't gonna believe this!" for you. To facilitate viewing on a search, some of the windows on our C-47's and C-54's had been removed and replaced with plastic bubbles. A bubble allowed the terrain scanner to insert his head far enough in so as to look directly below the plane, as well as outward.

I recall as though it were yesterday one particular search. We had been hunting for over a week. Time, running out hourly for the downed, ticked away. Harsh winter had frozen the land making aircraft difficult to sight on snow-covered ground. That's why the 10th painted wingtips red and fuselages yellow. Flying in a C-47, I was manning the port side bubble. Our co-pilot, *Captain Mustache*, hotfooted down the aisle from the cockpit to where Frank and I—bubble ensconced—gazed bleary-eyed at frozen terrain.

"Men, we are going to find those lost people. You stay alert and keep awake. The honor of the Tenth rests on your shoulders and your eyesight." So saying, he reached out and wiped the inside of each bubble to forestall icing up. Ordinarily this was considered a good idea except he had saturated his damn cloth with ETHER! Fortunately, although Frank and I, snoring something fierce, were nestled in the arms of Morpheus at the time, this story has a happy ending. A few hours later the missing were rescued safe and mostly sound thanks to a most considerate, cushioning snow bank.

Oh, that captain. He was the kind who persevered. No matter what it took, he was determined to learn to play badminton with a bowling ball!

Often, when the downed were sighted we could not land to offer aid and comfort. Reasons for this varied: No airfield located close by. Elevation too high, or distance from Ladd too far for our helicopters. Even ski equipped, a C-47 landing could be too risky. Unsafe to try a glider even though C-47's or C-54's could snatch them off again; huge rocks lie in wait beneath a deceptive covering of snow. Given those circumstances the trail crew, sleds and dogs were called into play. Frightening to view, watching a jump also checked out thrilling. Imperative for sled chutes to open, but no cause for alarm upon sighting a streamer. Most important for trail chutes to open as jumpers usually delayed pulling the ripcord until close to the ground; catch a streamer, but seconds remained for a quick prayer. Sled dogs—as though happy to jump—wagged their tails all the way to terra firma. Funny thing, I never saw a single dog volunteer for his leap. We always had to kick them out. Not responsible for pulling their own releases they were probably unconcerned over outcome, hence the wagging!

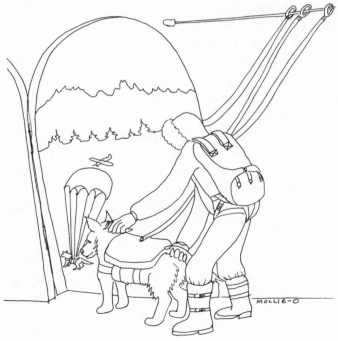

"I Never Volunteered"

Those were the best of times. If I ever ditty-bop this way again—in another life—ship my body to the 10th Air Rescue Squadron, APO Fairbanks, Alaska, and if you ever get lost, Frank, Mac and I will find you—guaranteed.

Author's note: I know that the Air Force is now totally based at Eielson. Ladd Field and the 10th no longer exist at Fairbanks. What was Ladd, is now Fort Wainwright and manned by the Army. Nothing remains the same.

Winter reluctantly eased into spring: longer days, melting snow and...*mosquitoes*. One of my first recollections of Alaska was a postcard which pictured a GI cook standing in his mess hall doorway, brandishing a meat cleaver, while two 'skeeters flew away carrying a side of beef. The caption read: "Now where'll we hide it so the big ones won't find it?" DDT was the rage in 1950. The base, frequently sprayed, was relatively free of the pesky little blood suckers. Not so the bush. Alaska abounds in tundra, flat boggy plains where "skeeters" breed and multiply, multiply, MULTIPLY! The prudent carried a sawed-off, double-barreled, twelve gauge to keep 'em at bay.

The long dark and deep cold was two-thirds over when I arrived in "Seward's Folly." Consequently, the sun for me, was not as earnestly desired as for those who had experienced the lengthy period of its absence. They, upon the appearance of the first truly sunny day, acted like a colony of squinting moles groping their way to roll call. Filled with overwhelming compassion for those having difficulty with sight, I offered the aid of my arm to my mole-like buddies reaching blindly for positions at assembly. Truly, one or two may have tripped over my foot during the time I kept searching for the rat who'd stolen my clothes, but those trippings were purely accidental. Short, or old timer, the warm sun felt good on the face. Spirits were definitely on the rise, and mischief free-floated in the air.

Skadorha (we'd tagged him Skidrow) claimed squadron honor of "scrounger." I never saw him involved in a lick of work. Nevertheless, if you were in dire need, he was the man to ask: he'd scrounge tools, engines, airplane parts, clothing, the rare, the exotic and the impossible. Skidrow on the hunt, traveled the whole flaming base, conning other squadrons, MP's, the army, anybody and everybody. In a matter of hours or days he'd return bearing gifts and he never paid for a blessed thing. Without doubt, heavy into magic, he was the Tenth's Merlin. If the desired object bulked too large or heavy to haul, he'd talk the giver into delivering it, usually with a little extra thrown in, like a case of canned hams! Skid was a remarkable man.

June arrived—summer does not linger in Alaska—and with it came much needed slack time. Planes were landing on runways instead of trees. Bush folk were axing logs rather than themselves. Mothers-to-be were not yet due or had sensibly already arrived in town for the lay in. The military, surprisingly, were also not damaging themselves. Not one Chechako had fallen into the river during ice break-up. As I said, a little slack time in a warming sun.

Skidrow desired a vacation, a couple of days would do and he'd take some buddies along. He wanted to brave the wilderness and camp out: a little fishing, a barbecue, laze, swap some lies. In other words, except for trekking the wilderness, what he always did. Could he pull it off? Give a listen.

Skid conned our commanding officer, a lieutenant colonel, into granting two days free leave to, *fifteen airmen.* I was one of them. He conned the motor pool into the loan of a two-ton six-by. He conned the quartermaster out of blankets, pots, pans, cutlery, "skeeter" repellent, sleeping bags and new shelter-halves (the quartermaster joined us). He conned squadron cooks out of food including a side of beef and a flock of dead chickens. Skidrow conned dark clouds out of rain and the sun into radiant shining. We tossed in a couple of rifles too. *Bear* roamed those flaming woods. Cameras and duffel in hand, we climbed aboard the truck, and like dead-end kids gleefully skipping school, headed out Ladd's back gate and into the boonies.

Other than standard fare in meat I've also eaten buffalo (old, stringy and tough), bear (strong, rich and gamy), moose (dark, juicy, tangy), elk (better than moose), venison (better than elk), caribou (outstanding but sweeter than beef or veal), and finally, Alaskan salmon: Sockeye, Silver and Chinook. There's none better—*anywhere!*

You couldn't care less what I eat. So why did I bring it up? Not to whet your appetite, no indeedy. Simply to report that all of the above tasted ten times better than that unfortunate side of supposedly cooked beef offered to the starving by our self-appointed backyard barbecue cooks. Hanging was too good for those dimwits! Pah-phooey! I can still taste it.

Realizing that a camping trip simply meant transferring cooking chores outdoors, the squadron's cooks were too smart to brave the boondocks with us. Thus our volunteers—all rejects from Cooks and Bakers School—proceeded to demonstrate what they didn't know. What they subjected that lovely haunch of beef to bordered on the criminal. First they trussed it up like a Christmas goose. Next, having formed a sapling tripod, they suspended dinner over high open flames. The result, a blackened, cinderous exterior married to a raw interior. It wasn't half bad, it was all bad! If you will excuse a bad pun—the chicken was fowl, too!

For two days we fished, forded streams, found Felix Pedro's abandoned gold mine, slapped at mosquitoes, swapped lies, ate pork and beans (not me!), got lost—found a trading post full of beer—slapped at mosquitoes, fished some more, played jokes on Skid, and then headed back to base slapping at more *mosquitoes.* All in all we had a wonderful time!

Skidrow failed us only once. He never successfully conned *all* Ladd's mosquitoes into permanently bugging the Army—on t'other side of the base.

• • •

"Sgt. Judge, AR-947's radio needs testing. I'm flying out to Tangle Lakes with supplies for the bivouacking research crew. Care to go along?"

Now you and I both know when an officer queries like that he's not requesting—he's giving a flaming order. What am I gonna reply, "No, captain, me old darlin', I'm plannin' on havin' a long lunch!"

I gathered my survival gear and climbed into the Cessna. Possessed of my own pilot's license today, flying was a joy for me and I truly liked to fly with Cap. A little later I'll add more about his piloting skills. What follows raises a possible question about other areas in his smarts department.

We flew together many times: through ice fog, forest fire, and frigid weather that iced the wings so badly that we had to set the plane on the ground in a hurry before becoming permanently attached to it. So, a little jaunt to a group of lakes in good weather; hey, slice me another piece of cake.

Cap loved to fish. You can bet his creel, fishing rod and waders got in as much flying time as did the fisherman.

In order to keep flight status current, pilots must "shoot landings." In Alaska they had to practice them on floats, skis and wheels, in fair weather or foul. This trip would involve a float landing and, of course, fishing. The radio worked perfectly so I settled back and smiled at the envious clouds who couldn't fly as fast as us. Cap's landing was a perfect "drop." His fishing line soon tantalizing those who travel around with their mouths open, I homesteaded a stump and proceeded to implant the view into memory.

Frank and a buddy were camped at Tangle Lakes for a few days, hence the need for fresh supplies along with determination of their welfare. Frank—ostensibly—was checking out summer survival gear, new equipment just in from stateside. Between you and me, I think he was goofing off. In fact, the only reason I'm cluttering up my story with him, as perhaps you might think I'm a touch inclined to exaggerate, is because he caught photo evidence of what occurred.

Fishing in Alaska could be described in one word—*fabulous!* If that state has decimated their salmon, as has Oregon, it cannot, and probably never will be the same singing reel paradise today.

The captain, having almost caught his limit and happy as a mosquito setting up to spear a fat, juicy arm, required my services. "Sergeant, I'm going to call the base and check in. I don't want to drain the battery so I'm going to start the engine. Hitch a rope onto the pontoon tie-downs, hold the plane snug to the bank and don't turn her loose. I won't take long."

What he planned on doing couldn't be considered a major brain teaser; consequently, I didn't foresee trouble, and to hear is to obey.

I tied a rope's end to each pontoon thus forming a loop. The bank at that spot appeared to be mostly gravel and possibly a tad slippery, so utilizing but a pittance of my incredible intelligence, I placed the loop over my head and slid it down to the middle of my justly envied, muscular back. In that way I could dig in the old heels, then lean back into the rope making a stronger and more secure human anchor. Pretty cool, huh? It worked like hot butter on popcorn until Cap terminated his message, at which time he GOOSED the engine! Scholars from around the world have asked why ever since. As for myself, I flat had no time to ponder—plane and I were headed out into the lake! Afraid I would drown me before my time, I did something foolish. Still entangled and being dragged, I flipped the rope up and over my head praying it would kindly not snap my neck. I recollected the lake's winter ice had

DON'T GOOSE IT !

Mollie-O

been gone but a scant three days. The shock of hitting that freezing cold water punched my breath out of me. Angels purely smile on idiots! By great good fortune my submerged body sank to only a depth of three feet and I managed to stand up. Then, inhaling and expelling air like a snorting polar bear, I made it back to shore in two and one-half jumps.

Cap was now floating in the middle of the lake. Ask me if I cared! After he quit laughing, Frank stoked the fire and we began to steam me and my clothes. Certainly my trembling wasn't from fear. Not much! Returning the Cessna to shore, the captain asked why the hell I'd released the rope against orders?

"Cap, you'll never believe this, but a six foot mosquito bit me on the arse and then spat me in the lake. If Frank will loan his gun I'll shoot the S.O.B.!"

Alert! We Have a Plane Down

A s all too soon summer waned, the airwaves waxed with frantic cries for the Tenth's services. Impatient to blanket fallen leaves, snow dropped in on an early reconnoiter. Approving of Alaska's, aesthetic surroundings, she slowly pulled up her blanket and snuggled down for a long winter's snooze.

Take a stretch and then settle back, friend. Borrowing from a *You Are There* adventure, I'm going to smuggle you aboard our C-47 and let you participate in a rescue from inception to—hopefully—a successful conclusion:

A bush pilot flying a DeHaviland Beaver inbound from Kotzebue is three hours overdue from a scheduled landing at Tanana. The last position report radioed in from Galena located him passing Hughes. At that time, the pilot had informed of snow squalls and icing. Nothing more had been heard from him. A veteran flyer and accustomed to harsh Alaskan weather, he'd have set the Beaver down if possible. This one doesn't look good.

Our pilot is also experienced in coping with bad flying conditions. He wears oak leaves. Captain Mustache (tall, good looking, quite vain about his soup strainer which decorated his upper lip in the classic style), co-pilots. The major commands and under his guidance the captain will, in time, become a skilled searcher.

Daylight lasts a bit longer in October. Alerted late, and flying in a C-47, we've just about two hours left before nightfall. If we strike out the crew will overnight in Galena and start the search again at dawn.

One word describes the people in the outlying communities in 1949-50—*superb!* I have no doubt they measure up just the same today. Homes were opened to the Air Force. Home-cooked food, good conversation—some of their wilderness stories were astounding—and comfortable beds were offered. No matter the hour of rising, breakfast would be ready. Hot coffee and plenty of chow were prepared, ready to fill hollow legs. Monitoring their radios, eager to pass on any new information or warn searchers of deteriorating weather, those people sat glued before microphones all day. Other bush pilots also flew, hunting for the missing; those guys always started first and quit last. Alaskans held and still hold them dear to their hearts.

The first full search day: visibility fair, no snow, altitude 1,000 to 2,000 feet, terrain remote and three-fourths forest; including bush pilots, twelve planes involved in search have covered twenty grid sectors; approaching dusk now limits hunt time. No word. No luck. (Most small planes were not equipped with emergency radio beacons in the early post-war years).

Day two: visibility fair, interrupted by snow squalls; terrain flat but rugged, altitude 1,000 feet. Some icing, do you hear it thumping off the fuselage? Thank God the de-icers are working; bless the guy who designed that lovely grid, we haven't mistakenly reworked any area and that has to increase the downed guy's chances. Another long day. No word. No luck.

Day three: Rested, full of hot coffee and good grub; raring, eager, off we go; visibility excellent, full sun; terrain open, flat, altitude 2,000 feet. Maybe today? Most of the grid's been covered, have we missed him? All that whiteness is making my head ache. We better get to him soon, temperature's dropping to 8°F. at night. It's much colder inside plane. Another tiring, no luck day. Good, the field lights are on. Damn, I wish we had better news.

Day four: Storm front due here in thirty-six hours. Grid numbers 48 out of 60 have been searched; terrain, intermittent forest and plain, some hills; altitude varying between 1,500 and 2,500 feet; visibility still remains good; time 0900 hours. (C'mon man, where the hell are you?) Check off grid 49. My eyes are blurring on me, I thought I saw a reflection in that grove of trees, probably the horns of a damn moose! No, wait, there it is again.

"Frank, take a look over here. Do you see that glitter? Looks like a wing tip. Major, make a 360, I think there's something in that small forest to port."

Losing altitude as we circle, at the 180 degree point it becomes easier to identify wreckage. Ski tracks have run smack into that grove. Looks like the fuselage is intact. One wing is canting skyward which accounts for the glitter. Bingo! It's a plane like the one we're after. Pray we're not too late!

Day four: 1100 hours. No way we can set this baby down that close to those trees, skis or no. Our trail crew medic (better him than me!) has to jump and check it out. Meanwhile, while we continue to circle, the major will radio base to recall one of our searching C-54's to refuel, load sleeping bags, sled, dogs and more trail crew. Three miles to the east there appears to be four or five level acres capable of landing a glider. If the pilot is alive, the trail crew will tramp out the landing zone and erect the snatch poles.

Safely down, the jumper's reached the wreck. Via walky-talky he radios the bush pilot has a broken leg, possible cracked ribs, is suffering from contusions and hypothermia and, while in bad shape, he is still alive! Fortunately, although now wing-less, the plane's cabin had remained intact, providing some escape from the cold; couple that with the blanket he managed to cover himself with and, knowing the Tenth would come, he'd hung on. If the wreck were not so far from a serviceable field, the trail crew could load the injured pilot on the sled and mush him to where we, having then landed, could take him aboard and fly direct to Ladd and the base hospital. No can do. We'll radio for the other C-54 to bring a glider. A C-47 could also do the job; but, coping with a heavy layer of ground snow, a snatch by a lesser powered plane could become a touch iffy.

Day four: 1300 hours. Here comes the plane carrying sled, dogs and more trail crew troops. Sure is pretty to see. Our major will sight a landing area for the glider while their crew prepares to kick sled and dogs out. Three more trail crew members will jump; one over the wreck so as to hitch up the dogs, help load the hurt man on the sled, and break trail to the glider landing zone. The other two will bail out over the landing sight and once on the ground, because of the heavy snow layer, tramp it down as firmly as possible. They will then erect the snatch poles for when glider arrives. There go the jumpers. Hot damn, I see three lovely open chutes! While we continue circling the wreck awaiting tow plane and the Tenth's glider, her work finished the first C-54 four-engine job dips her wings as she heads back to base.

Day four: 1400 hours. The injured man secure and well blanketed on the sled, the trail crew will now mush to pick-up zone. Fuel is getting low, but not critical; we'll stay and see the rescue through. The major continues to circle, waiting to spot the landing zone for the glider. I always enjoy watching dog teams race over snow when their services are essential and I bet they know it.

Day four: 1420 hours. Here she comes. And there, the glider's been released from the tow. Beautiful! In appearance, a down pillow with wings. Floating effortlessly, she side slips, sights on her mark and rushes for the earth. Cross your fingers. Oh, yeah, a fine landing. The trail crew position the poles quickly to allow the glider to face into the wind—that pilot will need all the lift he can get! Rescue dogs and their all important sled cargo approach rapidly. Lemme tell you, this is classic textbook performed by pros. I see the heavy tow cable is securely stretched between the poles, awaiting the hook. Another cable has been fastened from nose of glider to snatch cable. All is ready to drag our engineless sweetheart and her special cargo free of that clinging field of snow. The major executes one more slow circle. Patient's been carefully placed aboard; now load dogs, sled, and trail crew. A last look, nothing forgotten, our pilot boards and prepares himself for the grab.

Wind, still nose on, is picking up a little. Good. Our job done, we'll get out of the intended flight path and this time cross fingers, eyes and toes! The C-54 pilot, preparing to snatch, makes one final pass to gauge cable height, circles— engines roaring—and bores in again. Showtime! Make it good, guy.

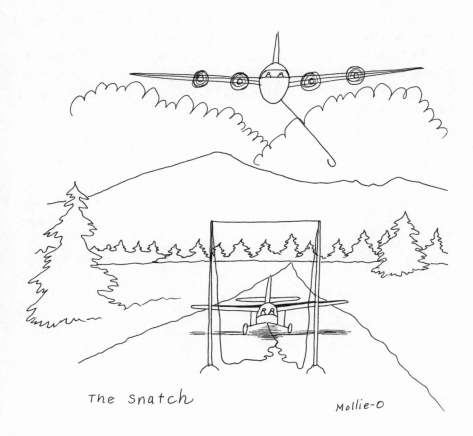

The snatch

Mollie-O

TWANG! SWOOSH! Right on the button. Away she goes riding the air to Fairbanks, and—for a lucky man—care, a warm hospital bed, loved ones.

What about the glider poles? When tempo slows and conditions are right our trail crew will hike back in to get them, or a trapper will hire out to transport the lot to Galena for pick-up. For now, to hell with them. Fuel is now close to bad news. This old hayburner is ready for some oats, and so is her crew. Everybody holler to the boss to throttle her up and boom her on home.

And there you have one example of an air search and rescue, conducted by the United States Air Force, Tenth Air Rescue Squadron, Detachment B, Fairbanks, Alaska. The fully recovered pilot is, for all I know—although most assuredly long in the tooth by now—still flying.

I'm sorry I forgot to fit you out in cold-weather gear chum, I hope you didn't get your nose frost-bitten!

We were not always that lucky or successful. If your blood pressure can stand a touch more excitement, after I've related a few more hair-raising adventures, I'll tell you about one of the Tenth's own real bummers.

Captain Popsicle

11

While the cold ground slept, winter threw a party, everybody came: Snow, Sleet, Ice-fog, those Whiteouts, the Silver Thaws, our playful triplets—Thirty, Forty and Fifty Below—not to mention, the Howling Blizzards. It was a wonderful party, lots and lots of fun! The effect on the dispositions of Alaska's teeth-chattering troops?

Let me try to explain it this way: I reside in Oregon. It rains in Oregon. It rains a lot in Oregon. It rains all the time in Oregon. Sure, we expect it in October, November, December, January, February, March and half of April, but—like this year—twenty-four days in *May*, 5.55 inches! Just once I wish I'd run into the Rain King. How I'd love to give him a knuckle sandwich! We felt exactly the same way toward that winter. One all the way from the floor uppercut, smack on her chin! It wasn't too much to desire. The Tenth staggered through those exhausting days, shell-shocked and dazed, while call after call for help came from Nome, Point Barrow, McGrath, Talkeetna, Willow, Bethel, Bettles and Tanana. And that was but the tip of the iceberg.

March, 1950. "Hello, Tenth Rescue. Point Barrow calling. One of our single-engine civilian planes is overdue. Will you help us search?" Within minutes rescue efforts were underway. Duties during this search were different for me. I was ordered to enplane for Barter Island to establish a radio station.

Flying the coast of the Beaufort Sea and further north to the Arctic Ocean, communicating with Fairbanks was difficult as signals had to surmount the Brooks Range. Voice communication became impossible. CW (continuous wave) intermittent at best. A relay station definitely needed, it became my job to install it.

Needed supplies and equipment aboard, an early departure scheduled—could a stay-abed ever depart at leisure? We rocked wings at the clouds and headed off to challenge those brooding, foreboding mountains. I buckled up tight, but not to fret, that flight was accomplished with typical expertise. After one pass to determine field conditions, our ski equipped C-47 settled smoothly onto the island's snow laden surface with scarcely any bucking.

Walking on iced-over terra firma considering several suitable locations for the all important communications shack, I stopped and took a look at Barter Island. From the air she was endless snow stretching in all directions, but with my feet planted on land, the viewing clarified. Ubiquitous Quonset huts—rounded and snow-bound to their roofs—sat side by side like prone sumo wrestlers. Eskimo huts made of all manner of wood and metal dotted the landscape. A rusted World War II LST, cable chained to the land—I thought unnecessarily—lay hopelessly ice-bound. An enclosed-cabin fishing boat, the dwarf to the giant, kept her company. In all, cold and barren Barter Island definitely would not be considered the year's tourist mecca.

Listed in order of importance, three questions required answers: Location and accessibility to the necessary? How far to the chow hall? And, where could I possibly install the flaming radio? The facilities— to one accustomed to a modicum of comfort—presented an utterly charming adventure in itself.

Barter Island, if I haven't made it clear, is one frigid son of an ice cube; hence, the troops two-holer required heat! Picture this. Adorned in arctic gear, one opens the door and steps into a blast furnace. Heat radiating from that oil stove would have encouraged a seal-hunting polar bear to remove his overcoat. Ensconced on the throne—trousers at half-mast—the opposite climatic condition prevails and one's exposed derriere freezes in record time. Above decks, sweat pours off one's blistering countenance. Below decks, all feeling gone, naught but numbness pervades. Let me tell you, one dasn't linger! Upon leaving, due to a frost-covered butt, care must be taken that one's trousers have not become entangled in the seat. Not only will progress toward yon welcome exit abruptly halt, a very delicate part of one's anatomy—absolutely in harm's way—could become a permanent addition to the Barter Island loo!

The chow hall, a larger Quonset, boasted a hand painted sign hung (should have been lynched!) over the doorway. "THROUGH THESE PORTALS PASS THE LARGEST BEANS IN THE WORLD!" That says it all.

Now it happened that sometime in the past a C-82 flying boxcar had made a good and a bad landing. No one had been hurt but the wings had parted company with the fuselage, as had tail and stabilizer. I suspect that along with the engines these had been scavenged. However, the derelict's empty and forlorn but intact body would be ideal—better yet, she was rent free. Radio gear stacked by my feet, I watched the C-47 equipped with JATO (Jet Assisted Take Off) for short fields, stand on her tail as the thruster bottles attached to her wings, emitting trails of white smoke, kicked her into the sky—a pretty sight.

Ever notice how some people are a touch shy when it comes to expressing gratitude after you've worked your carcass to a frigid frazzle for them? In double quick time one each antenna, firmly spiked in ice, stood eager and tall, thrusting into the air like a hermit sniffing hopefully for an early spring thaw. Chalk up radio receiver and transmitter benched cozily side by side awaiting a nudge from *Alec* (mechanic's parlance for electricity), which makes them talkative. I'd scrounged two comfortable chairs: American steel; backs frames and seats maybe a scosh chilly on the backside if 'twere ever apt to cool off. No danger there. Barter Island never drops much below minus fifty degrees Fahrenheit. Add a kerosene heater also courtesy of the installer. I even contemplated curtains for the windows. After all, long neglected, the boxcar lady was lonesome and could stand a little primp and fuss. And there she was, all made up, ready, eager to receive company. The old bag looked pretty good all spiffied up, if I do say so myself.

In flew two radio operators tickled pink to be the first to throw the switch.

"Barter Island calling Tenth Air Rescue, Fairbanks. Come in headquarters." Silence, then …"We read you 3 by 3, BI. How's the weather? Have you played slap and tickle with any polar bears? Fairbanks, over."

Hot smash! I'd just participated in the agony and joy of birth. My child lived! "Barter Island, repeat your last, you came in garbled. Did you say Judge was a genius? Fairbanks, over."

We were transmitting medium on voice, but CW (Morse code) would relay us just fine. Search planes will radio messages to BI. BI will transmit them on to Fairbanks. After study, headquarters will send back instructions which we will pass on to searchers. Ain't communication grand? Then, just because an occasional blue spark charging up hairy arms neoned their bushy eyebrows, those Morse key thumpers had the gall to gripe. True, I may have forgotten to ground some of the critical pieces of equipment; transmitters, you'll remember, were not my long suit. Besides, a teeny little zap once in awhile keeps 'em on their toes—nobody's perfect! Those bozos didn't even have the grace to express thanks for the walkway, freshly shoveled right up to Madam Boxcar's door!

• • •

Alaska is a glorious state. She overflows in grandeur, beauty and brave people, but she is not for the faint hearted. Nor, like all ladies of loveliness, does she enjoy being taken for granted. Never coy, what you see is what you get. Any mistakes made while courting the lady had best be small ones. Slight her, and the queen of the north is most unforgiving.

My tenure in Alaska covered two years. In that time we failed but twice to find downed aircraft. Regrettably that Point Barrow search was one of them. A month passed in the looking: an all out extensive two weeks by the Tenth, a further two weeks by bush pilots. Our final consensus: the missing plane's compass went haywire during poor visibility, not unusual that close to the Pole. Instead of flying inland the pilot headed out over the Beaufort Sea, possibly even on to the Arctic Ocean before, with no landmarks visible, eventually running out of gas and crashing through the ice.

No trace of him was ever found.

Engaged in mercy missions it's not unknown for rescue craft themselves to go down, be they bush or military planes. In fact that is exactly what happened during another of our most heartrending, all out, search efforts. I'll relate that episode for you a little later.

Looking so far back, two things remain most vivid: how exhausting and mean-minded the winter of 1949-50 was and how proudly we walked. I don't remember the number of rescues made, yet, we succeeded with all except for two.

Preparation and training should rate foremost with top-of-the-line outfits, and the Tenth Air Rescue was top of the line. Accordingly, we took advantage of opportunities for further training during the Point Barrow search. Barter Island supplied us the ideal frozen terrain needed for man to hone his cold weather survival techniques. We had to constantly ready ourselves to square off against Mother Nature and live to brag about it.

Lesson number one: Your aircraft has crash-landed on Arctic ice. What should you do? Picking up the phone and calling AAA isn't allowed, besides it's long distance. One had better possess the knowledge and skill to build a snow house. A touch of trivia: While my clumsy feet were sliding all over Barter Island's ice, I was informed in no uncertain terms by an expert, that an igloo is not a snow house. An igloo is a hut built by Eskimos from flotsam and jetsam and anything else that isn't nailed down, and is used as permanent living quarters. A snow house is formed of giant cubes carved from a really big block of icy snow. It is usually constructed for the temporary use of an Eskimo hunting for seal or—foolishly—polar bear. It includes a crawl tunnel added for one specific purpose, discouragement to that same polar bear who is also out hunting for a free meal. A snow house, skillfully built, can be heated by a single candle. True. I've tested that brag and it works.

Lesson number two: The GI version of Sterno makes a dandy

cook stove. Even K-rations become palatable if, one, you are desperately hungry; two, you've stepped through the bean portal door and run smack into the twin brother of a certain master sergeant who just happened to run the basic training mess hall at the lowly recruits alma mater, Lackland AFB. (Not a son of da barracks corporal?) As though it were yesterday I can still hear his dulcet tones: "Men, if you wuz home ya mudda would have youse put some of everthin' on yer plate an' 'nen tell ya ta try it, right? Now you boys jist pertend I'm ya mudda, while yer away from her apron strings, an' youse take an' eat some of everthin' the cooks—who've slaved away all day long—have graciously prepared fer youse. YOU FLAMIN' DUNDERHEADS GOT THAT!"

Lesson number three: Always, always, always carry a pair of dry socks, preferably two, and change often, often, often.

We erected snow houses all over Barter Island, learned, survived and enjoyed ourselves. Who said education is boring?

(Aside: If my informer, re snow house versus igloo, was wrong, perhaps dear reader you will take pen in hand and so inform me. No sense in asking my traveling companion, the poor soul has never even seen snow!)

• • •

Another cold weather chore assigned to the Tenth was the testing of new gear: clothing, electronic equipment and safety apparatus. Colder than a certain part of a brass monkey's anatomy, Barter Island fit the bill admirably.

I always breathed easier once we cleared the threatening, brooding, beckoning, and mainly human uninhabited, Brooks Range. It was one of the last truly remote areas in North America in 1949 and I suspect it still is. Any unfortunate pilot going down in that wilderness would be mighty hard to find—alive. Separating the Yukon Valley from the arctic slope, the range is an extension of the Rocky Mountain system. Some peaks reach a height of eleven thousand feet. The average width of the Brooks is eighty miles. Often forced to fly at heights from 15,000 to 20,000 feet to allow for a clear margin of safety, it was a real thrill listening to ice bouncing off the fuselage. The good news—at least the de-icers were working.

Hooty-tooty. Once again, we thankfully trod the frozen ground of Barter Island. Our assignment on this trip, twofold: test new felt boots, fiberglass flight jackets and pants, and test the latest model of the Gibson Girl. During World War II downed aircraft had no built-in radio emergency signaling devices, as do those of today. Flyers had to rely on the GIB girl. She was a box-like contraption, containing a hard on the butt narrow seat on one end, with crank handles inserted on either side. As Miss Gibson did not come equipped with batteries, transmission required cranking of the handles. Once up to speed a short range signal transmitted, which could be picked up and homed in on by searching aircraft. Two drawbacks: The range quite limited, searchers had to be close to pick up your signal, and she only worked when *constantly* cranked. That, of course, presupposes the pilot's in good enough condition to do the cranking after that sudden and unplanned landing!

Consider the predicament. If the cranker starts out a crank, then constant cranking makes him crankier, not to mention the off-pouring of perspiration engendered by the cranking—right? That action thus tends to make the crank, cum-cranker, a tad crankier, especially if no one shows up to rescue him!

Excluding the pilots, our test group was comprised of one captain and three enlisted men, Frank, Edgar and me. Having arrived fresh from a desk job in the Pentagon the officer stood, short, thin and terribly eager. Bucking for major, he charged right into the frozen fray—so to speak.

Wearing the new clothing, we set up thirty feet from a small hut inside of which burned a warm cheerful fire in one of those ubiquitous Alaskan oil stoves. Once outside, hopefully comfortably warm in our new gear, we were to take turns cranking the latest version of Ma Gibson to see if she would perform well in the *real cold* and how far the signal would range. That newer updated model was supposed to transmit a third again as far which would be a definite improvement.

The temperature outside that hut, in Fahrenheit degrees, fluctuated between forty and fifty below zero.

Taking fifteen minute spells each outside, eventually—as kind Providence often arranges—the captain ended up *out*, we enlisted three, *in*. My but it was comfy and warm; we lingered. From time to time, truly concerned for the outside guy, we peered out the window; the dedicated captain cranked on and on and on.

"Shouldn't one of us go and relieve him? He's been out there a long time."

"Naw," breezed Frank. "He's an officer, they get paid to climb and then ski down the higher, challenging mountains."

"Hey guys, look," warned Ed. "He's stopped cranking, his arms aren't moving and he's sure sitting awful still. We really ought to spell him."

"Yeah, Ed, you're right, pretty quick one of us will go. I do believe it's your turn Frank. Sure is mighty cozy and warm in here though."

So okay, you're absolutely correct, the compassionate should take pity on the freezing, surely they'd do it for you. Almost immediately—give or take another twenty minutes—we went out, chipped his hands free of the handles, carried him inside, and propped him up by that nice warm stove. Within seconds—he was that grateful—he started to cry. Of course, that could have been the icicles melting off his eyebrows. Regardless, when the last piece of ice slid off his jaw and he could use it again, Captain Popsicle expressed satisfaction with the testing, decreed an end to the festivities and announced he was ready to return to Fairbanks. Well, to be sure, total dedication is all. To a man we quickly volunteered to continue testing, should the need arise.

The new cold weather clothing tested out great, especially the boots. I'd no idea felt could be so warm. I've worn them in weather of fifty-eight degrees below zero and my tootsies remained as warm as a hot-buttered crumpet, except when the wind blew. Felt boots and wind get along like polar bears lunching *with* rather than *on* seals! Fiberglass thwarts cold superbly. But never get close to excessive heat, like maybe a red-hot oil heater or a mess hall cook stove. The fiberglass will melt first, promptly followed by the one wearing it.

Mother Gibson conducted herself in true Air Force fashion, sending out signal after signal, cold or no, like she was making free with her phone number to her two favorite beaus—the Army and the Navy. According to our pickup planes, her range had also, as promised, increased. Hey, we thought ourselves pretty hot stuff. I can't help but laugh at how primitive we were compared to today's sophistication.

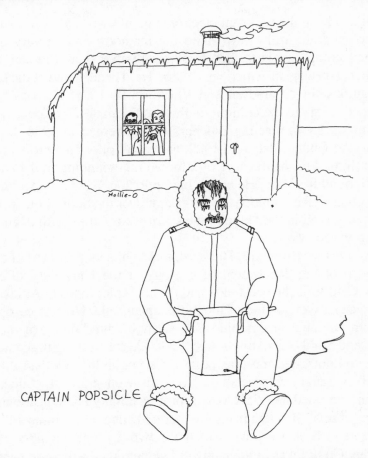

CAPTAIN POPSICLE

Oh, well, everybody's gotta learn to walk before they can begin to run.

After defrosting, test results clutched in his hands, the captain ordered us to pack up and we all flew back to Ladd. Bidding us a relieved and hasty good-bye, the future major, anxious to head stateside, his briefcase tightly clasped to his bosom, skipped rapidly up the stairway of his plane and flew away to sunnier and warmer climes. He was such a nice little guy—for a wheel! A dollar to a donut he retired from the Pentagon, a general.

Once in a while, Mr. Average Citizen is privileged to sit among the great. A flight to the North Pole was scheduled. I'm not sure why but I became a member of the crew. Given the usual conditions the radio had undoubtedly turned toes up. I probably went along to forcibly resurrect and keep the reluctant electronic mouth working. But that isn't the point. Yours truly flew off to the far north among very distinguished company. The pilot was the Tenth's own Colonel Bernt Balchen, Norwegian-American aviator. He'd headed one of the search expeditions for Amundsen and Ellsworth in 1925. He was also a member of their expedition to the Arctic in 1926. The explorer Richard E. Byrd, meeting Balchen in Spitsbergen in 1926, brought him to the United States. In 1927, as second pilot on Byrd's transatlantic flight, he was the hero of a forced night landing in the surf off the Normandy coast. He was chief pilot on Byrd's expedition to Antarctica which included the first flight over the South Pole in 1929. Balchen served in the United States Army Air Corps with distinction during World War II.

Add Father Bernard J. Hubbard, famed glacier priest. At one time the head of the department of geology at the University of Santa Clara, California, he was renowned for his explorations of Aniakchak, the volcanic wonderland of the Alaska peninsula. He also co-operated with National Geographic in a study of the "Valley of the Ten Thousand Smokes." In his words: "...in Alaska, nothing in scenic values is too amazing, too unexpected, for possibility. We had thought ourselves sated with years of Alaskan wonders; yet, Aniakchak Volcano revealed new. It is as awesome as mighty Katmai, abounding in bird, animal, fish and plant life that make it a world in itself."

Seated cheek by jowl with those two, a valid member of the Ignorant Club, I was quite happy to fade into the background and listen with pleasure to the intelligent converse. Unfortunately, that memorable flight was too soon over. Bad weather socked in. One hundred miles from the pole, ice playing a fandango on the fuselage, our destination now perilous, we had to do a "one-eighty" and turn back. Balchen made the right choice. A big disappointment to me. No matter, 'twas an eventful flight anyway and I've never forgotten it. Those two gentlemen imparted to me an even greater respect for Alaska.

Theah's a Beah!

A fter our failure at Point Barrow, Mammy (I called that winter Mammy Yokum because of her penchant for bouncing uppercuts off the glass jaws of the unwashed. Hey, she never let up, who had time for a bath!) eased off a wee tad. We figured she'd punched herself out so the boss let us catch up on laundry chores, pigging out, and lost sleep.

There blares the blasted phone! A MATS C-54 (Military Air Transport Service), carrying rotating airmen (those leaving Alaska to take up duties on bases in the interior or returning for discharge) including dependents and children, enroute from Anchorage to Whitehorse and thence to Great Falls, Montana, was overdue two radio position reports. The portends of this one added up calamitous.

Headquarters at Anchorage coordinated the grid search pattern. The Tenth Rescue covered from Fairbanks, the Chain (Aleutian Islands) and Anchorage. Canada also joined in the hunt. A week into that search a C-47 of our own, flying out of headquarters, went down. Scratch one plane! Fortunately she was found, sitting undignifiedly on the side of a mountain with her butt sticking up in the air, her crew having suffered no serious injuries. But naturally, the de-icers had quit, and the airplane had become one, huge, non-flying boulder, and then transformed itself into that fearsome Indian that citizens are always warned to be on the lookout for—"Falling Rock!"

During two weeks of intense looking, Dear Ma Yokum, caught up in a maternal quandary, co-operated; sadly, it was to be of no avail. We never found a single sign. One hell of a month, flying. We'd spent hours servicing, and again flying tired planes. We'd followed every lead no matter how erroneous or bizarre. Finally, sorrowfully, we had to admit defeat. It really hurt. Damn it, we were good at our job. Why not a single sign? What had we missed? Sure, terrain loomed mountainous, rugged, mean; settlers were few and far between; a blowing storm also muffles sound. Alaska displays lots of real estate and yet you'd think we'd find at least a trace of a plane the size of a DC-6!

Theory from the think-tank boys? Flying conditions far from optimum, MATS must have—even with their de-icers working— picked up some extra weight. If her radar was inadequate, enough altitude might have been lost to run her into a mountain. A resulting avalanche may have covered the plane, and fresh falling snow had probably then blanketed the scar created by the crash. That seemed to be the logical conclusion. Regardless, we carried the cross of failure again. It was a heavy load.

Finally longer days and a little budding appeared. We heard cracking, thundering, booming and splashing as winter ice departed the Tanana and the Chena rivers. Three hundred million mosquitoes, determined to draw blood, awakened and flew in to Ladd buzzing their battle cry, "Stuff your DDT!"

The boss, who'd worked every bit as long and hard as his men, decided all his "grunts" had earned a break. The darlin' man decreed a week's R&R for his troops, at Blair Lake, which would not come off regular furlough time.

I'll try to picture Alaska in words: hundreds of lakes, never ending forests, awesome glaciers, powerful rivers and streams, superb mountains, snow-blanketed valleys, endless Arctic ice;

the Aurora Borealis; sunrises placing joy in your step, brilliant sunsets coloring the sky and, not sated, that same setting sun, minutes later, popping right back up to warm anew. Add magnificent wildlife and you eyeball but a smidgen of her wonders. If she be Seward's Folly, we should all be that dumb! From the air, I never grew tired of drinking her in.

Claimed but not owned by a weather squadron squatting at one of her ends, Blair Lake was further homesteaded in her middle by the Tenth Rescue. Our trail crew had built a cabin capable of housing eight GIs, bunk-bed-style. Two windows, *one door*. Primitive? Yes, but most appropriate for a getaway from a never silent telephone. Complete with boat plus motor, and a dock for a floatplane, it checked out ideal for fishing, fun and *folly!*

Egress to the lake was by pontoon plane only. True, they had a weasel (like a jeep on tank tracks) but it had made its own trail in. There was no road. During winter a ski plane could also land there. The gang of "hit the bricks and find the lost" were always too busy during the frigid times to find out so I don't know if they ever did.

Floatplane takeoffs and landings are—to put it mildly—different. Consider landings: There are two ways to set down on rivers or lakes. When the water's surface is smooth and flat it is hard to judge distance from same, especially when one moves at speed over it.

Plan A: Continue your descent as for a normal wheeled landing, but if yon mirrored surface misleads as to closeness, results may well become an abrupt parting, due to running out of air and slamming into water, of pontoons, plane and in all likelihood— you! Thus, a real sinking feeling adds excitement to the end of your flight.

Plan B: Observing water's surface closely during descent, when one calculates he/she is just above (forgive me) splashdown, flare the plane, chop the throttle and drop onto lake. If faithful eyesight held true, water and floats gently kiss and landing is successful. Oh, joy, flight chalks up another big winner. On the other hand, if pilot's eyesight comes up boxcars, the drop— rather than a kiss—becomes a belt in the chops. Instead of retaining pontoons, the plane bestows them upon nearsighted pilot. In the long run, even if it puts a damper on their day, most pilots prefer Plan B.

Takeoffs can be likened to passionate kisses between lovers, the lake being the She, the plane being the He. Prolonged hugging and kissing, as you well know, involves a certain amount of suction. Embraced tightly, albeit tenderly, the He, anxious to try his wings elsewhere, concludes that the brief, fevered interlude must end. But how? With nothing but trees and wind for company, the She has no desire to part. Fact. Unless *joint release* be effected, hugee could end up hugging hugger forever. Concerned, lest He hurt She's feelings and not wanting to lose gentleman status, He lightly rev's his motor, floats to the far end of She, and then guns into motion. Throttle full on, He puts himself up on the "step" and surfaces rapidly over She.

Achieving "step" is akin to lifting one leg at a time free of thick gumbo and placing it on firmer ground; all walking proceeds better that way. A float plane achieves freedom when pilot abruptly rocks its wings which will, one at a time, lift the pontoons onto the water's surface. Naturally, such rising will break She's hold on He and air now flowing over the wings creates lift. Before reaching the end of Lake She, He springs into the air, climbs for altitude, circles, and fondly wags his wings farewell; He then heads off home to the wife and kids.

However, if prior to that, a friend of the lake—the wind—determined to help, shapes She's lips into those of an orangutan, trouble can ride the waves. I've never kissed an orangutan, but I bet it takes a lot of gorilla power to break that kind of suction; He will know it turned out a touch fine when, after a lengthened takeoff run, She's other friends—those tall, rapidly approaching trees at the far end—reach out and wipe her pitiful tears off the pontoons!

I reached Blair Lake via our float equipped L-5. The L-5, as previously stated, is a single-engine, slow flying, reconnaissance plane used extensively for artillery spotting in World War II, and soon to come into her own again in Korea. A canvas wrapped job, it provides absolutely no protection from ground or air fire.

Looking down as we circled, the lake made a pretty wilderness sight. My pilot, a major, elected to drop onto the water. He said it was about five feet. I say it was about two stories! This I know, if that L-5 lingers to this day it bears a perfect and impressive bow in the bottom of the fuselage from my butt! We hit so hard my backside passed my eyebrows on first impact before gravity tried to push the rest of me through the plane's own bottom. Fortunately, that old canvasback had been built rugged and we held together.

Wobbling, I wished a successful takeoff for the major and headed off the dock and up the stairs to home for the next week. I purely believed things were looking up. Frank, Charlie, Rosario, Gene and Ed were already there. Losing no time we grabbed poles and hustled to the dock eager to catch supper. The lake abounded in pickerel and you could snag 'em with a beer can opener. They don't put up much of a fight and often hug the lake's bottom before quickly surrendering; still, cooked fresh caught they are mighty tasty.

Fishing in the land of the midnight sun was dying and waltzing around in Heaven. Those lakes, rivers and streams back in 1949-51 were unspoiled, virginal, and crying for a friendly visit from anglers. To abate such loneliness, we wiped away their sniffles by visiting often.

Care to go for a swim, perhaps do a little boating, try your hand at water skiing? I have to be honest here. That last sport was invented about the time I was born (yeah, that long ago!). Nonetheless, we of the Tenth perfected it. No small thanks to us, water skiing made a big splash in the twentieth century. Accepting the challenge of the new and relatively untried, we disdained the curved tip ski. One four-foot by three-foot piece of five-eighth inch plywood sufficed. We looped a rope from one side to the other for a rein. A long rope led from front center of board to boat. Skier stood on back of board, holding its front free of the water by pulling on rein. Boat took off, board took off, rider took off. Smooth skiing unless boat curved in water and rider allowed front of board to touch, nay, *dip* into water. Boat motor not tower of power, and drag of ski through water causes

severe loss of speed. Groaning boat slows and stops, rider does
not although, now soaring through space, he could most certainly be accused of desertion of sinking ski! Encountering that
frigid water (it was June, the ice had been gone from the lake but
a scant week!) headfirst, quite unexpectedly and suddenly, was
akin to ramming one's sensitive skull into the side of an iceberg,
and you know what that did to the Titanic!

What the heck, didn't the Wright brothers have to contend
with glitches? Take a look now. Others, profiting from the
Tenth's pioneers have gone on to perfect sail boards, jet boats,
and fancier water skis. Thanks to us Florida's Cyprus Gardens is
collecting a chunk from the tourist. It purely makes one feel he
has made a contribution to the betterment of mankind.

Fishing had been good fun. Skiing had been jolly. Lookout
for the folly! A member of the trail crew was always in attendance at the cabin to maintain upkeep and, being medic-trained,
administer first aid to any of us dumb enough to catch a fish hook
in the eye. It was his habit of an evening to visit the guys at the
weather station at the far end of the lake, drink a few beers, and
play a little poker. As it would still be light at that time, he seldom returned much before two in the morning. One entered and
left our cabin through but a single door which latched on the
inside. As none of us desired to rise in the middle of the night to
let the trail guy in, on our second day in residence, we removed
and reinstalled the latch on the *outside*. The latch—a simple
affair of bar and slot—was quite easy to open. He could leave us
in peace and flaming well let himself in! Each evening before
trekking off to lake's end his last words to us were always "Keep
your eyes peeled for BEAR. They come to dig around in the
garbage. Be sure to bury it DEEP."

I have informed you, GIs constantly and unmercifully tease
one another. It has to be a macho thing, right? It is much more
than that. We flew and performed under stressful and dangerous
conditions. We bugged our buddies continually because humor,
including the dopey kind, helped to relieve stress.

Early June, 1950. We enjoy twenty-two and a smidge hours of
daylight, less than the two hours remaining darken only slightly to

dusk. No curtains on the windows; sleep had to be taken in the light. The sounds of cooling, creaking, cabin noises inside, chuckling trees swapping secrets outside. Anybody's nerves edgy?

Trying to sucker one of us into rising to quietly investigate each unknown noise, a louse among us would whisper, "I just heard a BEAR snuffling, he's right outside the cabin door!"

ANYBODY HOME?

"Har-har-hars," from the wise, 'cuz nobody bought that baloney!

I had captured a lower bunk. Rosario, a Portuguese, bunked above me. About midnight, just as I started to doze, he leaned down, jabbed me and hissed, "Theah's a beeg beah ovah theah by the doah. Theah's a BEAH!"

Now I didn't just come down in the last pine needle shower. True, I heard a slight scratching by the door, but it had to be the trail crew guy trying to get a rise out of us. Well, I'd soon put the "nuts to you pal" on that old boy.

I crawled carefully out of bed with a plan. I'd softly stride to the door fling it open, and bellow, "Welcome Mr. BEAR, kindly haul your furry carcass inside, there's always room for one more." Damn fool eager to sucker him, I quietly stepped to the door and...lucked out! Happened there was a fairly large slot between door and jamb offering a limited view of the outside. Hand on latch string preparing to yank the door open, I heard a soft snuffle and saw to my unbelieving eyes, the nose of the mother of all bears! *Whoops, his snout really was nudging the bleeding latch*! One serious upward thump of his nose, door opens, bear is inside, and where the hell are we?

Startled, okay, scared spitless, I choked out a half-strangled "DA, glub, DO BE IS A BEAR!" And *ursus americanus* split. By this time all bunks were empty and Frank had loaded our 30-06. The bear went round the cabin's left side to a large tree, stood, and dug his claws into the bark. We could see him clearly through the window. Adrenaline pumped and hearts thumped— he was a mighty huge carnivore!

"Shoot him, Frank. Shoot him!"

"No, he's too big!"

"He may come back. Waste him," we holler.

Frank shot him. Ursus didn't move. KA-POW, he fired again. Very slowly the big boy slid down the tree to the ground.

"Gimme the gun Frank," said the idiot of the group—me! "I'll make sure of him."

"Be careful. Dem beahs are known ta play possum," advised Charlie.

Not with Daniel Boone they won't, think I. When I'd stepped to within three feet of him the dead started to *rise*! I jumped ten feet in the air and shot him again on the way back down! Brave me! That poor old fellow wasn't going anywhere, his movement had been but a dying reflex.

Older, wiser, and looking back, I think how dumb could we get? A loud noise, beating on a pan, singing "Off we go into the wild blue yonder, la la la, da da da di" (off key as usual), would have sent him on the run for Mt. McKinley. City boys, we were also young and stupid and knew sick'um about how to behave with wildlife. I felt so ashamed then and I still do.

Hearing all the racket, the trail crew troop came hot-footing back and promptly turned livid. I think he actually frothed at the mouth. We had to drive the amphibious tractor—the weasel—around to the carcass, tie it to the hitch, and drag Mr. Bear off into the boonies where nature would take its inevitable course.

Our cheerful cabin custodian, now in the throes of apoplexy, yelled a long time about that broken window, too!

We'd been zapped by giant mosquitoes, scratched, sunburned, filled with fried fish and then yelled at long and loud. All in all, we chalked up a mighty fine week!

Operation Groundhog

13

June 25th, 1950. Figuring it was warmer in the south, the Commies from the north decided to vacation there permanently. Trouble was, they took their guns along and traveled in new hardtops, these were estimated to be—a hundred Soviet-made tanks! A nice little dustup ensued. Harry T. called it a police action; everybody else called it the Korean War.

Well, I'm here to tell you a little gun powder wasn't going to interfere with our upcoming Fourth of July midnight—sans lights—baseball game. Tradition is tradition. Besides, there is *no* season on war—excuse me, police action—and there is *only* one season per year on baseball. So okay, it is a war of sorts, but nobody gets killed unless you count the occasional umpire!

I played right field—a place of honor and trust I'd been told. It was only later, I found out that the team trusted not too many balls would be hit in my direction! A cruel thrust like that is enough to persuade a guy to take up golf. Believe it or not, I still have my 10th Rescue baseball jacket—it almost fits!

Korea turned nasty and Alaska began preparations for repelling possible invasion. By now, for Alaska, the Russians had realized who really deserved the title "Folly" and they could be planning on the old switcheroo. God knows, they'd sure stuck their big red noses into the Korean brouhaha.

• • •

I believe we went on the alert in Alaska due more to the lesson of the Berlin Airlift than nose-thumbing from Korea.

Bear with me. I promise just a few comments on an episode that turned out to be the greatest and most successful humanitarian effort by air in history, and *it was expended upon a recently defeated enemy.*

For far too many years, it has become popular for boorish countries to make rude gestures to the United States with the finger of one hand while holding out the other for the check. We are considered to be a nation of beer-guzzling rednecks, worthy only of contempt. Lest we forget, seventy-nine of those vulgar American and allied, slobs—unarmed—lost their lives smashing into the ground while flying succor to a city beleaguered by some *real rednecks!*

The Berlin blockade made plain to the United States the true intentions—total domination of Europe—of one of the worst butchers of all time, Uncle Joe Stalin. He and his hoods didn't succeed because, gathering C-47's and C-54's from all over the world we stuck it to 'em! Carried and safely delivered during one of the worst winters on record, 1948-49, the tonnage in supplies is unbelievable. Read about it. Learn about Halverson's Candy Express. It is a wonderful, exciting, proud chapter in our history which should not be overlooked. I believe May 12th, the day the Russians cried "uncle" should be declared a national holiday. Failing that, print a new stamp with a picture of a C-54 flying in to a devastated city. Berlin Airlift printed on top; below, "Up yours Joe!" Seems appropriate. (After all, we've got one of ELVIS!) *No nation in the world* has ever been as generous and giving of aid as the United States of America and, by God, you can also airmail that from the flaming post office!

Courtesy of Korea, operation "Groundhog" was born: Combat gear was issued, positions were assigned and manned around the field. Bunking on the ground; guard duty; K-rations; rifles and helmets. All that for the Army, sure, but for the Air Force, too? Oh, yeah!

The Army set up anti-aircraft gun emplacements encircling Ladd. F-80 air force jets were armed, fueled, readied. Doc Blanchard of West Point football fame flew his jet on combat training missions out of Fairbanks. The 82nd Airborne also scheduled a drop to test our defenses. It was an exhilarating but scary time. Young and green, we figured we were tough enough to handle anything. Against seasoned troops? Today, I'm not so sure. I'd qualified on the firing range with the M1 during Basic—but the range didn't shoot back and the only grenade I'd ever thrown never made it to home plate. Nonetheless, you can always count on the United States Air Force!

Surely you're familiar with those old rumors of how, for recreation on a pass to town, the Marines playfully slug the Army, the Navy belts the Marines and they all—joyfully—join together to throw the Air Force through handy windows; it's the outrageous gossip from some that's hard to swallow. Oh, there was that time Farmer and I, needing a break, stopped off in a Fairbanks bar for a steak. Members of our trail crew were already there and had been for some time. And, yes, they'd had a shot or two of sarsaparilla. It was only natural a minor disagreement might ensue. Two of the revelers even began to rearrange the bar furniture over themselves and others within range. The owner hollered for the intrepid to break that little scuffle up. I'm proud to say Ed and I immediately rose to the occasion and quietly moved to a back booth out of harm's way. Hey, the trail crew guys were all Neanderthals. Ed and I were gentlemen and besides, they were only playing!

Yessiree, I find rumors of inter-service rivalry preposterous and not to be believed. Are we not stalwart brothers in arms united against slime balls who disparage all we hold near and dear? Such gossip is fallacious character assassination of the lowest sort. I refuse to listen to it, which is why, when the Army major requested help from the Tenth Air Rescue, I knew we'd willingly and most happily hasten to provide it.

His need would be easy to satisfy. He, responsible for artillery placement around the field, merely desired to observe the Army's anti-aircraft gun sitings from the air. What could be simpler?

The captain (don't tell anybody but he was a hell of a good pilot) invited Charlie and I to go along. Old faithful, AR-953, a four passenger Cessna was chosen. Mac beat me to the cockpit and sat up front with Cap. I fanny parked in back beside the earnest major.

Let me explain something about flying: If *you* handle the controls, you'll know where, when and how the plane will maneuver; thus, *your* equilibrium enjoys its ups and downs. Go along for the ride and unless kindly informed of pilot's next direction, ninety percent of *your* body goes where the aircraft is headed, stomach flies off on its own. Usually, *one's* tum-tum will therefore be diametrically opposed to plane's capriciousness. "Oh, my, God!" will fit. A normal takeoff: altitude slowly and moderately achieved, gentle banking followed by lazy circling over Ladd. Purely a lovely day, not a cloud in the sky, perfect visibility. The major leaned over to me, "Could we perhaps climb a little bit higher? I can't see all our critical positions."

I relayed this most reasonable request to Cap.

Throttle shoved ahead full. Stick hauled all the way back. Prop screamed. Up and aw-a-a-y we went! My stomach wailed, "Oh, no!"

Amazing how distance flashes past when the just are having fun. Here we were seven thousand feet closer to Heaven. Simply lovely! The major leaned over again.

"I'm afraid we're now too high, can we go down and get a *little closer?*"

I passed his latest logical request to the driver.

Back came the throttle. Full forward went the stick. Over went the port wing. Up rushed terra firma. Run a picture in your mind of a runaway elevator heading nonstop from penthouse to basement. Poor stomach begs for mercy. In no time at all we were back down around one thousand feet. Major leaned over, almost as green as the color of my fatigues, and faintly inquired, "Do you carry a sick bag?"

I immediately transferred *his terribly important* question to wonderful pilot. Kindly, Cap snaps back, "USE YER HAT!"

The major carefully removed an immaculate handkerchief from a back pocket, gently spread it over his knees and, leaning over one more time, quavered, "I have seen enough. May we return to the field now?"

A definite Oregon, April green. He laid his head back and closed his eyes.

SWOOSH! Cap dropped us another eight hundred feet, side-slipped, lined up on the runway and our plane kissed the tarmac like a mom powdering baby's bottom. Having taxied clear of the run-way—an eternity for the major—Cap cuts the switch in front of the hangar. Still remarkably holding on to his cookies, our passenger tendered a shaky "Thank you" to our terrific pilot and wobbled off, desperate to embrace—oh so tightly—one of his stationary, land-locked guns!

Co-operation between the services? How can even a natural born skeptic harbor the slightest doubt?

Later—after a couple of his thinking days—Charlie trotted out a brilliant idea: "Lissen," he said, "Ina way a helpin' dem groun' poundahs prepare fa wah, I t'ink we really oudda test da bums defenses. Heah's how I t'ink we can do 'er." (He's from Boston— they talk funny!)

Like air wheezing from a padded bra, Mac, under a full load of garlic, leaned over to hiss his superb idea into my, I'm ashamed to say, receptive ear.

Cap was game and soon, all preparations for "test the Army" complete, the three of us were airborne and heading for a certain gun emplacement whose inhabitants had made rude gestures at us when—out of the goodness of our Air Force hearts—we'd flown over them in an effort to help *their major*.

I sat in back hugging the testers. Charlie was the exercise administrant. I say this not in an effort to affix blame, but as he had conceived and birthed the test, Charlie insisted upon administer's rights. Cap brought us in low, slow, and right on target. For shame! Aimed upwards at the innocent, here came those same uncouth ges-tures from those same loutish grunts.

Almost falling out the door, Charlie screamed like a demented banshee, "UP DA ARMY! HEAH'S A KISS FROM BEAN-TOWN!" Out and away went the instructional testers.

Score: two near misses and one bull's-eye. Altogether most satisfying and educational, as we had *filled three condoms with water and catsup!*

"Take a gandah at dat," whooped Charlie. "Dem nice guys is cheerin' an' applaudin' da aim of anudda loyal Red Sox fan."

Funny, I could have sworn most of those waving arms had clenched fists on their ends. Many of those cheers, too, sure sounded a lot like, "You rotten sons of bees!" But, they do say the hearing is the first to go.

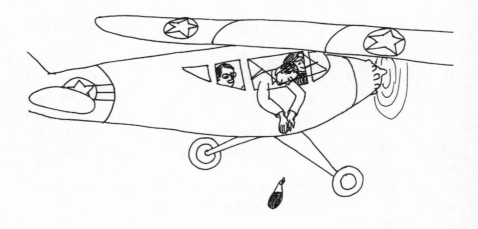

A KISS FROM BOSTON!

The Tenth participated in no more bombing runs. Back on station we were called on the carpet. The boss informed us in extremely descriptive language we were *not* at war with our own damn Army! The clincher: another GI rumor was rapidly circling the base. If a certain small plane—AR-953—were foolish enough to fly over a certain anti-aircraft emplacement—red in color—again, the lock and load ammunition fired would be—*live!*

Fiddlesticks! You know I don't set any store in rumors. Still…?

The 82nd Airborne flew in and jumped—a most impressive sight—sustaining only a few broken legs. They attacked and captured the base, so *they said*. It wouldn't have happened if a certain artillery major hadn't had his head in the clouds!

• • •

In late July, Fairbanks put on a big do called "Golden Days Celebration" commemorating the discovery of gold by Felix Pedro in 1902; the festival included arts and crafts, sports activities, food, a queen and a big parade. It was fun, and as summers were short led nicely into their "Winter Carnival" of dog team races, hockey games, Eskimo blanket tossing, and much more. Born a Canuck, I grew up involved with winter sports and would readily jump into the latest "guaranteed to break your fool neck" fad. Blanket tossing was a new one on me though. Certainly the Eskimos had a ball and many of the tossed reached good height. I couldn't help wonder, what if Lady Godiva were to ski past just as one of the tossed was reaching for the stars? Of course, it never happened and I really need to control thoughts such as those. Winter Carnival was also fun and I often dig out my slides to relive it. For GIs those festivities came as welcome breaks from duties and stress.

Operation "Groundhog" woodchucked (read that we lived outdoors on and in the sandbagged ground) from summer to fall; count that an eye blink in Alaska. On Sept. 15th, allied landings at Inchon canceled the Commies vacation. If the Chinese had kept their damn faces out of it, the red light in our faces would have turned to green. Truman could have swallowed his flaming police whistle and some thirty-two thousand Americans would be alive today.

Meanwhile, at the Tenth, it was business as usual. War or no, civilians in the Alaskan bush still got hurt or lost. We carried a rifle in one hand and searched with the other. Our recovery record remained high. In fact, there was only one outfit better. Under *battlefield conditions* the performance of the Third Air Rescue in Korea reads "superb." Ask those grateful troops that the Third kept the bad guys from grabbing!

The land of the midnight sun's favorite native blanket—snow—tucked the ground in for winter. What would the Air Force be ordered to do then? Dig foxholes of course. Uh-huh, I know what you're thinking. Why didn't we do that kind of excavating in the summer? Funny you should ask, the same wonderment occurred to us. An answer from our learned top kick: "Youse feckless bums (he was very fond of that word and used it often) pick up ya shovels, shut yer faces an' foller me!" Hey, that answer sounded perfectly reasonable to me.

You ever try to stomp a GI shovel into permafrost? Want a first-hand experience? Don't close out bank savings and fly to the land where beaver wear dentures. Go to your toolshed, grab a *decent* shovel, hike out to the highway, and then dig a hole in the macadam. Arms will fly, sparks will fly, shovel will dent and, yep, fly! You'll discover that macadam, like complacent, long-cooled lava, won't budge. Got the picture? If your luck continues, you'll find the chiropractor is booked and won't schedule you until tomorrow!

Using those old folding GI shovels, we dented the tundra down about two feet before hitting permafrost. Progress toward eventual heavy heat under the earth's crust halted. Being typical, intelligent and resourceful—the cream of American youth—we said the hell with it, climbed out, scouted up branches and, convincing ourselves we'd be protected, built barricades over those two-foot holes. Not that it mattered: An enemy with a good arm didn't need a bullet, he could've killed us with a snowball! Ready for the good news? Early next day they gave OUR foxholes to the *feckless* ARMY, moved us to virgin acreage and we started chipping our way to China all over again!

Cable! Defensive positions require communication capabilities; therefore, load a weasel (tank-tracked amphibious vehicle) with rolls of telephone cable. Engage that machine's gears, then track around trees (through the small ones), over stumps, up hillocks and down swales. Become fully aware the lousy weasel does not have a compassionate bone in its rotten mechanical body; nor does it have shock absorbers! Spend long cold hours feeding cable out and over the weasel's back. I guarantee that when a twosome, plus driver, climbs aboard one of those beasts, sooner or later one's eye will end up wearing another guy's elbow! Naturally, the only heat in that butt-busting sucker comes from GI swear words. Naturally again, it blows even colder with fresh snow. This is tons of fun! Eventually, they say, even the hanging cease to swing and sway. Thus, shuddering to a smoke-belching stop before the hangar door, we toppled off the tail of that miserable, body-crippling machine. Imitating Frankenstein's walk, we three frozen cadavers staggered inside to report mission accomplished. Next day *they* decided we'd laid the wire in the wrong sector and ordered us out to hand reel it all back up.

"Hey, Skids, some of this filthy wire is wrapped around a bleeding stump, I can't get the damn stuff loose."

"Gimme dem wire cutters kid an' move ovah, dere's gonna be a slight break in da line. We'll worry about splicin' it back when da invasion stahts! What ya suppose da brass uses fer brains?"

Barely before refreezing our tutu's, we gathered up most of that brittle, stabbing, frozen wire. I don't remember where the hell we re-laid it next day.

The Devil Laughs

14

A change of pitch in the engines interrupted my reverie, along with the hand of the port waist gunner shaking my leg.

"The Captain says to prepare for landing, buddy. Better grab on to a sky hook and hold on."

As there was no sky hook or any other kind of hook in that tunnel, lest I slide the full length of the tube and help the pilot land his B-29, I dug my knees, elbows and toes into the metal floor of my den and tried to hang on. I might have offered up a few Hail Mary's, too.

The pilot was an old pro and he set the big beast on the runway as softly as Mom's goodnight kiss. I didn't slide an inch. Stiff, thankful the engines had stayed *cool*, I stepped down off my first and last B-29 flight onto Fairfield Suisun's air base. I rattled my head to shake off engine roar, thanked the crew, and headed off to hunt up a GI bus eager to cough its way into Fairfield. From there, I caught a Greyhound heading south for Redlands.

I'd been in such a flaming rush to catch the plane for stateside,

I still wore my white felt boots and fiberglass arctic flight jacket over my uniform. In addition, besides carrying my B-4 bag, I was still toting my parachute and Mae West like they'd been woven out of strands of gold! You have any idea how much the military pays for one crummy *hammer?* I caught a few strange looks from fellow passengers but no smart remarks aired my way so I kept da lip buttoned, as Mac would say, and let 'em guess.

Some eight hours later after changing busses in L.A., I reached Redlands around two o'clock in the morning. Busses didn't service Yucaipa at that time so I knew I'd be stuck for a cab. Loaded with gear, my bones aching from the long ride, I lurched down the street toward the cab stand and met a fellow weaving and wobbling my way from the other direction.

"Sheez, guy, how come ya had to bail out? Wush anybody kilt?"

Four sheets to the wind, he was still serious and I really had to laugh. Admittedly, the Air Force is most efficient but on the way from sky to ground they don't take the flaming time to repack their chutes! I was still chuckling when I beat on the door to rouse the cabby. He said to give him a few minutes to lock up and he'd drive me home.

You can take my word for it, this country abounds in good people. My town, Yucaipa, lay about ten miles southeast. The cabbie had been a waist gunner on a B-17 during World War II and, kindred souls, we chatted about the service; some of the changes and some things that never change. Time flew by and before I knew it our front walk welcomed me. I dug out my wallet, but he wouldn't take so much as a shiny nickel.

"Young fella, Korea is now another damn killing field for Americans and you boys are doing the job we should have finished in the big one. I don't want your money. Merry Christmas and God bless."

As he drove off, I stood for a few minutes basking warm in his generosity before I walked up and rang the front door bell and nearly gave my parents heart attacks. A week earlier I'd written I wouldn't be able to get leave.

Ever notice how forty-five days of vacation pass three times as fast as forty-five days of work? True, I'd spent most of it either at the lumber yard or building chicken, rabbit, turkey and pig accommodations; now that'd been restful! I yearned for but a few days of leisure, so, as I still had accrued leave coming, I wired the Tenth for an extension to my furlough. I could see the colonel turning blue as he dictated his answer. Succinct, it read: "No! Get your butt back here on the next plane."

To read is to hear is to obey: Thus, still tasting Seattle's wonderful clam chowder, I stepped off a DC-6 on to, once again, the Land of the Long Sleep. Alaska looked exactly the same. Maybe she blew a dollop or two chillier after California's warmth, but all in all she felt like home. After checking in, I asked a buddy if anything untoward had happened while I was gone.

"Oh, hey, guy, have you been away?" he quips.

That hurt until I spotted the twinkle in his eye. Damn, I thought, even if he is a bum, he likes me. It's good to be back among friends. I'm ready, even eager, to practice the four R's once more: repair, rebuild, renew, recover.

Overseas tour lengths vary. Airmen constantly rotate stateside for re-assignment, while others arrive to take their places. I shook hands with three newcomers. A tech-sergeant replaced our radio department leader. The other two, staff-sergeants, were radio and radar operators. The radar troop did not *trust* helicopters. Dandy! We had a new pigeon to bug!

Came the day a radar set in need of repair required TLC from the facilities at Eielson AFB, about twenty-six miles from Ladd. Incidentally, the huge B-36 bombers demanded long runways and only Eielson could handle them.

Those expensive, ungainly, impractical bombers were soon replaced with that honey of honeys—the B-52. Having been the mainstay of SAC for well over twenty years, you know how successful they were!

Radar clutched to his chest, his face a wholesome shade of battleship gray, our pigeon gingerly prepared to board an eggbeater for his short flight.

"You're not really going to fly in old 'Body Bones Get Busted' are you, Sarge?" we groaned. Then sadly shook our heads when Ed added, "That's a fitting name for the ugly beast. Still, when the engine quit during that night flight last year, old AR-13 did land successfully on a gasoline truck."

"Yeah, and they'd a been okay too if dat dumb pilot hadna lit a match to see where they was! Ain't his brother flyin' dis crate today?"

"Also true," continued Mac. "*One* a dem eggbeater's has been recorded settlin' safely onta terror firmer afta da stahboad wheel fell off!"

"Remember when that pilot had him a heart attack flyin' Ol' Snake Eyes?" said Frank. "He splashed her down okay before he died, didn't he, Mac?"

"You mean da guy what dunked his whoilyboid inta da sewage disposal pond? He wuz one unlucky guy. We snagged his buns ez he wuz goin' down fer da thoid yucky time, but we wuz one dunk too late!"

Correct. The sarge was shaking so badly, it was our sacred duty to pep him up and offer encouragement for that itty bitty flight, and we did our best.

Strapped in, set residing in his lap and a panicky look in his eyes, Sarge waited for the pilot to complete pre-flight and lift off. Up they went, a good twenty-five feet before…*the engine quit* and they smacked back down onto the tarmac—KA-WHUMP!

Luckily, although spraining both legs and popping a few rivets, the whirlybird held together. Not so, Sarge! We had to pry him out of his seat. He wasn't hurt and only thought he'd died. Still carefully clutching his radar set, he wobbled back inside the hangar, told our section chief to stuff his helicopters, and then staggered over to the motor pool. Later, he told us he'd *ordered* the truck driver to keep the speed down to fifteen m.p.h. all the way to Eielson. No way was that vehicle going to get a chance to leave the ground! I think he exaggerated. After all, even if the Devil had laughed, twenty-five feet isn't far to fall…unless you happen to hit something solid!

He checked out a good troop; fun to tease and easy to like. He was also responsible for slipping me some info which resulted in a job as a waiter, working in the officers' club. I'd never thought of it. At every base he'd been for lengthy stays, the Club was the first place he visited to apply for a job as bartender. I'd always thought Club personnel were assigned that duty. Not so, and in addition the enlisted help were paid. Hallelujah! Extra dough. After that, the long Alaskan winter darkness rested easier on my mind as something different occupied my time during off duty hours.

• • •

A career master-sergeant managed the Officers Club. Affable and sharp, he, too, was easy to like. Radar Sarge—he of the helicopter incident—was one of his top bartenders and had advised me to also try for that position. The boss had no openings for such and he started me off as a waiter, promising to put me behind the bar as soon as an opening occurred. Actually, it was just as well, I knew zilch of mixing drinks and precious little about hustling grub.

With the club's limited menu, and sans too many of my normal goofs, I soon caught on and began to enjoy the work and the people. Don't ever let this get around: most officers are really not condescending and they even know a thing or two! Funny though, if you did run into a patronizing puke it was usually one of the officers' wives. Tips were as plentiful as hip pockets on a flaming kangaroo.

The uniform consisted of dark trousers, white shirt and black bow tie. No rank showed which made it nice as snots never knew if they were snotting on privates or sergeants. It's far easier to handle guff while but a lowly private.

Dances? Saturday nights, holidays and sometimes special feeds like "fish fries" or "burgers to die for" brought the homesick and the lonely together. Alaska wore hard on the wives, especially during those long winters. Festival nights and dancing until two (often in hopes of sobering those who'd bent an elbow one time too many) included an early breakfast. The master-sarge was too smart to send them home loaded. It simply wouldn't do for one of the sloshed to impale his car and perhaps himself on one of the Air Force's *landing jets!*

During one particularly rowdy bash, I was serving breakfast: sausage, scrambled eggs, hash browns, toast and lots of hot coffee. Glancing around for more customers, I noticed a pert, curvy little doll—feeling absolutely no pain—who'd decided she'd go up for more coffee. Her landing gear tried to go north and south at the same time. Sensing trouble on the runway, I intercepted her and offered escort service back to her table including, I hoped, the carrying of the desired extra strong java.

"Outa my way shonny boy, the Tenth Air Reshcue, shoarin' way up there among thosh shtars, flies tonight. Wahoo!"

Away she veered: one wing dropped to port, then the other dipped to starboard. Rolling about like flippin' Keiko, there was no way she could avoid pranging herself. Wincing, I took orders from another table all the while keeping an eye peeled for her return. Pretty soon she cruised into view clutching a brimful mug of boiling coffee in each hand and zigzagging like a merchant ship desperately trying to avoid a torpedo. During each roll, coffee slopped over from mugs to backs of her hands. The pain must have been excruciating, yet she neither hollered nor released her grip on either cup of liquid-lava-java.

"Wahoo! Thish ish the night for thosh Tenth Reshcue guys to eshcape thish ol' groun' an' reash for the shtars. Ya-a-a-hoo!"

Right on, babe!

Not long after that memorable evening, my boss put me behind the bar and I remember it all so clearly: He intercepted me taking off my coat and before I could pick up my tray, pen and note pad.

"No, Jack, tonight you tend bar. I think you're ready."

"Sarge, I've had no training. I don't have the foggiest idea how to do it."

"Not to worry, there are two more guys back there who'll teach you the ropes. It won't take you long. Besides, in this bar, the drink choices are limited and not complicated to prepare. Go on, go get your feet wet."

I thought that perhaps a poor choice of words. Nevertheless, shaking with trepidation, I raised the entrance door and walked timidly *behind* the bar.

Thus began my career as bartender. With your kind indulgence I shall refer to only three short incidents while I learned to hustle booze.

Say you request a highball: How hard can that be? Glass, ice, choice of booze, if requested, otherwise bar whiskey. Add soda and serve. Right?

My first order, a bourbon and Seven: Shakily, I choose a glass, add ice, pour bourbon, finish off with Seven-up and send it—via new waiter—to the customer with my compliments. I then turn to wait on other patrons. Shortly, an "ahem" tickles my ear. The flaming waiter's back with the drink.

"Mr. Bartender, the customer says this drink is flat."

What's with flat? I sniff it and it smells okay to me so I send it out again. Back it comes—this time born by the irate lady customer.

"This bourbon and Seven is FLAT, bozo! Kindly mix me another."

Just in time a *learned* bartender shows up. He tastes the belt, throws it out, apologizes to the lady, and mixes her another. Then he explains *flat* to me. "If the mix: soda, Coke, ginger ale or Seven-up sits out too long, it loses carbonization. There will be no fizz or sharpness to the drink. It tastes flat!" The lady listens, all the time nodding her head. By this time my face is the color of a setting sun and I'm desperately looking for a cubbyhole to hide in.

He adds, "Keep a close watch on your mixes. If you can't seal them to lock in fizz, dump 'em and open a fresh bottle. But nobody likes a flat belt."

Dear lady—wherever you are—mea culpa, mea maxima culpa. I didn't know beans when the bag was open. However, it was a lesson I never forgot. If we should ever run across one another again, it will be my pleasure to buy you a drink. God help the bartender that serves it to us *flat!*

• • •

A Pentagon general and his aides, on an inspection tour, came to visit our base's general and his aides. They dined at the Officers' Club. The master-sergeant asked me to come out from behind the bar, take their food and drink orders and then serve them. His reasoning?

"I want it done properly."

You're right, that's an outrageous brag, but sure as Doofus dances I've purely screwed up beaucoup times, too. The rare, but sincere, "well done" definitely strokes a bruised ego.

• • •

The major: A quiet, soft-spoken soldier and a gentleman. He sat at the bar—most nights—slowly drinking himself insensible. A heavy load of hurt was eating away at him. The world's biggest fracas wasn't too far behind us and now Korea was claiming more American blood. His loss? Perhaps a buddy, a lover, members of his family; he'd been summoned and found wanting; the horrors of war. He never talked about it and no one knew his trouble. The Club bartenders all kept an eye on him. He always offered too much tip and left too much money on the bar. Safely held, we would return it the next day only to have him repeat the process. Like a doting father, the sergeant-major never failed to show up about pass out time each evening and, gently escorting him upstairs to his room, put him to bed. None of us ever discovered the reason for the major's misery. Sergeants do not ask personal questions of officers and he never volunteered the unspoken. All we could do in simple ways was let him know he had friends among the enlisted; he'd nod and smile, thank us with true southern courtesy, and then order another drink.

I can still see him sitting there, that soft smile on his face—and no life in his eyes.

• • •

Three weeks later I received a pleasant surprise, I'd been promoted to staff-sergeant. Immediate benefit: No more KP! From that day on I sat at a table in the mess hall, cup of coffee at hand, counting the troops coming in for chow. Tomorrow, another deserving soul gets stuck with yo pots and pans! I was even ordered to taste test our cook's offerings. Notable in physique, "Crusher" Cookie resembled the Incredible Hulk; completely objective, my comments were never less than laudatory! Life. It was good, exciting, full!

Three days later, in the wee hours of the morning, the mess hall burned down. Don't look at me! Deep in the kip, I awoke to all the fuss and racket like everybody else. No matter the hour, our orderly rooms were constantly manned. In large outfits an officer of the day or OD along with a Noncommissioned Officer, or NCO (as they are usually on duty for a twenty-four hour period) will doss down on cots in the office so as to be readily on call for any emergency. Smaller outfits award that responsibility to NCO's with the OD but a phone call away. Requirements vary in squadrons, but in the main, duty personnel inspect squadron quarters on a regular basis. Think night watchman. They walk the premises, wake the poor souls stuck with KP, and man the orderly room phones so as to not miss an alert. Not a difficult assignment, it mainly requires one to stay alert and *awake*. Staff-sergeants and above perform as NCOD's.

Oil heat is prized in Alaska because it warms better, and when I served there the price was cheap. However, the stoves were dirty little twits that required frequent inspection and cleaning. Sooted stove pipes are dangerous. When a caked fire box, tired of blazing, belched, best call the base fire department in a flaming hurry 'cuz your britches are surely burning.

Our mess hall stove belched. Why? Someone missed an inspection? Heat not turned down when hall had been secured for the night? Oil? Dirty and not up to standards? The Devil had laughed once more and taught a dragon how to hawk spitballs? It matters not. At two o'clock in the morning the Tenth's grit palace caught fire in earnest. There was no way the duty NCO could have known the heater was in a burping mood. The fire was so hot and bothered, area snow melted rapidly. Hand scooping and then tossing snow on the flames induced them to hiss but did little to dampen the blaze.

The fire alarm roused one and all from their sacks and sent them outside to view, offer dumb advice, and cuss. Right away a fool—who fancied himself a wit—chanted, "Burn, burn, boil and bubble, the darlin' mess hall's turnin' into a pile of rubble! Har-har-har!"

"You think that's funny, do you, Judge?"

Our commanding officer, alerted hastily by telephone, stood directly behind the wit—*mouthy me.*

WHO FORGOT TO TURN
THE STOVE OFF?

"Uh...not really colonel...just tryin' a small Eskimo incanta-
tion...hopin' it'll bring freezing rain or a blizzard...heh-heh-heh."

Fortunately he had more important things to do than drop kick me
into the middle of the inferno. And inferno she was. Formed of flam-
mable wood, tarpaper and shingles, our dear supplier of sustenance
could conjure up none for herself. She burned clear down to her shorts
and was no more. I had thought to take my camera. Reviewing those
slides the other day, darned if I hadn't caught the old girl's demise quite
well. Counting five times ten years past, the pic's are still crisp, clear
and true colored. Kodachrome film of course.

More bad news. Chowing from then on had to take place way the
hell and gone over on the far side of Ladd Field and we were relegated
to eating in a huge mess hall serving a plethora of Army and Air Force

hungry. That close camaraderie at mealtime, enjoyed for so long among our smaller group of good friends, had just gone up in smoke. For whatever reason, the grub gracing our plates wasn't as pleasing to the palate either. It was only a rumor but Skids, who usually passed the legitimate skinny, informed us the cooks had all graduated from motor pool school.The "brass" sent 'em all to Alaska knowing everything was frozen up there, and we wouldn't be able to tell the difference between a warmed over wrench and a waffle! There is a lot to be said for family cooking and dining.

• • •

There are those who impress. There are also those who impress and influence. Such a man was the captain in charge of the orderly room. Quiet and unassuming, of average height, figure, voice, he'd have been overlooked in a crowd. That man was far from average.

A career officer, and caring about the men in his squadron, he oversaw all personnel records, promotions, furloughs, requests for emergency leave, duty rosters, commendations, and other matters of a personal nature. He arbitrated small differences of opinion including the occasional scuffle, (I cannot recollect a single court-martial while I served in the Tenth!). He performed his duties well. He also flew as all our officers were qualified pilots. Long searches required relief. Cooks, clerk typists, mechanics—any and all could be called upon to participate and often were.

I became better acquainted with the captain because he performed a service for me that he was not required to do. Remember way back during my narration of Basic Training when Bob and I had the choice of signing papers of citizenship intent or, waving bye-bye to the Air Force? Having perused my records, Cap called me in and offered to further that intent by helping me obtain my first papers. That way, he explained, upon discharge it would be only a matter of months rather than years before I could apply for final citizenship. I took that advice and have never regretted it. One small relatively unimportant service of many the captain performed for his boys.

Meet Steve Yapuncich, the Wild Hungarian, another who not only impressed, he wowed! A newcomer fresh from stateside—one more pigeon ripe for plucking—he was another radar operator. I haven't a clue why, but radar operators always served up well for our dumb gallows humor. Steve was older than most of us. Good-natured, he enjoyed the give and take which we "cautions to the Jay birds" readily gave. He often gave better than he got!

Six-one, slim, with flashing blue eyes and sporting an envious crown of jet-black hair, he was, in modern jargon, a hunk. When dispatched for punch at dances and returning glass laden, you and everybody else would find his girl clustered around the new Don Juan of the Tenth. Batting their eyes adoringly, cooing and sighing like a covey of mesmerized doves, it added up downright nauseating! Steve had to have swallowed a honeybee magnet. He never sent out signals, but ladies just seemed to flit and fly to his hive. Strangely—other than minor and rare cases of "Green Eye"—none of us resented him. He was genuinely liked by everyone.

Steve also rated recognition as a champion skeet shooter and during one of his contests he took a few of us along for a cheering section. Ha! Little did Hawkeye need our noise, he won with ease. He later showed us the rudiments. Deadeyes we weren't; still, we all managed to wing a few of the clay birds. I confess I found the sport challenging and fun, but *I never shot again.* My nephew, an avid collector of shotguns, under my urging, took to the sport a year ago. I'll be a squashed scuppernong if he hasn't won a few contests of his own. Who says it isn't in the blood?

Have you ever tried it? If not, here's how she blams! The shooter stands on a platform, yells, "Pull," and a midget in a little low house fires a clay disk from left to right across your bow or, vice versa. "Doubles" means here comes a disk from the midget on the left while another one from a dwarf (taller house) whizzes by from the right. One of the shooters in our group waited until just before the bird from the right hit the ground before nonchalantly firing and blowing its clay feathers off.

"Showoff!" hollered Charlie.

Showoff my sainted grandmother! I plain couldn't get the barrel around fast enough to catch up with that floating, artful dodger.

Forty-nine years later, Steve, you still linger in the mind as a valued friend.

• • •

April 10th, 1951. A clear, sunny day, visibility unlimited. No missions. This day would be devoted to maintenance and training. Ladd Field: clean, most snow long gone, no obstructions, runways clear. Army anti-aircraft gun emplacements situated around the base and close to landing zones, manned and ready. Military atmosphere: tranquil, lazy-tailed active, and peaceful.

Major assignment for the Tenth that day: Using a C-54, practice "glider snatching" off secondary runway. Piece of cake. During World War II, C-47s towed troop loaded gliders to Europe in advance of the D-Day invasion. They hadn't been snatched though; instead, already cabled to a plane, pilots towed them off. However, C-47s could also snatch. In a C-54 our colonel would often haul one glider off and— still towing it—circle around and yank off another! Personally—I think a C-54 does a much better job. For one thing the power of four engines makes possible a heftier yank. For another, your bigger plane is stronger and more capable of withstanding the grab and pull.

Bubba Bronco's rule to live by: Better to rope that big ol' steer with a big ol' horse; he who uses a li'l ol' horse to snag a big ol' steer can end up leavin' his li'l ol' saddle and flyin' arse over teakettle into a li'l ol' butt bustin' landin'!

Once in awhile, here in Oregon, we enjoy gorgeous days like that Alaskan one. Brothers and sisters I'm here to tell you, when the sun shines it *is* being reborn! Absorbing warmth that heavenly day, I was outside on the tarmac busy reinstalling an obstinate radio in one of the Cessnas. A glider snatch is exciting to observe so I paused in my labors to eyeball our approaching C-54.

The pilot, a captain who had logged mucho hours in four engine jobs, came in a touch high on his first pass and the trailing hook missed the cable. Undaunted, he grabbed some altitude, circled the big boy around, and brought him back for another try. Half concentrating on my work, one eye still on the plane, I saw—almost as though it were in slow motion—the dire events unfolding.

On this next pass the captain, much experienced in the glider grab business, brought the snatcher in lower. Looked like a perfect approach, perhaps a smidge low, but true on line with the hook.

Suddenly—before my horrified eyes—*the plane nosed over, hit the runway and exploded!* A ball of fire raced from one end of the plane to the other while we watched in helpless agony. How can appalling tragedy strike so damn fast? Conditions for the exercise were perfect. Aircraft maintenance was excellent and pilots were well trained. Regardless, the captain and his co-pilot (our orderly room captain), an engineer, radar operator (Steve Yapuncich), and four more skilled airmen had crash-landed. Screeching as though in human torment, skidding and scarring the runway, their plane in an eye blink had become a flaming melting wreck.

She slid to her final stop beside an anti-aircraft team. One of their members later stated he thought one of the pilots moved in the cockpit. Once they'd doused the flames and forced entrance fire fighters reported one of the plane's crew had his hand on the door. *They were all dead.*

Breathless from useless running and standing now close to the wreck, we could only stare as the fire died down. *Eight men were gone.* In seconds, a normal training exercise had turned into a catastrophe. In company with seven other brave men, the orderly room captain's concerns for his boys were forever over. He of the captivating smile, his shotgun at the ready, carefree, Steve would never bring down another clay bird. He was just thirty-three years old.

Military budgets were not as fat in those days and most training flights were not filmed from the ground. After analysis and careful examination of those parts still intact, the investigators formed the following theory as to why the plane crashed: The C-54, having been flown quite low, its trailing hook struck the ground before the snatch, bounced up and jammed the elevators in a down position. Too close to the ground, with no room for the pilot to work the yoke back and forth (a sometimes effective way to jerk the cable loose), they hadn't stood a chance in hell! Conclusion: Possible pilot error.

They were flat wrong. That pilot did not err. The bloody Devil had laughed again! I often think of the members of the Tenth Air Rescue, especially the Wild Hungarian, they were all good men: brave, dedicated, skilled, and compassionate. Full of the joy of living, Steve was a scosh more. Five will get you ten the line of female angels vying for his attention is so long they have to pick numbers!

THE DEVIL LAUGHS !

• • •

More than two exciting adventurous years had passed. I had learned plenty, especially from those of courage, and my Alaskan tour was ending. My new orders read assignment to Hill Field in Ogden, Utah. But first, I'd take a side trip to Yucaipa for two weeks. I knew I'd miss the Tenth, my buddies, work, climate (yeah, even that!) and the beauty of Alaska.

Here's a little "kitten on the keys" from some memories. When the local radio station turned off each night at midnight, the disc jockey always closed with a lovely instrumental version of "Bewitched, Bothered and Bewildered." Contentedly, I would scrunch down in my lumpy sack and nod off to that lulling, soporific tune. After an early number of mind and body numbing months in the far north, that soothing composition became mental security, like a kid's drag and hang-on to blanket. For four decades plus nine more years, I've missed hearing that song at day's end. Once in a long while a radio station will dust that old instrumental version off and play it for this nostalgist. Bingo, I'm back in my Alaskan Quonset hut, almost but not quite in the welcoming arms of Morpheus, knowing my services—never spectacular—had been welcomed and worthwhile. I give sincere thanks Alaska for the privilege and for my memories.

The motto of the United States Air Force is: *Sustineo Alas*— "I sustain the wings." Surely, steadfastly and honestly, it epitomizes the men of the Tenth Air Rescue Service.

Ahoy, me old matelot, pretty soon you won't need that jacket, unless you want to add more cushion for your derriere. The current's with us so I'm gonna sit for a spell and let this old dugout drift. Right quick, once we float around yonder wide bend, we'll be leaving Alaska and heading south, back to warm, sunny, Southern California.

Magic Made the Turkeys Disappear?

I arrived home just in time to become a murderer and a detective! Unpacked, I decided to stretch my legs and howdy up to Sweet Petunia. Of course, I'd forgotten she was no longer there so I decided I'd check the other livestock.

Cute, everywhere, and now fryer size, bunnies had become rabbits. Chicks, also fryer size, or hens soon to be laying eggs, had become chickens. This is it, farm life, I thought. No trouble, clean air, and *good fresh food!*

"It's good to have you home, Son. Let's celebrate and have fried chicken for dinner," trilled my Mom.

"Okay by me. When do we eat?"

"Well, first you have to...."

"First I have to do what, Mom?"

"You know...sort of get it ready for the pan."

"Get it ready for the pan? How do I do that?"

"Uh, well, you'll need to get the ax, then a small stump and ...."

It may surprise you, dear friend, but chickens don't commit suicide!

"You mean I have to kill it? What do I look like, Attilla the Hun? Why can't Pop do it?"

"He would, dear, but he ran out of cigarettes and had to run uptown to get some." I soon learned that whenever innocent victims for bonk and pluck time became chickens or rabbits, my old man always ran out of cigarettes!

"Why don't *you* dispatch the poor little guy?"

"Oh, no, dear, I'm just not strong enough. You'll have to do it."

Not strong enough? Ha! She could bite the ear off Mike Tyson if she flaming well had to! Trapped, I resigned myself to do the dastardly deed and headed off to guillotine an unfortunate chicken (somewhere I'd read that was how it was done). I sharpened the ax, situated a sturdy block inside the pen, then grabbed the first fool fowl who wandered too close. I laid a half-nelson on him, positioned his head on the stump, apologized, raised the weapon, closed my eyes, and...WHACK!

SWEET JESUS! Flopping, he ran all over the chicken yard hunting for his head! Appetite fled and the rest of me wanted to follow. Some time later, his body gave up the hunt and he laid down permanently. I gingerly tendered the carcass to Mom for plucking, cleaned the ax, housed the stump, and took a long walk. I opened a can of tuna for supper.

Two nights later the menu listed rabbit pie. Himself was out of cigarettes. Herself was too weak. Myself? Meet the Lord High Executioner!

"How do you bump off a rabbit?" I quavered squeamishly.

"I asked the butcher, dear. He said to hold him by his hind legs, lower his body until you can grasp his head, get a firm grip, twist his head sharply and quickly and that will then break his neck. It's really quite painless."

Offering more mea culpas I performed as told with one minor exception. Not knowing how hard to twist the little blighter's neck, I only gave it a three-quarter turn. OH-MY-GOD! Bunny SCREAMED like a guy who'd just been informed his mother-in-law had come to stay forever! Startled, I dropped him on his head which almost did the job. Totally ignoring double jeopardy, I repositioned bunny and tried again. This time I almost tore the poor little guy's head off, but it worked and...*he went quietly.* I could plainly hear my craven self begging for forgiveness at my next, long overdue, confession.

"Bless me father for I have sinned. I lost my temper with a ground squirrel. I swore something fierce when a rooster pecked my rear end while I bent over to fill the chicken feeder. Driving around trying to soothe jangled nerves, I nearly flattened a little old lady on roller skates and I swore at her, too. Oh, and I almost forgot—*I committed two murders!"*

That saintly man would have a heart attack on the spot. There had to be a better way to enjoy dinners of rabbit and chicken. I deposited the cadaver in Mom's arms for skinning and walked slowly to the house where I washed, changed clothes, hopped into our 1938 flivver and headed uptown for some cigarettes (I was also dumb enough to smoke in those days). Yucaipa was growing, and lo and behold I discovered a large, brand new, well-lit building frequented by many people. It portrayed a modern market. Huge lettering above the entrance read, "The Food Fair." Now you're talking. Wandering around aisles on the lookout for coffin nails, I came across a refrigerated section housing packages wrapped in clear plastic. I opted for two selections along with a bottle of Riesling, located the cancer sticks, and split. Arriving home, I asked Mom to unwrap one of the parcels, flour the contents, pop them in the oven, heat same to four hundred degrees and cook for thirty minutes. I chilled the wine, and though chow was a little late that evening we still rated it five-star gourmet dining. I've been axing and neck twisting all my chickens and rabbits the same easy way ever since.

• • •

Hoo-boy, turkeys were going AWOL. We'd started off with twelve and lost none to disease, yet they'd now reduced to eight. A PI (me) was needed to track down and recover Ben Franklin's choice for our national emblem.

Turkeys are quite capable of flying although domestic ones need a long runway and, when fat, are prone to overload their landing gear. With an idea surfing in my noggin, I searched the walnut grove. Even though their own hotel boasted a perfectly good roost, maybe they were hopping the fence and bunking in trees at night. Scratch turkeys among the nutty tree limbs or anywhere else in the flaming vicinity! Perhaps a thieving fox, raccoon, coyote? Uh-uh. No sign of carcass, feathers, beak, or feet, indicating a heinous crime.

Next morning at reveille, a roll call recount definitely totaled four plus three equaling SEVEN! I hunted low and high without sight or even sound of a gobble. Come late afternoon, frustrated, I volunteered to feed our two porkers their evening meal. Latching the gate upon exiting, I happened to look down and spotted a small object reflecting in the lowering sun. *Case solved.* Der Dumbkoff Acres Construction had flat-out goofed. I had built the pigpen directly adjacent to the poults digs and the turkeys, almost adult size, had roosted on top of the fence separating the two pens. Rating upper level in the IQ department, come daylight they'd jumped south into the pigpen rather than launching to the north from whence yodeled their brothers and sisters. As their neighbors had kindly dropped in for tea, the hospitable porkers *ate them*; feathers, carcass, bones, head, feet—everything!

A last minute bit of claw—the reflection I'd seen—lay silent, still, and oh so lonely, in my palm. A lifelong admirer of Erle Stanley Gardner, I called it the Case of the Gruesome But Gregarious Gobbler Gobble, and then I raised the dividing wall another thirteen feet.

• • •

One afternoon a few days later, our next door neighbor, Smitty called. He had a skittish sow in the field about to farrow. As it was going on for dusk, would Pop and I help him round her up and "chouse" her to an inside pen? Happy to oblige, as he was a good old stick, we reported for duty. Dad used a two by two as a herding staff. I chose to use my lungs.

Pregnant she may have been, but she still hared all over the field like a flaming greyhound. After fourteen tries at collaring her, short of breath—and even shorter of temper—my old man wheezed:

"Run the bugger by me one more time, I'll stop her!"

We did as bid. When Sea Biscuit raced by again, Pop jumped straight up in the air and slammed his two by two square on top of her thick dome. The staff broke in half. The sow pig grunted and her knees buckled. But undaunted, she shook her head, straightened, and galloped off into the sunset.

"A-hem, a-a-hem," croaked Smitty. "Let's let her be, guys. When the silly old fool settles down, I'll try to entice her in with a couple of turnips. Thanks for all your...*help!*" I laughed all the way home.

"I'LL STOP HER!"

Her piglets came the next day; two of them were cross-eyed!

• • •

A little over a week of furlough remained and there listed just one more item I desired to take care of before donning my uniform and heading away to serve.

Hill Field, Ogden, Utah, lay about five hundred and fifty meandering miles away from Yucaipa. 'Twas not really a long drive and besides, if I planned on visiting Salt Lake City, and I did, I would need wheels. Seemed like it tolled time for the purchase of my, all important, *first car*.

When one commits to a large goof, surely a calliope should play Dragnet's, dum-da-dum-dumb! Further, one should immediately dredge up a plausible explanation for the boo-boo, lest by snicker, innuendo or downright insult one be permanently awarded the honorarium, "Stupid!" Don't you find that to be so? The following is certainly plausible. Whether you buy it or not depends upon breeding, graciousness, sympathy, understanding and a double helping of rapport with—Lobotomy School—graduates.

I knew a whole lot of nothing about auto mechanics; my field was electronics. Pop knew a smidge about internal combustion engines such as: You poured gas in a tank, advanced the spark, cranked until she started or your shoulder broke, then ran around to the side of the shuddering, belching, smoking thing and hopped aboard. Armed with advanced knowledge like that, how could we go wrong? We set off to buy me an automobile!

In addition to booze and babes, GIs talk incessantly about cars. General consensus of my Alaskan buddies: The 1941-42 autos were first class. After W.W. II, Detroit's cars weren't rated as high (their opinions, not mine). Some time later I learned different; however, in 1951 I could not afford a new chariot—I barely had enough bread for an old one! Redlands or San Bernardino seemed likely places to start and perhaps find a classic.

Stepping onto "Honest Henry's" lot in San Berdoo, Dad and I spotted a Kelly-green, metallic, two-door, Fleetline style, 1941

Oldsmobile. Mighty pretty. New paint, no dings, dents or rust. For a ten year old, she was looking good. Raising the hood, we cranked her up. Pop, the learned, lowered his head close to the block and listened to the purring motor. Nothing appeared to be knocking. That smoke issuing from the tailpipe was—assured Henry—just her way of clearing her throat as she'd been sitting a spell.

"Sounds pretty good, son. How much you asking, Henry?" queried Pop.

"A steal at $550 clams," oozed H. H., halitosis wafting past yellowing teeth.

"A better steal at $500," ventured the retard of the group.

"Sold," hurried Ol' Hank. "Follow me and we'll just fill out a few legal forms. That is cash, right?"

My Dad following, I drove home, parked, and called Mom out to view and admire the new purchase. I had already christened my shining beauty the Green Hornet. She looked ever so jazzy parked there in the driveway. I hadn't bothered to check water or oil.

When you buy a new or used boat, what's first on the agenda? Go for a cruise, right? Next day, Mom, Pop and I, boarded G.H. and highwayed over to Lake Elsinore for a little shakedown jaunt. Atop that hill, you know the one, overlooking the lake, I noticed Hornet seemed to be spouting a tad bit of steam out from under the hood and the motor acted like it was suffering from a bad case of hiccups. Elevating the hood cleared everything up right away. Dear G. H.—possibly suffering from high blood pressure—steamed, spat and boiled. I hadn't thought the climb to be that strenuous on the sweet old thing.

After enjoying the lake view for an hour or two or *three*, my pride and joy had cooled down enough to remove the radiator cap and add-add-add, water. I thought to check the oil. *What oil?* Hoping to purchase one, maybe two cans of oil, I trotted back to the store at the base of the hill where I'd just been for the water. The Green Hornet, now additionally named S.O.B., inhaled *four quarts!* We limped home, stopping often for more *water*. One each shakedown cruise had left me feeling a touch seasick! Next day, a Monday, as there couldn't be much wrong, we decided to take my dear one to a mechanic. Pop knew a good man on Yucaipa Boulevard; surely, in no time, he'd diagnose and cure any minor imperfections. I still had a whole week of furlough left.

Yahoo! The patient having been poked, prodded and made to say a-h-h, would live if I consented to a complete overhaul: rebore, rings, crankshaft bearings, rear mains, and a new generator and fan belt. The radiator spouted enough holes to water the Garden of Eden, best to replace with new. The brake lining in close embrace with the drums had squealed passionately at every stop. Solution? Include new shoes and drums. Add heater hoses and radiator hoses. As the battery was close to its last surge, replace it along with the cables. The 1941 cars used voltage regulators, not alternators. The Green Hornet's was dying, install a new one, and don't forget wiper blades!

G.H.'s engine hadn't knocked because the piston rings, worn down to a nub, had anti-socially distanced themselves totally from the cylinder walls. Having thus severed all contact, ain't nothin' goin' to knock!

Pooped, the mechanic staggered to his desk, threw a truck-load of worn parts off it, and began to tote up the damage. Time passed. He licked the pencil's deadly end often. Simoleon total in Yankee dollars? As the song says: "Six Hundred Clamoring Partridges Besieging a Pauper in a Pear Tree."

Hey, it could have been worse, the rear view mirror was still good. And, good news, it was Friday. With one day to spare, the Green Hornet—reborn, eager to sting—awaited the challenge of one more beckoning road.

Tinted glass was foreign to pre-war cars. To block glaring sun from near-sighted eyes, and almost down to the lint in my wallet, I bought an outside metal visor which clamped on the gutter rails.

"So long Ma, Pa, I'll be seeing you soon." And with that, G.H. and I purred away heading first for Las Vegas and then on to Hill Field, Ogden, Utah.

Scooting along a flat, wind-blown stretch near Las Vegas, my sunvisor—no longer desirous of maintaining a lengthy and close relationship—tore herself free of the Hornet's grip and flipped gaily over the roof. Fortunately, traffic in those days even on two lane highways allowed for space and a taste of quiet, so no following cars or trucks were beaned. Regrettably, once my floating freely on the wind "Pep Boys" critter hit the deck, she broke every aluminum bone in her frame. I pulled onto the road's shoulder and sadly viewed the body pieces. Anxious to avoid the title, "litter bug," I gathered up the major parts of her corpse and stuffed her remains reverently in Hornet's trunk to await a proper military, trashcan funeral.

• • •

Hill Field was a MATS supply and repair base. I was given responsibility for a double floor barracks along with its sixty male residents. Comparing my six-man Quonset hut in Alaska to this, was like having an engine conk out while flying in fog! But, I had a room all to myself and privacy, my first in three-and-one-half years.

The work wasn't exciting. Food, certainly ample, plated plain. The flaming cooks were heisting most of the tasty grits, like steaks, out the mess hall's back door. Too much pork steak isn't even good for the pig. Succor finally came in the form of a three-day pass over Thanksgiving. I took three buddies with me to share expenses and made a quick trip home for turkey that *I wouldn't have to knock off!*

After the break, with one or two of my favorite sandwiches to tide us over, we headed back into cooler weather with snow forecast for the higher passes. Broke, as usual, I'd put cheaper alcohol instead of anti-freeze in Hornet. It got *cold* in Alaska; it doesn't get cold in Utah, does it?

Spelling each other driving, we lucked out cruising a high pass not far from St. George. Boomer, a heavy-footed driver, had the pedal to the metal when familiar red lights lit up the rear view mirror.

"Good evening," said a polite young man built like Man Mountain Dean and wearing a different kind of uniform. "Might I ask where you fellas are going in such a mighty big hurry?"

We explained to the officer our definite need to reach Hill Field before the eight A.M. roll call.

"Kindly step out from your car," that most polite of troopers requested of Boomer and me. "Please to do me a further kindness and slide your feet on the pavement," petitioned the big guy.

I scraped the road with my right foot and nearly landed on my butt!

"Correct, young gentlemen, *black ice!* You guys will never make it at the speed you're traveling. The highway is much like this all the rest of the way to the base. Your loving government has invested a lot of money in you and they want you to stay alive long enough to pay it back! I won't issue a ticket this time, however, slow this bucket down, and LIVE!"

Calmly, clearly and quietly, most grateful to Utah's highway patrol, I said,

"Boomer, slide your buns over, I'll drive."

Though snow now covered the ground, we reached Hill Field safely and there, I discovered all the alcohol had boiled out of the Hornet. She was drier than Death Valley. I had to let her sit outside and shiver until payday.

• • •

Not quite three weeks later on December 16th, 1951, I confess with mixed feelings, I bid the Air Force a fond final farewell. With a lump in my throat, I cranked up Hornet and slowly wended my way home. I was twenty-three.

• • •

Four months after my discharge and now living permanently at home, I was present for another fun time with a porker. Some time back, Mother had purchased a sow which now looked due to farrow. A mess of TLC had gone into tending to the wants of that old bag. She had been living, kindly excuse the expression, high off the backs of demised cousins. Well, Mom Nature obliged and we counted fifteen teeny, lusty piglets all scrambling for the same faucet. Don't you just love it when the newborn of any gender (rattlesnakes excluded!) elicit maternal oohs and aahs, sometimes even tears of joy, from viewers? My tears, quite brief on that occasion, soon turned to cries of rage. Be dipped in melted paraffin and hot waxed if that rotten sow, no doubt a touch peckish after all her hard work, *didn't up and eat her progeny, every dad-blamed, last, squirming, little piglet.*

No doubt you'll recollect that Dismus Dribble, that most learned of philosopher's, once said: "Some challengers having faced and experienced the bruising, harsh slam of a hammer are

GREAT EXPECTATIONS

eager to try again, while others—wiser—quietly knuckle under from the soft stroke of a downy feather."

Der Dumbkoff Acres, except for urging their hens to continue to produce eggs, promptly ducked away from that crushing ball-peen blow and retired from the raising of: chicken friers, rabbits, turkeys, pigs and cattle.

Not to worry, we rose in majestic glory from that ignominious defeat to accept the next challenge. Opting for the beezer busting feather—actually several wagonloads of them—behold Whispering Winds Aviaries. From livestock tomfoolery we were now knee deep in mother's next idea which was, literally—*for the birds!*

Whispering Winds Aviaries 16

S tuck for a money making idea? My Mother outlined another beaut! " ...parakeets, cockatiels, lovebirds, canaries. They make great pets, are prolific, and good parents; they're not expensive to house or feed. Best of all, these birds aren't costly to buy and they are popular with people. Why, did you know they can even be taught to talk! How can we lose? When you leave the service, we'll have the start of a nice little business. The money will roll in." Not only did it *not* roll in, it didn't even imitate a one-legged hop.

The above hard sell was penned to me in Alaska. I bought it. After all, as Pop was just wild about carpentry, he would be drafted to build the initial pens! Besides, I wouldn't have to knock any of those little guys off. I also liked the name; Whispering Winds Aviaries had a welcoming sound to it, much better than the effing Dumbkoff Acres. Look at it logically, if you put money in a bank, it will only gather interest and increase the flaming balance!

Before Pop could lay saw to board or hammer upside the head of a nail, Mom's idea was in full flight. Reading, trucking the byroads, chatting up breeders about their birds and then buying, she soon had ten pair of blue and green "shell" parakeets ready for aviary life, if she could only sell the old man on finishing the building of birdies inn. Pop was many things; a builder wasn't one of them. A southpaw, he could make a baseball laugh as it curved past your clumsy efforts to slug it. With a hammer, he usually hit his thumb. As a child, I'd learned some mighty interesting new words whenever that occurred. Eventually, after lengthy sighing and toe-tapping on her part, prolonged cussing on his, the aviary stood ready for inhabitants; while it may not have been Buckingham bleeding Palace, Mom's twenty birds, soon to be fourscore more, were happily chattering and exploring their new digs.

By the time I received my discharge, bid so long to the Air Force, and unlatched our bird farm's gate, we would have parakeets up the dump stump: Normals, Opalines, Albinos, Lutinos; also members of the parrot family, include Lovebirds: Peach Faced, Black Masked and Fishers; Cockatiels (one a house pet with a penchant for scrambled eggs). Add Canaries: white and yellow Rollers.

The head of "she of the ideas" was buzzing with more. Happily, as yet, we were not thrashing around in the red. Escalating parakeet production sure beat the foggy dew out of rubbing out the hare in the rabbit.

Parakeets mate for life and, though occasionally they belt one another, divorce is not a factor. With good healthy stock if, they are kept clean, out of drafts, and well fed, 'keets will raise at least four clutches a year (an average five babies per clutch). Some breeders go for more. In warmer climes where there is less danger of the hens becoming egg-bound due to colder weather, it's not unusual to breed year round. We bred four clutches only. Why? How would you like to be bare clawed of the feet and pregnant twelve months out of every year!

Both parents feed and care for the young. As long as the nest box is emptied and cleaned prior to the next setting, so that new eggs won't roll out of the concave nest bottom, babies hatch out about one a day; thus, there isn't great disparagement in size. All the young survive, fly and mature, then they mate. Who's got the flippin' calculator? Oh, how sweet it was, like learning the multiplication tables the easy way!

Whispering Winds soon learned to watch out for the guy who always over-bred and then—lying in his teeth—swore that overlapping beaks and crossed tail feathers were normal and to be desired. Some of those greedy jokers would even sell parakeets where the upper mandible aimed due north while the lower veered off to the south. Try picturing the fun those poor little chirpers have trying to crack seed with a mouth shaped like a Pushmi-Pullyu!

Mail call in frigid land, where I had just cracked open Mom's latest pitch.

"Dear, we also need to invest in the rarer kinds of parakeets: Opalines, Lutinos and Albinos. Cobalt-colored Opalines are really in today. Can we afford to buy some of the truly rare parakeets like those most desired Harlequins and Dutch Pieds?"

Busy helping to search the Alaskan bush for a missing logger, and aware that good old Pop, not this kid, would have to traipse off to the lumber yard one more time, I wrote to go for it and mailed my malnourished bankbook.

Opalines are not considered to be truly rare even though some have yellow heads and they sport lovely patterns on their wings which, to my mind, ratchets them a notch above Normals. Lutinos are a striking yellow with pink eyes and they grace any aviary. Albinos, another winner desired by all dedicated aviarists, are completely white and also pink eyed. Add one more large plus, similar to their Normal cousins rare parakeets are equally prolific.

Lovebirds are harder to breed and more expensive: parrot related, they border on being "squawkers" but picture a pretty sight for the eyes. During the day I always enjoyed listening to their gabby socializing. Whispering Winds succeeded in breeding and raising those constant jabberers although never to the same extent as our 'keets. There can be no doubt that the Almighty truly loved creating birds: observe their color, their joy, their song, their grace, the pleasure they impart, the way they make a gray day a tad less damp and dreary.

With the exception of the African Gray, my favorite member of the parrot family has to be the Australian Cockatiel. I have been successful in teaching a number of them to whistle and they do it well; however, I am more inclined to think I favor them because their regal bearing disguises a mischievous eye. The term "character" properly applies. No aviary should be without a few of these delights. Easy to breed, they likewise make good parents and lavish loving care on their babies. They are private birds and do not appreciate "nosy parkers" prying into their business. Leave their nest boxes alone, they'll let you know when they have babies!

Why canaries? Consider this: they are pretty (red factors rate the term, beautiful) they are also dandy singers, and even though wasteful of seed, bird for bird they don't eat much. A further blessing, they really enjoy raising babies. One can sell the babies. One might, possibly, make money. One might then buy more of the cheerful chirpers. Two of the three *ones* above are correct!

Rollers are entertaining, soft voiced singing companions and have been so for over five centuries. If breeders wish to keep their song pure, these tuneful little guys must be kept isolated from all the other noisy or singing birds.

Training the young to sing *true* is fascinating work. Only males sing. An occasional female will also rattle the windows, but such a happening is rare.

The training lesson: We have already identified our prospective students through their experimental chirping; sounds a touch like the adolescent who's choir voice is changing from soprano to sudden unexpected squawks. The adult singer or tutor, comfortable and happy in familiar surroundings awaits his class. Our young learners, housed in individual—completely darkened—cages, are placed close to and around the maestro. The front end of each enclosed cage is opened or lowered to allow the youngsters to see and hear Placido Domingo of the Roller bird world belting out "The Barber of Seville." Happy as a feathered clam, the tutor sings his chirpy little head off for the multitudes. Thus our novices, exposed only to he of the golden voice, begin to sing precisely in the manner of the master. Not all in the first lesson mind you, but it doesn't take long before Carnegie Hall harkens to the new kids on the block. Cool, huh? A little deeper into "fun with feathers" I'll twitter about Red Factor canaries as well as rollicking canary club adventures.

• • •

SHE was at it again: "Birds and plants belong together, dear. Don't you think we should have a greenhouse and grow African violets, Cyclamen, Gloxinia, Chrysanthemums and Cineraria? Don't forget those oodles of Begonia varieties? There's *money* to be made in selling potted plants." *Bet me!*

Why should I be skeptical just because we still weren't making enough MONEY to even qualify for the privilege of paying income tax! In addition, I knew of no available buried treasure. Glass houses cost bread, (the stuffed full wallet kind) to either build or buy. Ma's solution was a corker!

El Sol burns Yucaipa hot in the summer. In 1946, after building the house and planting fast growing trees, we'd also added a lath patio for shade. It so happened, an ad in the L.A. paper tipped Mother on to a hot clue which—as raindrops dripped few and far between on the bird farm—looked to be a winner. A company in the office fluorescent replacement bulb business offered, free for the hauling, their burnt out four and eight-foot tubes.

In the habit of traveling far afield in quests for the exotic in bird stock, this ex-airman and Mom had recently purchased, on the low down and small ouch a month plan, an *exotic* 1948 Chevrolet panel truck. Oh, woe in a leaky gondola, let me count the number of trips, on recap tires, we trekked between Yucaipa and Los Angeles chasing down defunct fluorescent tubes.

See, I figured to build us a greenhouse using long burnt out lights. What's the big deal? Well, no one else on the block had one; in fact, not in the whole state and possibly the whole flaming country! Guinness would have been proud! If I do say so myself, it crafted out downright pretty and I conned Mollie-O into drawing a picture of my enviable creation just for you. Once assembled and nudging their neighbors, on an occasional stormy evening— lightning and thunder—some of those old tubes would light up for brief periods. The effect was aesthetic, weird, and a smidge startling. If rain accompanied the upstairs angels noisy rearranging of their furniture, so what! I wouldn't have to water the plants all that day or evening. Water seeping past tube sides benefited without any damage to greenhouse or greenery. If I'd let Frank Lloyd Wright in on it, he'd have begged for plan privileges for the Whispering Winds Aviaries, fluorescent tube designed, experimental greenhouse. And you flat cannot overlook the fact that the price was definitely right.

Heating wasn't required as the sun's efforts heated the bulbs and they retained most of that warmth overnight. I installed water lines and besides providing moisture for the plants, they also permitted cooling of the gravel floor whenever the Southern California heat became excessive. Side opening windows allowed for cross draft and ventilation as did the screened door. Siding where needed was varnished redwood. Inside, I built three-tier shelving on the south, east and west sides. The rockery then arranged nicely on the north end, which formed the only solid wall. The medium-pitched roof was formed of both eight and four-foot tubes on each hip. Four-foot glass lengths comprised the other three open sides. Most winters were not severe enough to damage the plants although it actually snowed on

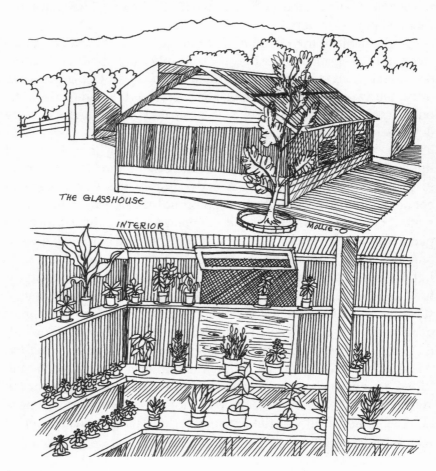

THE GLASSHOUSE

INTERIOR

MOLLIE-O

one Easter Sunday! Fortunately, given the privilege of cleaning pens every day, I wove a mess of feathers into cloaks and right quick slipped them over the potted pots!

Pleased with our greenhouse, we hied back to Los Angeles about another forty dozen times for additional loads of those burned out jobs and I then proceeded to remodel the old lath patio with them. And that turned out every bit as pretty as Lady Godiva's frock—and just as cool!

Every year after that I'd put in a formal request for prolonged thunder storms in late December. I was sure, once the demised tubes lit up, they'd save me the trouble of putting up the Christmas lights.

I hadn't been involved in building for ten or fifteen minutes so I could hardly wait for the *next idea*. Here it came:

"Dear, according to my bird magazine, red canaries are really catching on. Not color fed—color *bred*. Groups have organized clubs; they hold meetings, socialize and put on shows. Awards are generous, show winners garner good money for their stock and a lot can be learned from other breeders, especially how to avoid pitfalls. The prize birds breed as efficiently as their common canary cousins and will raise two to three clutches during the season. The breeder can count on three to five babies per clutch; a trio—one male, two females—may produce as many as thirty birds a year. We're talking *real money* here! Sounds like fun. What do you say, care to give it a go?"

"How much for a trio?"

"Not a whole lot, dear. *Three hundred for a good trio*. We'll also have to join a club and go to meetings, but dues can't be too much. I believe they rotate hostess duties, so we will be able to entertain club members here."

As you can imagine, I could hardly wait to entertain a bevy of old broads!

• • •

Breeding and raising prize birds lessons out somewhat more complicated than introducing parakeets to one another. For instance, foster mothers are used with your expensive stock. Right, it behooves me to explain foster mothers:

To begin, Red Factors are pedigreed birds which necessitates keeping accurate records. To properly and correctly register them, the birds must be *close-banded*; such can be accomplished only when the babies are quite young. Additionally, the well-bred of the canary world do not take kindly to overwork. Raising an active clutch of those finch kids adds up beaucoup work for ze leetle bird. To ease the load, a normal momma canary is conned into becoming a foster mother. Here's how she flies including how, unlike life in the wild, the babies in each clutch hatch at much the same time: Normal hen and pedigree hen having posted the banns, exchange vows and get it on with their respective swains. In the natural course of time each hen—housed separately—builds a nest, then eagerly expectant (I presume) awaits the arrival of her eggs, one per day. At this point, the human breeder becomes a ripper off of the eggs! Each day, foster's egg and pedigree's egg are removed and in each case a child's marble will be substituted. You can wander away confused here, so pay attention. Foster's own egg is deep-sixed; pedigree's, retained, is then carefully placed in a cotton-packed chicken egg carton. Both hens are now *each sitting on a marble they think is an egg.*

These two are going to be first time mothers and they lay four eggs apiece. When no more appear on the fifth day, the marbles under foster mom disappear and are replaced with red momma's heisted eggs. In turn, Red's marbles are removed and she gets nothing back; this dastardly act so confuses her, it probably gave rise to the phrase, "She's missing her marbles!"

Naturally upset, Red chases all over her cage hunting for her missing eggs. In the process of searching, she'll likely tear her nest apart, but hoo-ha, rots of ruck, 'cause she never will find them. Much twittering and gnashing of her beak. Finally, as all birds are philosophical, she chirps "to hell with it" and hops over to the male where she warbles: "Let's get it on again, Dad. I can't find our damn eggs!"

Meanwhile foster mom sits contentedly on Red's eggs counting the days—fourteen—until her little millstones arrive. Soon, sweet cheeping emanating from her neighbor's cage doesn't do a whole lot for Red's disposition.

If you have ever observed Ma Nature's bird program, you've noted that those babies do not all chip through their shells at the same time; therefore, birds hatch at different times and this results in size variation, which means that the last one to kick a hole in the shell is certain to be the first one that brothers and sisters stand or sit upon. Here comes momma with a fat worm; the bigger kids hog it all. Junior gets nuttin' and pretty soon—numbered among the absent at table— mother can only hope he's being fed by the angels.

Nix to that happening to pedigree birds, hence the marbles. Other than a brief marble chill homing on mom's tum-tum, nobody tumbles to the breeder's con. Slick, huh? Don't get your water hot, a frustrated Red swearing at innocent Pop and bending her beak on cell bars is not desired. Accordingly, although we continue the marble routine to control time of baby arrival, we permit her to hatch her next clutch without interference. Believe it or not our machinations are for her own good. Allowing too much hatching and feeding of bird babies isn't smart. It's not unusual for a tired mother, sick of gaping mouths, to flick it in, leave the kids to whomever's tender mercies and more than ready to kick back, hop the first red-eye leaving for Miami!

Proper feeding plays a large part in successfully raising those pedigree babies; for that matter, any birds. We fed the mothers our own formula, derived from discussion, reading and experimenting. Recipe? Sieved, hard-boiled egg, crushed cracker crumbs, wheat germ and Gerber's dry baby food.

It worked like slickum; much-a-many years later—still breeding and raising Red Factor canaries—mother, at ninety-seven-and-a-half, continues to feed with that same formula. Even as I pen this, the little chirpers spaced about the dining room, are belting out arias behind me. Tends to choke a guy up.

Members of the canary club, Whispering Winds joined, were all long in the tooth. I, young, suave and devilishly handsome, became their prize pigeon! My titles? Number One Gopher; Number One Toter of Caged Birds; Number One Slugger in of Seed; Number One Arranger of Caged Birds on Tables at Shows; Number One Master of Ceremonies at Shows; Presenter of Awards; Leader of Applause for Winners; Supplier of Nose Blowers for Losers. Why the honor of number one? Including others who'd conveniently forgotten to bring their ear trumpets, I was the only male of the group who still retained all his teeth! That's not really true—but I like the part of martyr.

Whispering Winds folks were never called forth to receive the big gong for best bird of show. However, we garnered our share of ribbons, had fun, enjoyed the chatter at the socials (my, what some of those old gals would haul out to discuss!) and learned a great deal about raising color bred canaries.

A word or two about color bred versus color fed: A coloring substance, available in pet stores, when added to color fed birds' water will, once imbibed, deepen their feathers' color. This can be done to an already light orange Normal canary. Having been shopping around in pet stores for a bird exhibiting a deep shade of red and, upon sighting just *the* one, you become oh so eager to purchase the radiant fellow, yes? No! All birds molt. Canaries start in July-August after the breeding season when most males also stop singing. Not to worry; molting can be compared to buying a new pair of shoes, as soon as you break 'em in, your feet stop hurting. Same can be said for your birds. New feathers tend to itch and irk them for awhile. Come September, nature has salved that itch and serenity, floating into Pavarotti's cage on a mellow fall breeze, tends to lighten his load. Time to serenade the cute little hens again; they, of course, have been itching, too!

Beelzebub! Cry you who bought the bird of the deep shade of red who is red no longer. He looks more like orange faded by a mean sun! What the hell happened? When you bought the bird you forgot to ask was he *color fed or color bred?* If you got him for a song (I couldn't resist that) he was probably CF not CB and his feathers no longer bear the deeper color. What to do? To be able to once more call him Red, instead of My-God-He's-Fading-Fast, you start color-feeding again. Regardless, you'll never achieve better than second best nor end up with the color bred bird you desired and thought you'd bought! Color bred means just that. From the time a Red Hooded Siskin from South America successfully courted a good looking canary, Red Factors have deepened in color, generation after generation through careful selection. Varieties today are almost unlimited. Unlike color fed, after baby's first molt he'll feather out again a deeper, richer, orange-red.

How the galloping fantods do you tell a CF from a CB? If possible before buying—yank out a feather (gently). CB goes all the way to the root of your colorful subject!

How about money in the old kick? Did we fatten the flat bank account breeding and raising canaries? Now why did you have to go and ask a fool question like that!

"Dear, you've noticed we are selling a few plants. Parakeets and cockatiels are also moving and I sold two Rollers and a Red Factor last week. Shouldn't we expand? What do you say to including German Shepherd dogs in our venture?" Here we go again. Naturally, wampum is waiting in the wings!

"We have already been offered a female, Dear. Do you mind having to leave early tomorrow morning? Our appointment is for seven in the morning and her owner, Clint, as you know, lives over fifty miles away."

By her so saying, the first tiny problem rolled over the cobblestones. I am a dedicated night person. Don't misunderstand, the only fault I have to find with morning is that it occurs before *noon*. Seven o'clock is, of course, the middle of the night. I had absolutely no desire then to even think of arising at that ungodly hour nor, do I have it now! Civilized stirring of one's body should never, ever, be contemplated before the early hour of eleven!

• • •

This seems like a likely spot for you to become acquainted with Clint. I say acquainted because, if you had known him, you'd have liked him. His life had not been easy. Suffering from polio while young he'd overcome it with determination, weight lifting and exercise. Clint's heart—outlining the physical here and not the giving—had been slightly damaged by that filthy disease. And he also walked with a slight limp, but his regimen of exercise, adhered to faithfully, had rewarded him with a strong athletic body. Like Whispering Winds, he, too, was into birds, many of them hook-bills.

I've stated parakeets are prolific. That fact had led to our meeting Clint. 'Keets also follow a regimen; the little chatterers lay their eggs, hatch 'em and raise their babies; lay their eggs, hatch 'em and raise their babies; lay their eggs…see what I mean?—regimented. With good food, care taken not to over breed, clean and large pens for exercise, *abundance* is what you get. So what's the connection? Clint was also a bird fancier. Rugged and tough, he was anything but what you'd expect a bird lover to be. Once we got to know him and learned some of the details of his past life, his present occupation, that of owner and operator of a bird farm, became harder to believe. For many years he'd been a bouncer in a gambling casino; eventually he became manager and part owner of one. That kind of life had begun to turn him hard and mean. He began not to like what he saw in his mirror. One day that mirror heard: "That's all, no more." He told his partners, "Cash me out, I'm outa here!"

One month later he purchased prime property in El Monte, California, constructed some pens, installed a phone, fastened a sign on his front gate, established contact with Chicago and New York buyers, took out ads, and announced he was buying and selling birds.

We had sold a few of ours to a store in Compton but the buyer was a shyster. Neither Mom nor I liked the way he kept and handled his stock. Spotting Clint's newspaper ad and having a goodly supply of birds on hand, we took a run into El Monte to check him out. We hit it off right from the git-go, beginning years of friendship, a business partnership and South American adventures. (I'll relate more about "Bring 'em Back Alive Jack" a little later.)

While a young lad, I was required to eat that which had been placed upon my plate. Often it resembled those rotten *peas*. Abhorring those miserable little green spheres, as you know I do, I would push them all around the plate in a futile effort to divide and conquer, all the while hoping SHE would think they were going through the process of subtraction! I've stated, resembled, because I vowed never to taste the nasty, mushy things. Latching on to a glass of water in desperation, I would swallow them like pep pills which put paid to that particular vexation!

Gabbing to you, me old punting partner, I just noticed I've been pushing peas all over my plate. Some eight paragraphs to the rear I started out talking about German Shepherds and then I hung us up on a snag for a brief spell. I suspect I had better follow through on that canine topic now.

Meet Jet, a female German Shepherd. Clint owned her and was in the process of trying to locate a home for her in the country, thus our seven o'clock appointment. From her name you have surmised she was all black. She presented all beautiful, too. Approximately two years old, she had but one teeny, tiny fault, which friend Clint, the dirty rat, neglected to mention. Jet rated pedigree but lacked the required papers; that was not the fault. *She was death on cats!* I don't mean she disliked them, no indeedy. I mean she killed them—*dead!* And absolutely no appeal for mercy worked. We all know cats wander, and that they totally ignore "No trespassing" signs. Many a travelin' kitty came to visit Whispering Winds Aviaries and never left. It wasn't that we adopted them, as cats and birds are seldom buddies. No, unless I could quickly effect a timely rescue, I ended up psalming 'em, and then planting 'em! I once spied a snarling Jet climb halfway up a tree after one. I expect that's called fixity of purpose, folks. Amen and R.I.P.

Jet became most honorable matriarch of our Whispering Winds puppy clan. Royal of blood, she was courted, won, and honeymooned with Big Duke, top German Shepherd hunk of Yucaipa.

Harken to soothing, encouraging music, and maybe toss in a few pickles for those in the family way, while time for the expectant and expecting, drags.

I'm sure I've mentioned most winters in Southern California are not severe although a sharp chill will often invade, come evening. Heed the day when a restless, pacing Jet, foretold of impending activity. Approaching darkness decided us to bring her into the warmth of the house kitchen. My knowledge of mystery of bird and bee extended as far as knowing that the fish were also in on it! I had to laugh when my mother asked what needed to be done for dear Jet? Purely beat the foggy dew out of me!

Fortunately, abetted by Mother Nature, the slightly confused dog, even though 'twas her first litter, knew the routine. Almost immediately she presented to the world an ugly little pink rat! Jet knew enough to clean it, but right away cleansing was interrupted by the arrival of another. Ignoring the first she began to wash the second. Oh-oh, like shucking flaming *peas*, she and we were staring at six more squirming pink rodents. "*Finem respice*," whined their poor mother, beginning to show definite signs of panic.

What to do? Four of her initial presentations were now growing cold to our touch; time for ER for a mess of rats! Mom wrapped each one in swaddling socks and I popped them in the oven. Relax, we had only set the oven on WARM, not a bleeding 350 degrees! A long two hours later a plumb tuckered Jet settled for ELEVEN of the little buggers, they looked like a long row of sausage rolls warming on the bottom rack of the oven. Their mother lay whacked-out and sacked-out on the floor. To hell with maternal duties!

Wearily, I elevated my bod and went in search of a LARGE box for the new mom and her brood. Sleep on, Jet—joy-filled days await.

An hour later, I couldn't help but sympathize with her and the confused expression on her face as she lay in her cardboard den overwhelmed by a mewling, squirming mass of pink! I wondered how long before she accidentally squashed one or two?

Nothing eventful occurred in the nursery for some weeks, though Jet disagreed. One feeds only so many kids and changes only so many diapers before one finds out all that fun is beginning to pall. Gaining rapidly in size, weight and length of tooth, her pups—she'd lost nary a one—were also becoming a large pain in her gluteus maximus. Constantly feeding, cleaning and counting, the pups poor mother was saddled with enough domestic duties to maintain a regiment in the Army. Something purely had to give.

Turned out to be the garbage man! Frantic to escape from those constantly demanding mouths, Mother Jet was outside her pen, seven weeks after eleven sausage rolls in the oven arrived, peacefully taking care of her own immediate necessities, when the clashing of gears downshifting, and roar of a large truck motor, intruded.

Whether the arrival of the noisy garbage truck—possibly equating to the constant cacophonous racket of her six plus five rowdies—set her off, never will be known. What is surely known is the hullabaloo which ensued when innocent garbage man met enraged dog!

After arriving on the battlefield on the run, what had sounded like tragedy to me pictured a comical sight. Snarling mother dog and hollering man had separated. He, with his pants down around his ankles, was desperately trying to look past polka dotted shorts to see how much of his butt was missing! Jet had *teeth-pinched his derriere*; thankfully, not seriously. Offering profuse apologies I carefully iodined his wound while Mom got the dog the hell out of sight! Later, I gazed nervously down the road as the truck, driven by the then painted and patched driver—hopefully mollified—raised what definitely appeared to be a huge question mark plum-

"YOW-W-TCH!"

ing out of heavy dust.

For two weeks we waited apprehensively for the letter from: TROUBLE, TROUBLE, SUE and HAD—Attorneys-At-Law; *Thankfully, no legal letters ever arrived.*

Not long after the pinched fanny incident Whispering Winds weaned Jet's pups. Profoundly grateful she didn't knock off another cat for almost a...week. When our now leery garbage man paid his weekly visits, although always obnoxiously vocal, Jet was safely slammered out of sight, but wisely, he always carefully checked before vacating the security of his truck.

Some extol the joys of motherhood in song, poetry, sonnet, essay or play. Such phrasing may word gamut from costly to expensive to highly extravagant. Others, frugal, settle for but two words—stuff it!

It is only fair to remember that those ecstatic mothers who sing at length, also don't field enough at one time for a flaming football team! When sold, while no reward to Jet, the pups did pay for their keep and a tad bit more for the Whispering Winds poke. If asked, I'm sure the reluctant mother would have readily admitted that her offspring had turned out handsome and sought after. Couldn't hurt to throw Big Duke a bone, too.

Why not expand a touch further toward the select? AKC registered German Shepherd dogs could play the wonderfully exciting music of the cash register further up the scale, and considerably longer.

Breeders of German Shepherd dogs were not numerous in Southern California in 1953, but we located one in the San Fernando Valley which at that time proudly boasted, country. After a thorough scan, we decided; Sachem and Bailereina left one valley and took up new residence in another at a place called Whispering Winds Aviaries.

Sachem, black and tan, stood wide and tall. A proven breeder at the age of three, he displayed the big, gentle, lovable goof. Jet, certain he was Jack London's "Buck," cozied up to him almost before he'd unpacked his suitcase.

'Reina, but eighteen months old, portrayed a beautiful queen. Close your eyes and picture German Shepherds at the Westminster Dog Show. Reddish brown, streamlined of body, sloping at the hindquarters; add a proud head and there stands a champion. In English you'd pronounce her Spanish name "Bailereina" as Ballerina; how appropriately she had been named. Though a teensy bit high-strung, 'Reina was a sweet, gentle girl, easy to love.

In a definite attempt to water up a down situation, Whispering Winds Aviaries was soon awash in puppies. The dry spell came when we tried selling them. AKC registered canines for purchase emptied the wallet in a hurry. As the breeder's investment is greater, puppies, in turn, called for considerably higher fees. All well and good if the public agrees to your needs; not so good if they don't. Remember hearing on radio that famous tobacco ad, "Call for Philip Morri-i-ss"? We called—'till our faces turned blue and the dentures flew out and landed in the fish pond—but nobody answered our paging.

Why? Pet economy rated just so-so for those times. Moola was hard come by. Most folks decided eating and paying the rent was more important than buying the kids a classy dog. Sayonara to the breeding and raising of German Shepherds. Aw, what the hey, at least a pauper's purse won't wear a hole in his pants!

• • •

Hook bills were hot, especially those ubiquitous parakeets. Price of feed, for normal production return, rated reasonable. Given proper care they were, as you know, truly prolific. Of all our ventures to date, we had realized the most money from our birds. Accordingly, when friend Clint called with a proposition, we listened, considered and accepted.

His proposal read like this: Whispering Winds would furnish the land. He'd supply the money to build a *battery* of pens; in addition, he'd furnish the stock and share costs for seed. For a monthly salary we'd house, breed, raise and then transport the saleable young birds to El Monte. Once expenses, bound to be picayune, tripped lightly off the top, we'd split the profits. Wanta bet a vacation in Hawaii wasn't just around the corner?

The battery was constructed so as to include one twenty-four foot wide, twenty-foot deep exercise pen at the upper end. Each breeding pen measured six feet wide and twenty deep. There were fifty of those. We boarded half of each pen on two sides. Then, except for an eighteen inch wire section located high across the back for ventilation, the balance of it was boarded from foundation to roof. Hinged shutters could close off the wired back during cold or inclement weather. (Draft is not healthy for birds.) The front half of each pen, ten feet, comprised of half-inch hardware cloth—a wire resistant to predators— remained open to the elements on both sides and the top. A five foot high three foot wide door, of the same sturdy wire, and framed of one by four, allowed egress through the front of each pen. Sheet metal—sloping six inches front to back to allow for runoff—formed the roof for the boarded section. Each enclosure, including exercise, was bolted to a one-foot high and four-inch wide concrete foundation. Nest boxes, enough for thirty pair, adorned the wooden sides. Perches were fastened to walls and wire. Every pen contained a spigot from which dripped a constant flow of fresh water.

Water dishes sat upon wood sided and wire topped grates, allowing overflow to spill onto recessed gravel beds, eliminating the mess of a muddy floor—unless it rained, which naturally called for the issuance of birdies rubber boots! Large, wall-mounted feeders required filling but once per day.

We bred approximately three thousand parakeets at any one time; another four hundred happily vacationed in the exercise spa. We planned on breeding five thousand eventually. Unfortunately, Clint suffered a heart attack which, while it didn't lay him out, left him bedridden for a lengthy period. Prognosis was excellent if he obeyed his "croaker" and played it cool. To relieve pressure, he'd hired a manager to oversee, handle, buy, and ship his birds. Remember, *he* was to supply the stock for Whispering Winds new battery.

I don't know why, but the manager palmed a lot of junk off on us: old birds, some egg-bound, some over-bred, and some just plain over the hill. They took a long time to weed out and necessitated numerous trips to El Monte where a quiet but firm word out of Clint's earshot, he didn't need the hassle, would be held with the manager. She was a flaming cow and needed a swift kick in the backside, which I was aching to supply! At long last with the help of Elva, Clint's wife, the clod got the message with Clint being none the wiser and gaining strength every day.

Ever wonder if birds of a feather do flock together? Ha! Do fleas practice multiplication on canines? With that as a given, you're ready for class and a smidge of bird farm economics: Small of body, parakeets become bottomless pits when it comes to depleting a filled feed dish. Tinier members of the Psittacine family, they eat a seed called millet. Millet, comes in one hundred pound sacks, and a flock of hungry 'keets snacking their way through a feed dish soon diminishes that seed. Ma Nature obligingly adding more mouths to the crowd puts paid to a hundred weight of millet sooner. No problem in itself unless, like the lady trying to fit into a sweater two sizes too small, too much is going out and not enough is coming in! Solution? Sell a flock or two and purchase even more seed. If done right, in addition to acquiring seed, a buck or two will also return to crowd the moths in your purse. Naturally then, if a breeder desires to waltz to the bank whistling "Ze Prolific Parakeet Fandango", his parent birds must be young, strong and healthy.

• • •

Whispering Winds Aviaries began to garner a tad bit of attention, probably because no one else was dumb enough to try as many, *sure winners*. Word has a way of getting around and soon, in addition to selling 'keets, we also found ourselves buying them—wholesale of course. A large number of fanciers called "backyard" breeders had surfaced along about then. These folks were avid to latch on to a good thing. Most, breeding around six to eight pair, pursued it as a hobby, as well as a chance to pick up a little pocket money. A few knew what they were doing, the majority did not. Consequently, over-breeding ran rampant. Not bothering to band or keep accurate records, brother was bred to sister. You know what they say about that: "Incest begins at home!"

The result is disastrous: throwbacks, malformed beaks, crossed wings, mature young unable to fly, and weakened stock: brother buyer beware!

One of the smaller breeders who did know what he was doing was the sales manager for the finest Chevrolet agency in the state of California. I ought to know—I went to work for them. I seldom mention names in my scribblings; in this case I will, I want you to know of them. Also, be sure not all automobile dealers worship the almighty dollar! Regrettably—as I'm talking 1954 here—their dealership no longer exists. Nonetheless, and I confess to waxing nostalgic here, it is with pleasure that I introduce to you, Lange and Runkel Chevrolet Agency, Redlands, California. *Their word was their bond!*

Bill, the sales manager, informed me that Lange and Runkel was in need of help. Broke, per usual, I applied for the, job was accepted and started work as the assistant parts manager. Whoa! Before you start banging on symbols and sounding the trumpets know that there were but two of us in that department, you can guess what the other guy's title was!

Most of the employees: (Sam, Stu, Tuby, Glen, George, Eric and Clay) had been with them for many years which spoke of good service and contentment. Mr. Lange, best described as a courtly gentleman, had recently retired. Mr. Runkel and his son John now ran the company. Lillian, the office clerk, and I were the short timers. These people were capable, honest, hard-working and good neighbors. Lillian was a delight even if she did think thirty-five was middle-aged!

With the exception of Stu, Clay and John, most of them have left us now. If they've conned the angels into playing poker with Glen's deck you can rest assured those pasteboards won't be marked! I honestly admired and respected those people. Perhaps in small payment I've conveyed that.

I have more to share about Lange and Runkel, my sailor friend, and I'll get back to them, but first, in the next few chapters, we're going to take a trip out of country. You did bring your passport?

Whispering Winds Aviaries

Su Pasaporte No Es Vuelve Aqui!

I have been moaning about empty pockets for quite a spell now and that, perhaps, has caused you to wonder from whence came the food for the table? Mein Papa brought home the Braunschweiger. While Mom and I fussed over feathers, he put in the eight to fives and half-day Saturdays as an office manager and salesman for a local lumber yard. He'd been married for a long time and planned on continuing to honor his contract, so while he figured the rare avis business was akin to roller skating up the freeway blindfolded, and profit as likely as finding oil in the back forty, he let Mom do her thing. In the process, he also shook his head a hell of a lot!

I see I have to be square with you. I wasn't broke in the sense of truly broke! I could take in a movie, date a girl and buy her a burger. What I couldn't do is add up the interest in my bank account. You cannot add to that which doesn't exist. With that cleared up, let's get back to relying on a wing and a prayer!

• • •

Gracing the bird farm now, include Parakeets (Normals, Opalines, Albinos, Lutinos, Harlequin Pieds), Cockatiels (Normals, Lutinos), Lovebirds (Peach-faced, Black-masked, Fishers), Canaries (white, yellow, red), Finches (Cordon bleu, Strawberry, Cutthroat, Zebra, Society, Green and Cuban), Troupials and Paradise Whydahs, Pekin robins, Rainbow buntings, black and red-headed Lady Goulds, Painted buntings, Toucans and Toucanets, Grenadier weavers, Brazilian cardinals, Bleeding Heart doves, Conures, Cockatoos, Lorikeets and Java Rice birds. All day long the farm tone sang the power and glory of birds at song. Sheesh! The cash register likewise rang although not as long. An additional "something" was surely needed. Like maybe a Kookaburra from the land of down under?

The next "idea" turned out to be Clint's. To this day I blame it all on his deep state of mesmerism induced from drinking too many cups of Mom's tea!

"There is moola to be made from gathering and selling exotic animals: monkeys, jaguars, ocelots, coati-mundi, reptiles, tropical fish and parrots. (The ban on importing hookbills had recently been rescinded.) How about you and I traveling to South America where *you* will set up and run a compound: where *you* will buy the exotics, cage or crate them, and then *you* will air-freight them on to *me* in Los Angeles? Together, *we* will really become known and MAKE MONEY!"

I know damn well you, too, have eased around the bend a yard or two and also a time or two! So, how come you're shaking your head at me because I did it? There were two good reasons for saying yes to the venture. I really do enjoy delving into the unknown when traveling, and I was a tad bored.

Thanks to my mentor, the orderly room captain, whose foresight had helped me obtain my first papers, I had applied for my final papers not long after my service discharge. Then, after hitting the books and taking the test, I'd been awarded citizenship. It was a simple matter to present those papers and in no time I received my passport. Today, naturalization papers which indicate clearly the dates of birth and citizenship will not suffice. Only an authenticated copy of the birth certificate will be accepted. "So what? No big deal!" you say. Think so? Try getting a copy of your birth certificate if you've been adopted and the adoption papers have been sealed!

Regardless, with *my* passport in hand, it was on to the next tiny little step—SHOTS! Oh, boy, seemed like there were myriads of anti-social bugs doing the big-buzz-around in South America. So, what would I need? Boosters for Tetanus, Typhoid, Smallpox, Cholera, and one I had never had before, Yellow Fever, which I discovered only after I returned home had not taken. Traipsing hither and yon in a bugged up jungle, dumb and happy, I was not even reasonably close to being immune to it!

My bag checked, ticket in hand, and apprehension drying my throat, I boarded the plane with Clint. Ah, you wonder about Clint, "Hadn't he suffered a severe heart attack?" Your memory's good, he had. Having followed the Doc's orders, and also Elva's loving threats, he was now back displaying in the pink—almost!

The airchine (that's the latest term for an airplane) smoothly hauled up its feet as we left the ground, but definitely a good omen! First scheduled stop with a one day layover, delightful Guatemala.

The landing uneventful and slick as only Pan Am could do it, we cleared customs and grabbed a cab heading into Guatemala City and our hotel. After a quick wash we tootled off to check out the sights. Mindful of Clint's still mending ticker, we'd elected to stay close to quarters for the nonce and settled for a leisurely two block stroll.

The capital was rated "pretty city and pretty people" and it was easy to see why. Her people were friendly, often laughing delightedly when, trying to converse, you loused up their language. Guatemalan attire, artistic, colorful and tasteful, made a refreshing change.

Settling for dinner at the hotel, we dossed down early as we planned to visit the zoo on the forthcoming day in order to familiarize ourselves with the kinds of animals we hoped soon to be buying.

The next day in that lovely city, the people continued to enchant with smiles and directions and we soon found our way to the zoo. It was there I first sighted the snake that would forever disturb my dreams. Not much thicker than a Ball Park wiener (I don't think he'd plump if you cooked him!) and four to five feet long, his forte was to hang from trees or vines and drop onto victims as they passed under. Called the "green snake" the ugly sucker was poisonous and hard to spot in the foliage. That stealthy, mean, slithery little critter scared the living fire outa me! I snapped a quick photo—thank God he was behind glass—and vowed, while traipsing about in the jungle, to keep my eyes aimed skyward at all times. Oh, sure, then I'd probably trip over some other varieties of lethal heart stoppers snaking across my path! Knowing I'd be heading into the jungle in other countries, where he and his cousins lived, I truly hoped my passport would be refused, for any reason!

Clint and I enjoyed a full day identifying, learning the habitats and totaling those animals it was permissible to catch and export. Though we were presently in Central America, much of South American wildlife was also present. I filled several of my notebook pages with pertinent information and then promptly lost the flaming thing in Panama!

Scheduled to depart on the morrow, we concluded that informative and educational day by enjoying another excellent dinner at our digs and again crashed early. During the night Clint suffered another *heart attack*. Of this I knew nothing until morning. Some people sleep like the dead. When I sleep, I am dead!

Fortunately, it was Clint himself who informed me of his attack. At the onset, he'd quickly taken a mess of his pills. Luckily, these had effectively controlled the trauma. Incautiously, we had both put in a strenuous day at the zoo, and my partner had paid the price.

"Keep a damn shoe on your nightstand after this," I snarled. "If you even suffer a gentle burp, bean me with it. You're the one with all the bread and the contacts, I'm just a flaming gopher!"

That scary episode put a definite crimp in my physiognomy. Keeping a constant watch on Clint, my right eye began to bug out. Attempting to keep track of our wanderings, the left eye soon suffered from divergent strabismus and warped walleyed. I trod forward walking backward. On to the Jungle!

Our next three stops: El Salvador, Nicaragua and Costa Rica stayed brief, allowing only enough time to clear customs and reboard. El Salvadoran and Costa Rican officials were gracious and pleasant; Nicaraguans, arrogant and rude. Was it something we Yankees said, or neglected to do?

Panama, where we overnighted, was hot, humid and *dirty*. While embarking the next morning, we were sadly informed a young stewardess from a major American airline had soloed from one of the hotel's balconies; her landing had turned out bad. Why do young people give in to despair so quickly?

Ecuador—little did I know—was ready for me! We'd scheduled a longer stay there. Our anticipated business would possibly headquarter in Guayaquil; investigation, chatting up the locals, would determine yea or nay.

After a butt-busting landing and having once again cleared customs, we taxied to our hotel eager to look the city over. Dripping, after dunking my mush for a quick cooling, I hollered to Clint to get the lead out and then I stepped outside into South America. Coastal, tropical and equatorial, Guayaquil was hot, humid, and—wonderful!

While absorbing produce stalls, shops, costumes, odors, climate and language of the country all at once, my thoughts carried me back to how gracious Lange and Runkel had been to me when, deciding to go trekking off to the other America, I'd quit my job. They had come through for me when I needed work; in payment, I'd left them in the lurch. I felt bad about that but Mr. Runkel, knowing the blood of youth flows hot, held no rancor. Rather, he wished me luck. I think he halfway desired to go himself. Me? Just naturally, when adventure hollered in my ear, I had to go find it.

After an Ecuadorian steak dinner, that turned out to be as enjoyable as trying to chew a hole in a truck tire tube, followed by a brief constitutional, we happily inhaled the perfume of a tropical evening while formulating plans for the following day. Early next morning, upon consulting government officials, we decided I should apply for a business visa and license which would allow me to conduct affairs in the Ecuadorian jungle. That turned out to be a slight goof which, cruising the friendly neighborhood on a balmy breeze to sail through the open hotel window and deck me in the eye! Why? In order to obtain the license I had to surrender my passport. Enclosed with the permit it flew away to Quito—the capital—for *prompt* processing.

While awaiting action on the requested papers, Clint hired a car and driver for a countryside exploration; we ventured out to look for a site for the compound. While thus engaged, a deserted area crossed our bow ideal for the sighting in of my .38 caliber, 4-inch barrel, Smith and Wesson revolver. In those days one could transport a weapon by plane without being accused of trying to hijack it. Some folks were willing to tip-toe, unarmed, through what is playfully called "the Green Hell," but this old boy wasn't one of them!

Clint and I became aware of two pertinent facts: Our compound would have to be established in the jungle proper, and we'd need to engage a guide as escort; preferably one who spoke English, knew his way around on the eastern side of the Andes, and would protect you know who's butt!

We returned to the hotel and Clint inquired of the desk captain if such were available? "Si, señors, we gots lots of thees guides in thees Ecuadors," replied Esteban. "We 'ave thees Norte Americano 'oo alzo espeak of thees Spanish; he's leeve but uno kilometer from thees 'otel."

A quick phone call and George—but recently returned from a trip to the hinterlands, those of mucho calor—appeared at *thees 'otel*.

Resembling a tall drink of water, he pictured six o'clock straight up and down and weighed just about as much. His gaunt, deeply tanned face, sported a long thin nose like his Adam's apple, and crinkled batwing ears supported his steel-framed spectacles. He was almost as good looking as me.

George was a gatherer and shipper of jungle orchids. Hailing originally from Miami, after a failed first marriage, he'd taken up permanent residence in Guayaquil. There, he'd married a native Ecuadorian lady much younger than himself who was unwilling to leave her home. Strange how domesticated the independent and adventurous become when collared by the "cute and clingy!" George's wife pictured a living Ecuadorian doll. He was operating on the high side of forty-five in age but, in her vicinity, he honey-tongued, "Si, mi dulce esposa" so often that the balmy tropical air dripped flaming treacle! Dying to bug him about "Sweety" I noticed he also wore a holstered "mas grande pistola" and decided upon discretion over a loose mouth.

Due to buyer contacts made while still a resident of Miami, and because living was cheaper in his present location, George made a fair living with his orchids. Add to that, he was working and living the way he wanted. No fault to find there, at least not until he opened his big mouth again after we'd dispensed with preliminaries.

"Ecuador is a poor country with many government restrictions. To accomplish your aims will require paying off bureaucrats from the lowly to the high, and it won't take any longer than forever to get anything done."

Clint and I expressed confusion as to his meaning, so he elucidated.

"Most state workers in these South American countries don't prosper well off the public largess. In short, they don't make much bread! Consequently, a system I call "the bite" flourishes in all areas of government. For example: You desire a contractor's license. Appearing at the office of issue you request to take the required exam. Before the test papers are produced, you'll have to place a small "bite"—unobtrusively of course—into the clerk's palm. Having acquitted yourself well on the exam, you then carry the paper to an eager clerk in another office for his stamp of approval. Behold, one more wee "bite" warms another palm. Test passed and stamped BUENO, it's off to the next office for issuance of that must have license. Ouch! That guy's fat palm chunked off a bigger "bite!" Stagger to the next bandit. A big shot, he will benignly stamp APPROVED on your pretty, new, now legal license. You suppose he gets a chunk, too? Not that it matters, by this time you have been bitten so many times you haven't enough energy left to build an outhouse!"

"There you have the system that prevails on this continent," said George. "But I have good news. Peru is a better country for y'all to go get bit! They are more efficient, and they move quicker in Lima. I'd get your license there. Besides, I don't really recommend taking a non-sched plane over the mountains. Charter flights are often poorly maintained and leave only when full; thus, they do not set a certain time. Flying over the Andes is much safer via Panagra, the South American branch of Pan Am, they stick to listed schedules."

"Okay, that's what we'll do," decides Clint. "George, you're hired. Jack, let's get packed and get outa here."

"Uh, Clint, me old pit boss, we've got a slight problem here. My flaming passport's gasping for air, 9300 feet up, in Quito!"

"Damn, Jack, so it is. Well, you'll have to stay here and wait for it. George and I will launch for Lima, we need to make some contacts right away and get this show on the road. Get a plane ticket and follow us quick as you can. In the meantime, try some of their great Guayaquil pineapple."

Eight days later, after calling Quito twice a day and always hearing, "Joo gots it comin' mañana, señor." I got my passport back and vowed we'd never be parted again. Guess what they can do with Guayaquil Pineapple!

Lima imaged pretty from the air. They say it's a city where the sun she's a shine, but rain she's a don't. Other than the occasional damp from dew, *she* never had her face washed while I was there.

My passport secure, the anticipation of progress coupled with the beauty of Lima put me in a positive frame of mind. Disembarked from the airchine, I entered the custom's office for baggage and passport examination. Forty some arriving passengers selected chairs, sat and waited. Hey, when in Rome. I sat. Soon an officious little twerp waving a paper in his hand thrust his torso past an open door. Like a frog in a hurry to lunch on a room full of bugs, he rattled off some spanish and then, turning quickly, retreated within. One by one the seated rose, walked over, and disappeared past that open door. Each time, the pop-out guy with his paper reemerged and spat out more Spanish, I recognized only a few of the names he called: Pedro Gonzales, Jorge Valdez, Juan Hootgay, Felipe Hernandez, Dolores Escobar. I fine-tuned my ears but never heard mine called. With only ten passengers to go, I began to get irked. Finally the last—excluding me—exited through that lousy door, *never to return*. The paper waver didn't return either! To hell with this. I got up, walked over and through that flaming doorway.

Sitting at a desk, motor-mouth was chatting up a cute little senorita. Shoving my passport under his nose I said, "Hola!" He took a gander, his eyes lit up, he smiled like a hungry caiman and said, "Ah, si, Señor Juan Hootgay!" Can you beat it, that's John Judge in flaming *Español!* Bienvenidos á Lima.

Everything now seemingly serene, I reached for my passport. Enough time had been wasted and I was anxious to get to Clint, George, and dinner—not necessarily in that order—at the hotel.

"No, no, señor, su pasaporte no es vuelve aqui, en tres dias, a su 'otel."

"Run that by me again, bud!"

The cute little dish came to the rescue: "Señor, thees man ees a-tellin' joo el pasaporte mus be peek up at joo 'otel in uno, dos, tres dias; no can 'av eet now. Ees hokay, Señor, ever' zings bueno. Usted 'otel 'av eet pronto."

I'll be a ticked off candidate for political office suing for a vote recount, if my passport hadn't flown the coop again, taking with it my GOOD MOOD! Mad, cussing every foot, I cabbed to the hotel. Reunited with those two laughing hyenas, each busting a gut at my rantings, I *almost* saw the humor.

"After Ecuador, I knew you'd get fired up," hee-hawed Clint. "Don't worry, as promised it will be here in three days. You'll have it back in plenty of time for you guys to make the flight over the Andes."

• • •

It was 4:25 P.M. Thursday, April tenth, 1955, and while this small insert has nothing to do with the gathering of animals unless you are fond of eating and, when you do, you have a desire for sauerkraut and wienies, knowing the following may well come in handy. The absolute best dish of the above ever placed before me and which I then had the salivary pleasure of devouring, was presented when I lunched in a German restaurant in Lima, Peru. Wieners: Big and fat, sweet and juicy. Kraut: Presenting itself not as long thin strings, but chopped. Sour? Indeed. Yet, it did not pucker the lips like sucking on a lemon will. Rather, think of that taste as though I had prepared myself to whistle; the inhaling had added the melody and the exhaling sent it back in full song.

Remember, not Bar-S, but—bar none—the ever lovin', drop me in the pan and brown me lightly, best you ever tasted. Don't ask! I can't remember the name of the wretched street; however, if you go to Lima, breathe deep then just follow your quivering nose and please, take me with you!

Two Cases of Malaria—
One of Leprosy

Seeing my .38 mm S and W, George shook his head and related the following tale: "The jungle growth where we are headed spreads thick and is tangled. Unless following well-worn paths penetration is quite difficult; there are no long fields of fire. A few years back while out in the bush I spied a lovely strand of orchids hanging just about shoulder height on the back side of a large tree. Pushing through thick brush at its base, I reached out to capture my prize. Uncoiling from the far side of that deceiving tree a huge boa constrictor, in turn, reached out and captured me!"

"I managed to pull my pistol and fire all six shots into the squirming bugger. I never hit a vital spot. Scared and desperate to escape I pulled my knife, cut his damn head off, and finally broke myself loose. The point I'm trying to make is that a pistol is of no use in the jungle. To be safe, and even then maybe not sure, carry a sawed-off, double barrel, twelve gauge shotgun. That baby will take care of anything with the possible exception of an untimely meeting with an adult jaguar! For that, teach your feet to run fast."

"One more point: You *will* catch a disease of some kind. There are enough bugs out there to sicken half the earth's population. Not to worry, we have sulfa drugs and penicillin. Remember to take your quinine for malaria and anything else you catch we can cure—*in most cases!"*

After he retired to his room, tremendously reassured by that little homily and now more eager than ever to find a way out, I carried my passport over to Clint and said, "Oh, shoot. Guess what old buddy? Right down here at the bottom in the fine print it says length of stay limited to five days. That means I've gotta dust outa here in a paltry ninety-six hours. Sure won't leave enough time for an exciting trip to Bugsville! Reckon I'll have to grab the next flight out. I'm ever so disappointed and I'm truly gonna miss you."

Clint gave me a long, searching look and said, "Jack, I know you are scared (You can bellow that one out loud and long.) and I understand. If you want to call it quits and head on home I won't hold it against you. However, consider this, if you flick it in now you'll always wonder. Life is full of these prodding tests. If we run from them, will each of us ever know what he is truly capable of? And only you will know if you measure up as a man."

Well, hell, after that little pep talk there was no way I could split. The ironical part was, due to his bum ticker, that S.O.B. would remain behind in Lima! In simple truth, his lousy pep-talk that evening, because he was absolutely correct, has stood me in good stead all my life.

• • •

Ka-chow, brr-ump-brr-ump; I listened with a practiced ear as the engine settled into a familiar roar. Strapped in, George and I waited for the other ancient one to start. Our flight over the mountains would be via DC-3. In military parlance a C-47 and fondly called the "Gooney Bird." I wish I had a nickel for every safe mile I've flown in one of those old loves. Of course I purely hoped touching Heaven while flying over the Andes wouldn't prove to be the big exception! The cabin wasn't pressurized on this baby.

Though I'd been as high as 18,000 feet without requiring oxygen in the past, at the summit on this flight we'd reach 22,000 feet. Panagra's system? An oxygen tube (hopefully sterilized) that each passenger would insert into his mouth. Quaint but serviceable, it checked out a-okay upon reaching the altitude demanded for crossing the peaks. Feeling like I was puffing away on a hookah, I settled back ready to enjoy the grandeur of those jagged Andes. Take my word for it, the view was worth the trip. We flew close enough for me to want to slide open a window, reach out, grab a handful of snow, mold a snowball and whip a fast one back at Lima, aimed in "Monsignor" Clint's direction!

At 22,300 feet our chariot's engines wheezed asthmatically as we slipped over the top, but they never missed a beat. Lord above, I truly loved those ageless piston-pounders.

Descending all too soon, mean-visaged crags and spires long behind, our supplementary oxygen no longer a necessity, we soared down and then over a carpet of green distinguished by countless tributaries. From above those strands of silver, like soothing tears, gently furrowed an endless verdant face. Children born of the mountains, oxbowing, entwining, enlarging; forsaking material ties, eager for play, they rush to frolic and sport in the sea.

Playing the memory game as I pen this, I recall that during the flight to Iquitos, opinions differed as to the actual source of the Amazon. Researching for geographic accuracy in the local library in 1998, I hauled some fairly recent investigation from off the top shelf. I enjoy geography, do you?

During the 1970s, a young couple along with their dog had been led to a permanent spring—17,000 feet plus—on Mt. Huagra in the Andes; their local guide, a man well versed in the area, claimed that the waters from that spring began the tiny flow that eventually becomes the driving power of the mightiest river on earth. In the mid 80s, a group of kayakers offered an ice cave, over 17,000 feet up on the same mountain, as the true source.

No matter. Beginning as the Apurimac the Amazon changes its name four more times to the Ene, Tambo and Ucayali. Finally, where the Ucayali joins the Marañón just above Iquitos, behold the Mighty Amazon!

From its source the Apurimac—meaning Great Speaker—flowing to Atalaya, *drops 16,000 feet in 600 miles.* From there to the Atlantic ocean it descends but *a scant 700 feet more over a distance of 3,600 miles!*

Rio Amazonas is fed by over 1,100 tributaries, ten of them longer than the Rhine. One, the Medeira, is 3,000 miles in length and collects ninety tributaries of its own before joining Big Mama. Ocean going vessels navigate 2,300 miles from the Atlantic as far up as Iquitos. Iquitos, 715 miles from Pucallpa by river, is more than twice the distance than if she followed a straight line. The breadth of continent is equal to 2,800 miles; yet, the length of the Amazon is over 4,000. At Iquitos, the river is still 120 feet deep. The daily tide from the ocean can be felt at Obidos, 500 miles upriver.

"Thees rivair's mouth ees mas grande than alla joo rivairs een thees 'hole a-worl' aroun',", said Manuel, the busboy at our hotel.

Seems to be a slight exaggeration there; however, her mouth is *200 miles wide* at Belem and her force is so strong, she powers fresh water 150 miles out into the Atlantic ocean. In spring, the river can rise fifteen to eighteen feet in two to three hours and the water flowing seaward from that mouth would, *in one day, supply New York City for approximately nine years!* Her great sprawl drains over three million square miles. The number of fish, insects, birds, animals and reptiles, boggle the mind. I could hardly wait to see and greet her!

Our gooney bird's wheels bussed the runway in friendly fashion and, dodging terrain imperfections, crowhopped up to the terminal. Iquitos lies in the frontier province of Lorito. El pasaporte inspection was required. Never fear, I hung onto the sucker with both hands! A perfunctory look, thump of stamp, a slight nod followed by a polite "buenos dias" and I was outa there.

The wait was over. There I stood on the river bank above Belén, pulse pounding, viewing and smelling the mighty Amazon. I have to think it's the most impressive and powerful river in the world, and yet she flowed serenely by giving no hint of that driving force 120 feet deep beneath my feet. Coffee-with-cream-colored, occasionally rippling lazily, she journeyed quietly on to the sea.

A floating village, Belén, part of Iquitos, is a small water-craft port. The huts of this floating village were built on stilts, a precaution against heavy flooding during the rainy season. They provided none of the amenities which we take for grant-ed, but the people, busy chattering and laughing, certainly seemed content. Primitive, hot and colorful, Belén both repelled and delighted me.

Vessels including rafts and canoes ply the river; Indians bring baskets, fruit and small animals to barter or sell. Because the down river current rules, they often hitch a tow from larger motor powered riverboats when traveling back upriver to their villages. That system works well; those same boats are in the habit of stopping off at villages along the river as well as its tributaries to also buy, trade and sell. The Indians, recalling the labor saving tow, greet in friendly fashion rather than laying a shillelagh upside the captain's head!

Friend, I don't know about you but every strange place I visit, be it city or village, I always hunt up and browse the local farmer's markets. I derive a great deal of pleasure from the sights and smells, the unusual, and the people. Belén was the market place for Iquitos. No question the produce—bananas, papaya, pineapples, and mangoes, having just arrived by canoe—was fresh. Caught on the way, fish still flapped in the bottoms of dugouts. Although also assured they were fresh, I was a touch dubious of the monkey, tapir, snake and caiman meats as absolutely nothing was being done about the pesky, ubiquitous FLIES!

George knew a lot of people in Iquitos and after registering in our hotel, we set off to check out his contacts. The town housed about 20,000 people—today, make that 450,000—and boasted the *Malecón*, a colonnaded promenade along the river. The square included a fountain and a bandstand where the band serenaded strolling young lovers. Elegant statues of explorers and heroes added decor as did large ornate park benches. A few streets were paved, most were not. Surrounded by jungle and truly obliged to the Amazon, the city supported a first class hospital; her people were friendly and hospitable. All in all, I found

IQUITOS

myself enamored of Iquitos and occasionally, I'll trot out my slides and pay Belén a return visit.

George and I strolled to a much poorer section of town because he said he wanted to check for local information on animals and conditions. By and by he stopped in front of an ugly little shack, the door of which gapped open on sprung hinges to disclose a wizened old crone who, when she opened her mouth to respond to George's greeting, displayed an alarming lack of teeth.

Jabbering in Spanish my guide, "Hola'd, buenos dia'd, donde esta aquied and muchas gracia'd." Madam jabbered a bunch back; George, in closing, *"Hasta la vista'd con muchísimas mil gracias"* and we vamoosed—like in, split.

"George," I said. "Your employer does not speak Spanish. So, me old son, what was that all about?"

"That old bag is the poor man's local *madam*. She rents her bed of an evening to ladies practicing a rather ancient occupation. I asked her about current conditions of the local area's health."

"What did she reply?"

"Not bad at all," replied the one I trusted. "She informed me that there were but two cases of malaria and one of leprosy on her block for this week."

I bet you'd have agreed with me, because I wanted to whippy into a U-turn and accelerate right back to the airport, frantic to book a seat or even standing room on the first flight out. You must understand. It wasn't that the old cow was renting her bed. She could have rented it to the Army and the Navy for all I cared. It wasn't the two cases of malaria, quinine could put that on hold. The concern, bouncing around in my head like a BB in an empty boxcar, was that case of leprosy! It sent an urgent message to my feet, "Let's get the hell outa here!" A frantic call later, nothing, not even a broken-down crate headed in any direction, would be leaving for three days! Resigned, I asked Jorge (George in Spanish) to excite me with the next item on his agenda.

"We are going to pay a visit to the post office."

It would seem, for those planning on trekking the netherlands, the prudent should—before leaving town—avail themselves of the first opportunity to cozy up to the post mistress/master. If you happen to neglect postal dudes in South America, or rub them the wrong way, they might accidentally lose your mail or, more conveniently, feed it to their pet macaw. Therefore, George firmly believed and always practiced buttering up dem dudes.

A post mistress ran the office in Iquitos. And, a touch of nepotism here, her sister checked out as number one helper. We polished the dear Eve's apple to such a high luster that the worm left in disgust. Both sisters were amply endowed, putting it politely, and delighted in having their picture taken. I wasn't sure my lens was big enough to cover the subject(s). I've a slide of the three of us. Placing me in the middle, the shot looks like a mighty thin slice of ham flanked on either side by a half loaf of sourdough! The irony? We weren't in Iquitos long enough to worry about receiving mail anyhow.

Amenities tendered, credentials accepted, and sisters photographed, Jorge and I finally tramped the surroundings on the hunt for animals. Our first prospect, a German trader, exhibited and tried to sell me a Red Saki monkey. The fellow wore heavy work gloves while displaying this unusual mono. Heavily furred in red hair, the monk's face—clear and deep red—displayed like that of a little boy caught in the act of watching his older sister taking a bath. The thick gloves were a touch off-putting as was the mono's smile. After a closer inspection of the canines, I figured El Mono Rojo would bite like El Hell'o. He was already adult sized which meant he was most likely set in his ways—bite first, then negotiate. I passed.

Continuing to investigate possibilities over the next six days, we ran double smack into bad news. Competition was going to be too tough. Two brothers—I'll call them the Bamboozle Brothers— owners and pilots of two C-46's (fat cousin to the C-47) regularly flew in from Miami and New Orleans. They were buying up everything in sight including tropical fish. There was also another well-established trapper/buyer at Leticia, the tiny tip of Columbia which touched the Amazon. He, too, benefited from the services of Avianca Airlines airchines, readily available to transport his animals. They say that for recreation he liked to travel along the river banks, capture an anaconda and then wrestle it! Ask me, he'd spent too much time in the hot sun sans his hat!

Purchasing was possible by paying much higher prices. Unfortunately, that would only be the tip of the jaguar's tail. We still had to pay to fly the animals to Lima, pony up the export license squeeze, and then fly them on to Los Angeles—by commercial airline, which was bunches of miles further than Miami or New Orleans. Freight costs would be considerably more and stock would be confined for longer periods; this meant a higher mortality rate. Faced with higher costs, we'd have to charge lots more bread for our exotic animals than the public might be willing to pay for us just to break even.

Confronted with such news, about as welcome as a skunk at a garden party, it became imperative to have a little chat with Clint. No phone line to Lima! Luck lassoed us. We located a ham radio operator who was willing to call another ham in Lima who, in turn, would phone Señor Clint at his hotel and arrange, at a specified time, for him to use the Lima ham's set and call us up on the Iquitos ham's set. Piece of cake as long as I dun't 'ave to 'splain eet espeakin' een thees ah Spanish!

All came to pass. Faced with our dilemma, buying el monos, George had recommended backing up to Pucallpa and trying there. Through the static and oft repeated, "'allos, are joo zere señors?" Clint finally got the gist of my message. He concurred on Pucallpa but suggested I take a riverboat for the 715 mile journey which would take about two weeks. The captain, stopping often at remote villages along the way to barter would (for only a teensy "bite") also make it possible for us to buy animals direct from the source. Sounded good at first until I began to think about it. Riverboats are not long on quarters; passengers, bug besieged, slept on deck. Where do I get and store cages to hold the animals? The captain wouldn't wait while we built 'em. How would I feed the little critters? they don't all eat bananas! A fair-sized jaguar, perchance spurning his quarters and strolling the deck, could, in a hell of a hurry, help control the population explosion!

His idea seemed to me to be one where the cost would outrun the gain. Clint and I did not always agree and this was one of those times. After a few more days of fruitless investigation, the situation still a no win, Jungle Jack and his faithful guide boarded the plane and beat it for romantic Pucallpa.

The same ancient, rivet-popping, old love deposited us safely on the potholed tarmac. Understandably, there was no passport inspection, anyone arriving couldn't help but improve the place. Supporting approximately 8,000 people (push it up to 220,000 today), the town's houses were roofed in corrugated metal strangely angled and rusted. They were examples of where a tin man had peeled his oranges and hammered them into bananas. The riverbank blossomed with typical Amazon crafts: canoes, rafts, dugouts and small riverboats. No ocean going vessels here. Pucallpa was a wide swath hacked from that green carpet, one lengthy edge bordering on the Ucayali river. No sewers. Contaminated wells. Depending on rain, streets were mud or dry earth. Primitive? Oh, yes. Pigs wandered the streets and companionably lodged inside with the owners in their huts. A small aside here: The people of South America are very fond of their pets and take excellent care of them no matter if they are city, urban or jungle dweller.

PUCALLPA

Pucallpa did offer accommodations in the form of a barracks-like, share the bathroom, hotel. There were no fans in the room, but extra perspiration was free of charge. If one was unconcerned about combating bugs and opened the window of his room, the jungle grew right outside. The noise was cacophonous: twittering birds, buzzing insects, squalling animals and screeching parrots. Interspersed, I could hear howls like some poor unsuspecting soul had just been given a hotfoot. Later inquiry determined that they were Howler monkeys. George told the inn's inhabitants I was a "Científico" and that impressed no end, resulting in only-slightly-mud-discolored-red carpet treatment for Senor Hootgay. Oh, si, El Señor Juan ees lap eet oop!

The local's colors, way of life and people, intrigued me; they had so little yet laughed much. My sensibilities in a culture so foreign to me, clamored to explore and absorb. Truly, here lay a jungle town on the banks of the Ucayali: No dearth of mosquitoes and enough roof-perching vultures to man Congress. Want more? Close by, lived a tribe of the Jivaro—headhunters! While wandering the town, I happened to notice some Indians and more than one of them wore paint. Jorge decided they were probably tame, even friendly, Jivaro. All the same, I elected not to go over and introduce myself.

Pucallpa was a dump. How I loved the sight, smell and sound of her.

In short order, travel dust washed away, we set off to taste village flavors so tantalizing to our senses. Bingo! Almost immediately things began to look up. I met Dave Pent. He would play a large part in helping us obtain our first shipment of animals. Dave was the son of a missionary. He was about twenty-three years old: blond, blue-eyed, strong of frame, he was a good-looking lad who spoke Spanish plus some Indian dialects fluently. He was knowledgeable, honest, and a great find. Dave introduced us to the Jefe (a town mayor). Looking askance at the surroundings, I wondered if he'd truly been honored by his constituents. Gracious and quite friendly, El Alcalde offered whatever help he could. David started the ball rolling and before long we began to buy from villagers living along the river. The message sped:

"Norte Americano ees goin' pay mucho dinero por el Monos, joo call 'oncle Pedro an' cuzin Pablo to be bringin' all they gots."

Soon we had monkeys: Spider, Woolly, Saki, Squirrel, Howler and Owl, plus Lioncito and Pygmy Marmosets; Kinkajous; Ocelots and Coati-mundi. I wanted a jaguar in the worst way (cage-contained that is!) but one never came my way. We weren't equipped to handle tropical fish—a major over-sight—as the area absolutely teemed with hundreds of varieties. Once more, all hookbills were back on the banned list in USA so we couldn't *legally* import any. A flaming shame, as the jungle abounded in Macaws, Conures and other parrot types, big and small. (A touch of trivia: Turkeys are more prone to psittacosis [parrot fever] than are parrots.) I believe that as of this writing the ban has once again been lifted as it should be.

Live Caiman would have emptied the wallet to ship, so we passed. Still leery after our sojourn to the Guatemalan zoo, I acquired a crick in the neck craning upward on the lookout for Leptophis Ahaetulla—the green snake—in every tree I passed under. I still walk with my head tilted like the bent end of a bow. Some unkind people say that's because my stomach sticks out. Don't you believe 'em. The squirmy little feller fair gave and gives me the jim-jams!

One day the natives brought us a twenty-four foot Anaconda. This giant worm was a potential chunk of bucks for us but before buying him I asked Dave to tell the natives the sale would have to be on hold while we queried zoos in the States for interest, as shipment costs would be horrendous and the purchaser had to agree to pay the fare in addition to plenty of cash for the snake. If they cared to leave Big Wriggles with us we'd see what transpired. The Indians agreed and tied their offering to a telephone pole. I messaged Clint, via an airline captain, to get on the horn and sell the huge sucker!

'Condas eat about once every two weeks depending, of course, on the quantity, not quality, of what's on the menu. He was no problem except for raising hell with the eastern long distance telephone line. Whenever his jaws snapped closed on the pole, he got the Brazilian operator. In Portuguese and

English, she'd ask, *"Number please?"* He'd never answer. If she'd spoken in his native Spanish he'd probably have replied, "Two pigs and a goat!"

Oh, all right. The telephone pole, grown old and tired of standing, had surrendered to time and lay prone in a row of banana trees above the riverbank making it easy for the Indians to fasten the snake to it. Just as well, as that acrophobic anaconda was afraid to climb any of the upright poles! Besides, AT&T had raised their rates and the phone had been discontinued.

Ever ponder the merits of being suffocated over the pleasure of being squeezed to death? Well, many a midnight with nothing in store but peaceful sleep, I've considered crushed bones over slowly running out of breath, or vice versa, and you know what, I purely can't make up my mind.

I finally do understand why caiman with whom I was acquainted were bug-eyed. I'd studied a photo picturing one unlucky caiman all rolled up in an anaconda and, according to the explanation printed below the picture, every time Señor Caiman exhaled, the Big Squeezer kindly added more squeeze. After awhile, appeal denied, no oxygen for the caiman went in; likewise, he exhaled nuttin' out! The poor, long-snouted reptile was well and truly wrapped up in the throes of a fatal dilemma. Resolution? Aired out and thoroughly bugged-out—it's amen to the caiman! Wasn't that interesting?

We'd been in Pucallpa for three weeks, the time had now come to arrange transportation for our animals by airchine to Lima. Again my friend Dave was up to the task and muy rapido steered us through airport requirements. I wondered if Clint had made the sale, would the pilot have invited the 'conda to ride up there with him?

Meantime Ol' Clint, wheeler and dealer of the month, had located and also rented a building suitable for holding our livestock pending needed export permits. Naturally, he experienced the ubiquitous South American "bite" while quarters hunting; still, in the process, he also made a valuable friend. Paco owned and operated a large number of florist shops in Lima. Familiar with bigwigs and knowing the routine—including shortcuts—he smoothed the bureaucratic—'oldin' out of thees 'ands—path for Señor Cleent.

Señor Hootgay was rapidly running out of Peruvian loot. Through Paco, Clint could arrange to send more and I knew that. However, I had a decision to make. Out wandering the jungle I'd seen firsthand that we were up against tough, established, well-financed competition. Any fella owning his own plane will transport a great many more animals than could we via commercial carrier and do it for a lot less. Distance traveled to our animals final destination measured many more miles. That would definitely affect mortality. Anyone who has ever been involved in the care and production of livestock knows exactly what loss does to the owner's wallet, let alone his heart! Too many people in our operation would continue to be involved, thus escalating costs. The difficulty and expense of building a first class compound and maintaining same in the garden city of Pucallpa loomed about as large as our tree-tied-snake. The trapper/buyer based at Leticia already had hunters plying the areas up and down the Ucayali and Amazon rivers. Dave Pent knew the location, language and habits of the local and jungle people, and he was far more qualified to gather the animals for us than Juan Hootgay. Additionally, Clint had had health problems which could turn severe again. He funded our operation. I hadn't a farthing to bail myself out of trouble. If, due to unforeseen vultures perching on the headboard of my broken bed, I came up short of the bread needed to pay the natives for their offerings, they might well elect to tie *me* to the unoccupied side of that certain telephone pole!

Standing there on the riverbank playing that feasible, non-feasible, ballgame in my head, every time I swung the bat I whiffed!

To hell with it. I decided to go play golf! So, I collared George, left final instructions with Dave for shipping our first load of captives to Lima which was but a day or two away via a cargo plane. One more time, we caught my favorite two-engine wheezer and flew back over the Andes.

Regrets? Yes. I never visited Cusco or Machu Picchu. The source of the Amazon remained hidden (from me) as did Manaus and its opera house. Belém and the Amazon's humongous mouth never had the chance to overwhelm me. Finally, I never sweated buckets tramping the heart of the "Green Hell." Believe it or not, while the notion of doing that still gave me the galloping scram-a-rosis, I wanted to give it a shot. But, as they say: "The novice, walking barefoot, shouldn't pick up porcupine quills with his feet!"

Having since answered the call of a totally different vocation and performed successfully, I'm confident that back in 1955 I made the right choice.

• • •

Back again in Lima, while making preparations to receive our animals, I met Paco. Within minutes I found out how generous and thoroughly pleasant a man he was. I must mention an act which illustrates this quite touchingly: Clint, George, and I had been invited to his home for dinner and to meet his large family. I've mentioned he was a florist. His immaculate house displayed vase after vase of gorgeous flowers generously perfuming the air. It reminded me of the long ago days when, coming home from work in 1945, I walked along the residential section of Hollywood Blvd. and inhaled the aroma of orange blossoms and night blooming jasmine.

After a delicious dinner, Paco's wife rang the kitchen and requested dessert. It pictured an elegant surprise!

As new friends becoming acquainted do, Clint and Paco had shared confidences. During those pleasantries Paco had learned of my partner's upcoming wedding anniversary. Behold, servants entering from the kitchen bore a huge cake to the dining room table. An artist had made that cake. It portrayed the continents of North and South America; a candle symbolizing the number of years of their marriage stood at the northeast end. Two hearts— one reading "C," the other "E"—resided respectively at Los Angeles and Lima. A scarlet ribbon, in the center of which rested a two-headed silver arrow, tied the two hearts together. The truly touching gesture moved Clint. Tell the truth, as I knew just how fine a lady Elva was, Paco's kind gesture brought the wisp of a tear to my own eye. Paco was a true gentleman.

Dave Pent accompanied our shipment to Lima and in celebration, we all went out to dinner. No big deal except what I
chose was not what I ate! The restaurant rated elegant but was
not posh. Always eager to try new taste sensations I ordered the
usual, *a steak!* Both the waiter and Dave threw me pitying looks
and my pal recommended Antecuchos which turned out to be a
huge form of Scampi. Dave requested a side dish of Ahi along
with his order. Ahi, I was laughingly informed, was finely
chopped red and green *hot* peppers. That information truthed out
totally incorrect. Hot it plain wasn't—molten lava it surely was!

¡MI CASA ES SU CASA!

How come I tried it? Blame the waiter. Most politely he informed me the dish was the special of the day and not to be spurned. He said, "Señor, joo pleez 'scuse for talkin' een front uv joo face. Thees deesh ees bestus een 'hole worl', an' joo gots 'hole een mucho grande cabeza eef dunts try eet." He also said if I'd take a flyer and hated it, a steak would come my way free of charge; no way could thees El Señor lose.

Buddy, that scampi was the absolute best I've ever had the pleasure of eyeing, tasting, chewing and mailing to my stomach; that includes all the years in between. Enjoying that gourmet delight flew me off to Heaven. Converted, I decided to go for it and I lathered Ahi on the next morsel. Halfway down my gullet it kicked in and damn near killed me! There were four glasses of water on the table—I drank 'em all. The flames continued to climb, curling and coiling me through an attack of the bends. Now, I like salsa and always reach for the container that reads *hot*, but that Ahi would've brought tears to the eyes of a mummy! One more gallon of water dampened the inner fire into smoldering ashes. I slid my dish of flammables over to rotten Dave and dove happily back into the balance of my scampi. Ready for this? He ate Ahi by the *flaming* spoonful and never even broke into a sweat!

Toodles

Returning to my hotel one night, a few days prior to departing for the States, I made a terrific buy; matter of fact, I stole it. A sad-faced but pleasant fellow accosted me, offering to sell—at great personal sacrifice—a rare, gold ring. The design depicted that revered Inca god Konga-Tiki. Dressed decoratively in a gold cloak of Macaw feathers, the image was eating a banana. It was positively rare, and definitely a beauty.

The gloomy fellow, a tear trickling down his nose, stated he was handicapped and unemployed. He swore he could handle it, but pleaded his wife and ten children were suffering undue hardships forcing him to sell the family heirloom. What the hell, he had a nice honest face and considering the figure quoted was almost reasonable, I bought it. It's a dandy gold ring and a great memento. On special occasions, I wear it still. Strangely, though, it always turns my finger *green*. Guess I've got a lot of acid in my system.

Time for me to head for home. Dave was to continue shipping the few animals he would still be able to garner from the Pucallpa area on to Paco in Lima. Paco would house, acquire licenses, pay fees and then send them on via commercial carrier to Los Angeles. Clint would stay a few more weeks to smooth out any sudden wrinkles in exporting, and to also look for some Peruvian gift items which we'd import and then sell. By tracking the exotics progress, I could then accept and clear the shipments through customs in L.A. and transport them to El Monte.

After a quick trip home to Guayaquil to cuddle his "cute and clingy," George planned to venture back into the jungle for another load of orchids.

Bidding a fond farewell to Dave and Clint (and an *oh-no* to Ahi), I boarded a four-engine Pan Am job heading for Brownsville, Texas. I'd left my .38 S and W with Señor's of thees Cleent so I anticipated no problems reentering the Estados Unidos.

Brownsville burned hot and humid as the hinges of Blisterville. Thankfully, customs was a breeze, then it was onward to the drier heat of Yucaipa. Seemed like a long time had passed; in reality I'd been away but two months. Did it feel good to be surrounded by caged birds once again? Bet a ham and cheese on rye, it did! Why, I was even looking forward to cleaning out the pens, maybe even building something.

• • •

You've got your questioning face on again and I'll bet I know what you're just dying to ask. WHAT HAPPENED TO THE ANACONDA?

Tell you what, I'll just brace the pole against the current and slip us into idle for a brief spell. Allow me time to catch my breath and then I'll explain what happened to the big fellow.

You'll remember, that the twenty-four foot squeezer had been tied to a telephone pole in the Amazon Jungle while Clint, in Lima, and Elva, in L.A., made inquiries of various zoos around the country for their interest in purchasing him. Lobonda represented big bucks for us and we purely hoped for a salivating buyer. Snakes, especially large ones, have to be handled carefully as they can sicken quite easily. Before you know it, a coiling investment can become a stretched out cadaver. Zoos are wise enough to take out insurance against such happenings and we would have to do the same until his safe arrival and buyer acceptance. That meant further digging into the rapidly shrinking exchequer.

Regrettably, with no purchase offer forthcoming, we had to release the giant. The truth is, George, Dave and I picked straws for the honor. They don't call me Shorty for nothing! Not to worry, given my superb physical condition, it wasn't truly dangerous. Edging slowly up to his involuntarily restrained snakish length, I patted him on the head then gingerly cut the ropes. The 'conda had been tied up for some time and now free of that cussed pole, he moved a tad bit sluggishly. It took him about five seconds to react, and by then I was half a football field away shifting into afterburner. He missed his first snap! Today, I can verify, he also missed his second!

I was truly disappointed that the Big Squeeze hadn't sold. Unless we had a deep desire to give him away, he didn't even garner enough interest from European zoos. We all indulge in fantasy and I could see Lobonda happily slithering from pond to bank to tree and back again in the San Diego Zoo. I would convince all the guys at Lange and Runkel to pay him a weekend visit. Just like a proud papa I'd holler, "That's my boy!" Naturally all my friends, not to mention tourists, would be awed. Sure as shootin' though, when that fool 'conda saw me again, he'd probably turn all affectionate and wrap himself around everyone in sight. I guess things really do work out for the best.

• • •

After the relative quiet of jungle sounds, the clang and clatter of busy Southern California commerce rang loudly in my ears, though not too unpleasantly. And soon, back to normal, I took no notice. Tack on forty plus years and I now find myself fighting to ignore the roar and clamor of the nineties. I lose!

What sound—other than verbal usage of four letter words—is heard most often today? SWISH-SWISH-SWISH, the rude, constant and lingering message of passing automobile and truck traffic. Springing full blown to my mind comes a picture of calmer days of yore.

Behold the *Mountain Man*: What racket did he have to contend with? The roar of a bear! The squall of a mountain lion! The drumming of rain on his head! The stampede of buffalo *coming in his direction!* The screech of attacking Indians! The zip, zap and his *ouch*, from pesky mosquitoes! Come to think of it, maybe we don't have it too noisy after all.

• • •

During my absence, our parakeets had been multiplying like tax increases and a great deal of the Whispering Winds workers' (Mom and me) time had to be devoted to their care. I purely wish I had a nickel for all the time I've spent cleaning bird cages! Up to then I'd not had the pleasure of handling monkey pens, was I ever in for a treat!

While waiting for our exotics to arrive we were also preparing for the arrival of some new feathered friends. Right on! Before I'd had a chance to fall off the aircraft, Mom had sprung her latest idea on the one who never seemed to learn. And yet, I gotta admit it had possibilities!

Happy as a clam spitting on those who dared disturb mollusk slumber, I was feeding our most recent arrivals, the Pekin Robins (Chinese nightingales), a mess of meal worms. I'd just raided the worm manufacturing bucket for a quick fifty. You can buy the worms in a pet store, but it's much cheaper and easier to raise your own. How does one go about doing that? Drop a half a dozen from your original purchase into a jar or plastic container filled with dry oatmeal. Punch holes in the lids for air and let nature take its course. If you are feeding large numbers of birds, work several batches at a time and keep the surplus in the refrigerator—not freezer—until needed. As you can see, it's quite easy. Besides, free is cheap!

We imported from Belgium and also Holland (Netherlands). Our latest shipment included: Shama thrushes, Orange Weavers, Whydahs (related to weavers but with long tail feathers), Cordon Bleu and Strawberry finches, Java Rice birds, Rainbow Buntings and—the Pekin robins.

Bird importing is quite similar to that for animals. Health certificates are issued at point of departure and live arrival is guaranteed. The shipment, after Custom's inspection, is then immediately available for the receiver to claim, and quarantine isn't necessary, but the sooner the buyer claims and releases his stock from cramped quarters the better for both. Filing reams of paper, claiming and receiving for loss, takes forever. It is strictly not for the birds!

The little feathered guys are always shipped in containers equipped with ample food and water. However, after truly close encounters with your own kind over a lengthy period of hours, a bath and a chance to stretch the wings sure feels good, not to mention improvement in social hygiene. Those countries of origin deserve high praise for excellence in shipping. Now housed in totally foreign quarters the mortality rate, several weeks after the birds arrival, was still less than two percent. Would that our animal shipments fare as well.

Feeding for the day complete and pens freshened, myself now cleaned and presentable, I'd just settled comfortably on the garden couch with a libation, when our shrilling phone rang loud enough to energize cadavers. According to the airport wallah, our first animal shipment from Lima had just arrived.

The airport, quite close to the Hollywood Park Race Track, lay some eighty-five miles distant and those Whispering Winds folks needed to flit and git! Mom called the El Monte bird farm advising 'em to prepare quarters and food. Then management gassed up at the local Pour and Ignore and headed for old Highway 99. (Seems to me, 1955 was the last time I received *any* service at a gas station, other than the terribly taxing effort required of the over-worked attendant to insert the gas nozzle into the tank's neck, while holding out his other grimy paw for the money. Call me cruel, but how soon, Lord, before long range electric cars, cruising by, stir dust over deserted stations?) Thankfully balmy the weather boded well for our newest residents. Airport officials helpful and considerate, U.S. Customs obliging, we completed the paperwork as quick as your new car depreciates upon leaving the lot. Boxes and cages were loaded in the truck even quicker; then, as ducking engine pistons tried to escape exploding gas, we rolled the roads to El Monte. Uppermost in our minds: Free these animals from confinement—pronto!

Uncrated, our first shipment consisted of all monkeys: Woollys, Spiders, Squirrels (alias the Green Monkey), Pygmy and Lioncito Marmosets and one White Saki. I had just, momentously, met Toodles!

Thank you for asking. Forthwith a description of the White Saki: He presented the living picture of a wizened, highly learned, white-bearded old man. His thick body fur, black and gray, including his head and tail, suggested he was larger and weighed much more than he did. The owner of a non-prehensile tail he made up for it by possessing human hands and feet; that is, five fingers and five toes each on both hands and feet. His face was completely furred in white. His unclipped canines, like most monkeys, were long and pointed. In an attack mode he'd fake a rush, scream and, baring his fangs threateningly, appear ready to bite. With humans, if the threatened didn't buy his bluff, he'd grip the hand, lay his cheek on it and chirp in friendly fashion. He was a total passivist! When first we became acquainted he didn't chirp for, even though he was a monkey, Toodles was sick as a dog.

It figured out later that the poor little travelin' guy had picked up the mother of all colds which now bordered dangerously close to pneumonia. He was so weak he could barely lift his head and ate and drank nothing. With the majority of the shipment fed, safe, and bedded down in clean quarters in El Monte, I dared not leave him. I wrapped him snug in a blanket and along with several of his Woolly and Spider cousins we headed for home.

Don't ask me where the idea came from (probably Mom!), I haven't the foggiest. Just know, for the next week where I went Toodles went. Using an eyedropper at regular intervals I also trickled honey down his throat. A trip to the vet, the first of many while we handled exotics, resulted in a penicillin shot for the wee mono with me learning how to give them; I wish I'd had a big kiss for every one I've flaming well popped into unsuspecting animals since; my lips would be permanently Ubangi puckered!

Carry me to the Bullfrog Ball and teach me to dance the Calaveras Hop if that sick little monk didn't come around. Count another few days and he was eating and chirping like a momma canary feeding five nestlings. By that most happy time we had become lifelong buddies. Toodles was—without question—the sweetest, gentlest, most loving monkey I ever handled. A touch later I'll relate more about him and also that which shames me forever.

So far so good. I had built strongly wired pens for the monkeys, and they were acclimating nicely. Toodles had turned the bend and was now bunking in with me. The main house was really quite small and had necessitated the building of a bunkhouse a short distance away. I wired it with lights (no heat) and my pal and I were quite comfortable unless it snowed which as I've already stated it only did once, on *Easter Sunday!* At night, when I retired him, he'd crawl under the bedspread and sleep sitting up. When I entered he would pop the spread up off his head to see who it was, chirp, and drop it back down again. He was a clean little animal. His droppings resembled those of sheep only on a much smaller scale; this was surprising as he, too, ate fruit. Although not potty trained, neat he was and would never foul our quarters. When I fed the big battery of parakeets he climbed upon my shoulder, clung to my neck and chirped to the birds as we entered each pen. They soon learned to ignore him and, temporarily, contentment reigned over the "boidy" farm. "Hey Ma, what wonderful and thrilling new venture will we be delving into next?"

"Dear, as we've decided to inquire of pet stores their interest in purchasing our monkeys, don't you think we should dress them in doll's clothes so as to stimulate interest? The babies are so sweet and cuddly, I'm sure they'd look darling all dressed up," suggested "She" of the ideas.

By George, there was a *good* idea! Away to the five and dime. Load up on dresses, bonnets and diapers! If I do say so myself, dressed monkeys are that cute. Ready? Grab a handful of those Dior-garbed cuddlers, crank up the Whispering Winds chariot, and off we go on the pet shop circuit.

No matter how I try to ease the shock, the following is bound to surprise you! The pet-selling populace as well as the pet-minded populace do not line up to buy exotic birds or animals. In fact, I can attest it gets downright lonesome all by yourself up there at the head of the line. Wonder why, matey?

Tell you what, I'll pose your question in the form of a multiple choice, the kind you'd find on professor Bomb's test, like the one he hadn't warned was coming and so who'd bothered to study; you only get to check one.

QUESTION # 13:

Why is it that the public will seldom choose to purchase exotic animals such as monkeys, parrots, or snakes—for their pets?

__ A. Dumb salesman.

__ B. Public does not know how to care for them.

__ C. Too expensive to buy.

__ D. Remind you of many members of Congress.

__ E. All of the above.

I see you picked "E" then erased and chose "A." Thank you very much!

If I have to get serious, "B" and "C" come closest to the reason. People tend to shy away from that of which they know very little. You ever hear a school administrator discussing—at length—the fine points of an instructor's life in the classroom? Come to think of it, you ever hear one discuss classroom life at all?

By the time we pulled up in front of our third pet store I was beginning to question the wisdom of dealing in exotics. It wasn't that the owners didn't like our tiny critters. No, they were simply plain afraid to invest. To be fair, which at that time I had no flaming desire to be, pet shops operate on close margins. Take away dog and cat foods, bird seed, aquarium fish, puppies, kittens, the odd canary or parakeet and your average pet store would dry up and blow away. Not their fault, it's just the way of that kind of business—feast or famine; usually more fam than fea with a couple of fie, fo, fums thrown in—gratis. They won't take a chance on unknowns and, while that didn't help us, I'm not sure they are to be blamed.

Anyway, reception was the same in the third shop until...a lady entered through a side door. She walked right over to me, oohed and aahed over the doll-dressed baby Woolly monkey nestling in my arms, reached out for him and walked (I followed) back through the same door to the outside where her husband (smart fellow) sat in his car out of harm's way—he thought!

"Ooh Honey," she cooed. "Look what I want you to buy me for a pet!"

Hubby grinned feebly and tried to slide down the front seat out of sight. After a few more, "He's just adorable, I truly love hims," we re-entered the shop where the unconvinced owner still shook his head, "No."

I left our card, gathered up the baby monks, and Mom and I split. Heading home in the truck, I groused, "That lady really wanted the Woolly. If she'd spent a few more minutes working on her old man we'd have had a sale. Wanna bet the pet shop owner won't call us?"

Half an hour after putting the truck to bed, stock watered and fed and my feet up relaxing a tired bod, I harkened to the squall of the telephone. Yep, it was the store's head shaker. He wanted the monkey. We'd offered the monk to him wholesale and, while I might have talked the lady into buying, it was his business establishment she'd entered. For us to be honorable it would have to be his monkey to sell. Cost to him eighty clams. Cost to the guy who couldn't disappear fast enough, one hundred and thirty clams. The pet shop owner had, because I'd really sold the monk, made fifty clams profit without so much as feeding the mono a flaming banana! And, afraid to take a further chance, he didn't buy another.

If I were quite willing to spend my days sitting and selling monkeys to customers entering his store, then, and only then, would he buy them. At the same time he'd flat take for granted his non-involvement and—with nary a qualm—count his profits. Sheesh! *We sold very few exotics to pet stores.*

• • •

Delivering a shipment of 'keets to El Monte we picked up a fresh supply of animal arrivals. This time we became acquainted with Chico (saddled fits better) a gray spider monk, some owl monkeys, and a Kinkajou (honey bear).

Ever notice how some incidents stick in your mind regardless of the passage of years? That day had been long, we were both tired, peevish and peckish. In the truck headlights I spotted a lit neon sign on Foothill Boulevard, "Affie's Neapolitan." Sawdust on the floor and heavenly aromas, it was a place for human homing pigeons to coo, then land in a plateful of pizza!

Dining at Affie's, besieged on all sides by exciting, enticing, beckoning odors, the kind which sway and say, "See, dying for a bite of our pizza really ain't bad, ready for seconds?" The taste buds celebrated sensual freedom.

That pasta at Affie's had to rate the best I've ever delivered to my eager tongue and happy stomach. If he's still in business, try him. If you find I've not lied, how about airmailing one of his Supremes to Oregon? I'll pay!

Foothill Boulevard wasn't overloaded with street lighting in those days and it hadn't been built wall to wall from L.A. to San Berdoo either. Mom and I, replete, and in complete darkness, each opened one of the panel truck's doors prepared to continue on our way. Within, *A wildcat, in a killing rage, screamed!* Completely undone, I landed flat on my butt in the middle of the Boulevard! Mom, back up on Affie's front porch, ended up hugging a pillar! What the hell was that? *That*—was the kinkajou. Absolutely the most docile of creatures, its defense—hoping to scare away intruders—is to scream like an attacking jaguar. His message damn sure convinced us to hit the bricks!

By the time we cautiously opened doors again and he let loose with another of his deadly squalls, we'd figured it out and retained door handle holds. All the same, nobody was in a hurry to jump into the flaming truck! The honey bear, a meat eating mammal somewhat like a raccoon, has soft yellowish-brown fur, large eyes and a long prehensile tail. Gentle and easy to tame, once you get by that frightening screech, they make fine pets; including tail an adult grows to about three feet and weighs not much more than your lap-warming tabby cat. One barely noticeable problem, they're *nocturnal*.

Would you like to meet Chico?

The little S.O.B. was something else! As tame as he was he had to have already been someone's pet in South America. Upon reaching home still savoring the taste of Affie's Supreme, we caged kinkajou and owl monkeys together but took Chico into the house. Holding his head, the poor little guy scampered right over to the fireplace hearth, then crying, "oooh-oooh-oooh," he rolled over and over on the flagstone. Turned out he was car sick and just like your kids, his stomach said, "throw-up!" Chico—if you haven't already guessed—was more human than monkey.

If you believe comedians who say, "The devil made me do it." Or, "No my fault." You're well on the way to understanding

CHICO

that imp of a spider monkey. Mean he wasn't, mischievous he surely was and—smart.

Example: The screen door to the house closed via a loaded spring. If you remember, the patio had been formed of burnt out fluorescent tubes. The rafters had been nailed to the studs by using 45-degree-angle-cut two by four brackets. Employing his prehensile tail, if outside and wanting in, Chico'd wrap that long appendage over a bracket, reach out, open the door with his hand, and drop down inside onto the kitchen's tile floor. The first time he tried it the screen door snapped closed on his tail before he made it all the way in. His screech was heard in Redlands—ten miles away! Worry not, that brilliant little sucker studied the way the door

opened, figured out he'd have to open it wider and, during the next
hundred times he entered the house on his own, the quick-zapping,
tail-crunching door never caught him again.

Example #2: Chico excelled at climbing trees. Beg pardon,
being a learned person, you already know monkeys are good at that.
Jet liked to stroll carelessly under trees (unless, of course, she happened to spy a cat lazing on a sunlit branch). Jet had a nice long
bushy tail. Dropping out of an Elm tree being quietly passed by the
canine, the pest would grab and bite that lazily waving tail, then
scamper back up into the safety of sheltering foliage. Howling, the
startled dog would spin and snap viciously at a totally innocent
bumblebee! Ho-hey, the bee was willing to play that game and
promptly stung her on the nose. Clearly not one of Jet's better days.
That bloody Satan of a monkey would scratch his bum, thumb his
nose at the dog, and—laugh.

Example #3: Toodles was a dedicated non-scrapper. He faked
attacks well but there really was no fight in him. Afraid he might
wander onto the road when not with me, I tethered him to the umbrella tree, placing his food and water within easy reach. Many a time,
alerted by his angry squall, I'd run and find Chico had rendered
Toodles immobile with his prehensile tail wrapped around him.
Totally impervious to the pathetic cries, he'd be calmly laying on his
stomach in front of the little guy's food bowl, busy pigging out!

Came the day he tried it with a new resident, a young female
Brown Saki. Chico put his move on her and she came unglued.
Ever see a spider monkey in a definite hurry to reach the top of a
tree—alive? The Whispering Winds mono pest never messed with
that sweet little lady again.

Example #4: Using the electrical line, furnishing light from
bunkhouse to pens, as a swing-over pathway, he, safe atop aviary
roof, would hurl insults at Sachem, 'Reina, Jet and any other
passersby. End result, his swinging weight eventually shorted the
wires and set fire to the pens which—when first viewed through the
kitchen window—we thought was the rising moon! Fortunately, a
handy hose and quick feet doused the fire with no loss of bird or
animal life and but minor damage to the pens. Mr. Innocent crawled
into the security of Mom's arms, his big brown eyes eloquently say-

ing, "Don't look at me guys, I ain't guilty of doin' nuttin!"

Actually, it was mostly my fault. I had fused the line into too high an amperage and, once the wire shorted, the fuse failed to blow. Still, it felt altogether righteous to blame that rotten monkey.

So you see, he wasn't bad even though he truly did try our patience. In truth, while his antics drove us all up the wall, he also furnished us with many a hearty laugh. Why do you suppose I yearned to bust him one in the nose?

Is it possible a parrot could sing opera? Whispering Winds boarded a female Panama: yellow head, green body, red on tips of wings—larger than an African Gray, smaller than a macaw—who sang up a Wagnerian storm. That bird would have given Beverly Sills competition. She could also *bite!* I have no idea where Clint ran across her. Perhaps she was born and raised here in the States. I would opt for Mexico or South America. Certainly she had been a revered pet. The human, or bird, coloratura doesn't master opera overnight.

I absolutely believe birds *do sense* when they are being teased faster than any other creature. Our parrot had to have been bugged by human males; any female that cruised by she'd cozy up to, males were anathema. I would often watch my Pop trying to coax her into becoming his buddy. He planned carefully: Selecting a choice morsel, one of her favorites, and crooning—oh, ever so sweetly—an Irish lullaby, he'd kindly offer it to our feathered soprano. She, perched upon her stand, eyes half-closed pretending sleep, waited until the proffered morsel was a tad past safety range and then—like a striking cobra—she'd bypass it and grab the closest—his vulnerable finger—every time! The air around immediately turned blue as Pop praised, at long length and in depth, the parrot's pedigree. You don't suppose Mom and I cracked up? Did I ever attempt to crumble her walls with choice tidbits? Butter up the wee, feathered creature? Let me say this about that: That mean-beaked, song-belting, close relative to an ugly faced buzzard, could go feed off the dole for all I cared! Do parrots fly? Perhaps lumbering like B-29's carrying full loads and needing long runways? Yes, they certainly do fly; some imitate jets.

One hot, bug infested day, too warm to eat inside, we were lunching under the umbrella tree. Pest attacked on all sides—

frustrated—I slammed my hand on the table and bellowed, "ROTTEN, SODDING, BLOODY BUGS!" Somnolent on her perch from summer heat then rudely startled, her wings flapping madly, our loud-mouthed parrot vacated her stand and took off for the oak trees at the end of our property. It gets better. Rewarded for being soft-voiced I had the pleasure of hiking, in the blazing sun, to that grove, climbing her chosen tree, prying her feet loose from a branch and then, bark gashed, sliding to the ground. Pouring sweat I placed Panama Hati in Mom's arms and limped to the house. Might have been worse—she only bit me four times!

Sailor, I salute you sitting so long without complaint. I'll bet a whoopy cushion wouldn't have gone amiss though. Hang in there, I see some familiar landmarks, just a few more twisty turns, and we'll have come full circle.

Mollie-O

Toodles

Monkey Business at the Fair

20

L ooking forward to crashing after another long day in the Yucaipa zoo, I opened the bunkhouse door and entered. Toodles, as was his wont, popped the bedspread up, chirped hello and ducked under again. In that brief span I detected a slight odor. "What ho, Toods my man, got a wee touch of gas have we?" If you recollect, I've stated he was a clean little animal and never fouled his own nest. Thinking no more about it, dead tired, trying to ignore pesky kinkajou and owl monkey antics outside, I hit the sack. Fortunately, I am not a thrasher in sleep. The bunkhouse, narrow in width, allowed but little room. If I'd been a kicker, Toodles would have become part of the wall!

Next morning, carrying him out to his tethering tree, I caught another whiff. I recognize Chanel # 5, that wasn't it. Making a mental note to dunk and rinse him that evening, I tied him up, left his food and water and took off to tackle the problem of Kinkajou and Owl monkeys. Both are nocturnal. No problem unless one desires sleep. *They* slept all day and raised

a holy ruckus all night. Six monos and a kink' bouncing and rattling off their wire-sided pen hour after hour discouraged rest
for the weary. After a second cup of tea, an idea from my head's
hard drive screened to the surface. Eager to try it out I entered
the monks' pen and, collaring all seven of those now daylight
sluggards, I put them in with the squirrel monkeys. Squirrel
monkeys are not nocturnal. Sensible animals, they sleep at
night and raise hell all day. It was a rare old treat to watch what
happened. THUMP! A squirrel monkey landed smack in the
snoozing kinkajou's middle. BOINK! Two more bounced off
the comatose owls. RATTLE-RATTLE-BOING resonated from
vibrating hardware cloth. Nobody, but nobody, slept through
the commotion. Consider this: If you were a kinkajou, and a
jumping up and down banana scoffing squirrel monkey repeatedly landed on your belly, would you be able to zonk? I'd
doubts about zees for him. As for me, I bet I'd sleep that night!

In the evening, satisfied with the accomplishments of the
day, I headed over to free and then tuck into bed, my pal,
Toodles. When I picked him up, he stunk so bad my eyes
watered. "Hey, Toods, what have you been rolling in? You
smell like a GI barracks full of dirty socks! You suppose a double dose of ipecac is called for?"

That stink had to be telling me something. Accordingly,
away from the tree and out in the light, I gave him a thorough
examination. Damn and flaming blast! His stomach was literally rubbed raw, and *it had turned septic!*

While stepping about in Iquitos and Pucallpa, I'd observed
the way the local people restrained their pets. Most, with monkeys, had tied a soft cloth around the middle which then fastened to a tether line. I'd asked why and the answer seemed logical. A monkey, frightened or just plain energetic, running to
the end of its line could—at the abrupt cessation of movement—snap its neck. Behold, a dead pet! Better, they said, to
restrain him around the middle. Stopped suddenly, the mono
might then suffer a shortness of breath but that, provided the
cloth had been tied properly, should be of short duration and
monkey, retaining health and head, would survive. *Comprendé?*

Put that way, the system seemed sensible and foolproof. Nobody mentioned that the cloth, tugging on a tender stomach, might chafe and irritate the skin, resulting in infection and septicemia! I bathed and then sulfa powdered the little guy's belly and then, because he had been so good during the patching, rewarded him with a shot of penicillin. A visit to the local pet store and a cat harness, just his size, took the place of that lousy cloth. Luck, plus my terrific skill with adhesive tape and needle pulled him through. In a few days a healthy Toods was once again suffering indignities from Chico!

That night, we both enjoyed undisturbed slumber. The kink' and the owls were too traumatized to cavort about their pen. In fact, both night and day gangs, totally tuckered from the squirrel monkey daylight prankishness, completely zonked during our blessed period of darkness. How sweet it was!

· · ·

New arrivals from tropical America: White-faced Capuchin monkeys, so young we had to feed them from a dolls' bottle. Prehensile tailed, the cute, smart, little tykes, when not clinging to one another, liked to dangle from a human finger. They were fun to have around. We sold one or two of those. Toodles thought they were kissing cousins until one of them wrapped his tail around my little buddy's head and tried to crack it like a nut!

Thus, our menagerie had grown: birds, varied in kind and large in quantity. Animals: Whispering Winds handled puppies, cats (temporarily!), monkeys, kinkajous, ocelots and—more human than not—Toodles and Chico; we never handled reptiles, Mom couldn't cut them. In fact, more than once I heard her hollering for help while batting hell out of a tiny mouse with her broom!

Add the greenhouse full of potted plants and everything on the joint, but for the human inhabitants, was for sale. Most of the time, the exotic birds, animals and special plants were for sale over a lengthy period of time.

"Have you been to visit the Yucaipa Zoo?" the locals asked

of kith and kin. "They've got quite a variety, you really owe it to yourselves to go."

Strategically placed on Yucaipa Boulevard, we had recently erected a large sign which advertised our live offerings.

That sign along with word of mouth garnered us beaucoup lookers. I spent oodles of time holding Toodles and showing folks around. *Seldom did they buy.* We even had school teachers request to bring their classes to the farm for a field trip. *Whispering Winds never charged admission!* To this flaming day I don't know why. It flat out would have helped with that trunk full of bills.

• • •

Clint came up with the next hilarious idea. It was another doozy!

"We need to become better known. How about you two manning a booth at the Pomona Fair? We'll stock with parrots, 'keets, cockatiels, monkeys and South American souvenirs; we can hand out cards and maybe...convince the public they really need to take home one of our special exotics."

The Pomona Fair was the largest and best attended fair in Southern California, comparable in importance and prestige to our own State Fair held here in Salem, Oregon. And there was an idea presenting just bunches of possibilities. How could we lose? What could possibly go wrong?

Showtime at the Big One: Whispering Winds was assigned a booth in the favored garden center. This, a huge, enclosed, atrium-like structure contained concrete paths weaving in and out of sections devoted to artistically arranged plantings advertising the best wares of local nurseries. That building also furnished a series of booths on the east end. The overall aesthetic effect always pleased and it drew big crowds. Could the location be a good omen?

Egress to booths was via individual doors opening into the back of each stall from an enclosed hallway running the length of the building. The doors all padlocked, the key to be retained by the renter of cubicle. In addition, security patrolled the center and hallway daily and also at night. Behind the door to your booth, another provided entrance and exit to the outside so as to allow seller to bring in or remove his stock without having to run the gamut of crowds; that door was locked by officials upon daily closure of the festivities.

Our initial stock consisted of two tame macaws on stands— a scarlet and a blue and gold—a large cage of parakeets including rares and another one of cockatiels; add Amazon, Panama, and Double Yellow head parrots. Include native crafts from Peru: dolls, stuffed animals and carvings. Finally, add a large carrying box full of squirrel monkeys. We also brought cages and travel boxes for the birds and monkeys we were bound to sell! Packaged seed was on display as well. Hey, a buck is a buck whichever way she comes floating over your counter.

Opening day we planned issuing raffle tickets with each purchase. Winner *had* to be present to collect his/her prize on closing day; a genuine—bound to liven your days—Amazon parrot. We're talking an eighty-five dollar value here! Of course there wasn't much chance of the lucky holder of ticket, out of the hundreds sold, being there at gate closing time on *drawing day*—right?

Before the fair opens and after they've set up their displays, sellers usually cruised around other booths to check out the competition and to also see what was new and selling on the market.

Except for un-boxing the squirrel monkeys and installing our come hither sign, we were pretty well set up for action when a tall skinny guy, with a twitch, an overbite, and a wart on his nose, stopped in front of our stall.

"Those are beautiful birds you have there," he said, indicating the macaws.

"We think so," replied Mom.

"Are they tame? I mean, do they bite?"

"Naw, these old loves are quite gentle and friendly," said Mom.

"Look here, my name is Shelwood Borkid. I own and operate Borkid's Orchids. I also have a garden arrangement of potted plants, ferns and orchids here in the atrium. Would you be willing to place some parrots in cages and then hang the cages from light poles in the fresh flower section? Then, to add extra live color to my orchids, would you also be willing to allow your macaws to wander freely throughout my display? They'd be ever so lovely."

"Shel, me old son, I'm agreeable to hanging caged birds for you, but I don't think turning the macaws loose is the hot thought for the day," I burbled.

"Oh goodness, gracious, yes," gushed Shelwood. "They'll look ever so charming, I'll definitely take and share with you some of the lovely pictures I'm bound to get. Surely nothing unwarranted can happen. They're seed eaters aren't they? Oh please, do grant permission. I'd be eternally grateful."

Now, the darlin' Blue and Gold had a wee bit of a bad character trait. He possessed what you might call real determination, a severe case to boot!

Parrot stands look like flattened out satellite dishes sitting up on metal poles. The pole inserts through the dish's center to a length of about eighteen inches. Bolted upon the top of the pole is a thick, round, wooden perch. Molded metal cups, with permanently fastened protruding bolts, drop through holes drilled at each end of the perch and are then tightly secured with wing nuts. The cups hold sunflower seed and water respectively. The wing nuts are used so as to allow removal of cups for cleaning and replenishing.

That takes care of the description, now for the action. I've stated Goldy had a tiny bit of a flaw; here 'tis. He'd wait until his filthy stand had been scrubbed clean, he'd also wait until seed and water cups had been emptied, freshened and refilled; *then*, using his bill, the sod would undo the wing nuts, grip each cup in turn, pull them free with his beak, and dump 'em all over the tray!

"Naughty, naughty, Goldy, you wrench-billed clown, I've more important matters to attend to besides cleaning your flaming tray, ad nauseam!"

Everything serene once more—wing nuts *well* tightened—knowing I could trust him, it was away to tackle some other delightful state fair task.

Clink, thump, splash. Damned if he hasn't taken the cups off again!

"Goldy, dear. If you do that once more I'm going to yank one of your tail feathers and stuff it up your nose!"

Perch recleaned, cups reinstalled, and the wing nuts now very definitely secured because I'd used my never-fail tool—pliers—I started laying out packets of seed and arranging the Peruvian souvenirs on the counter.

CLINK, CLINK, THUMP, SPLASH! Aw, the hell with it!

Knowing the above you can understand my reluctance to turn Goldy, and dear Will Scarlet, loose in a fresh, carefully arranged prize garden. Borrowing a ladder, I hung four cages, each containing a colorful parrot, from lamp poles in the flowered area. I must say they surely dressed it up nicely. Then I left Will and Goldy up to their knees in happiness among Borkid's Orchids.

A short twenty minutes later, Mom and I had just finished hanging our sign, when up raced Shelwood holding his head and hollering like somebody'd put a hot rock in his helmet! *"Come and get your macaws! Come and get your macaws,"* he screeched. "Oh, oh,

MACAW
Mollie-O   ORCHID SNACKS

oh, *they're eating all my orchids!* Oh, run quickly, oh, dear me, chase them away, oh, get them OUT of my garden!"

Will and Goldy—now mostly stuffed—were ready to come home. I don't know why Shel was so upset; how'd I know those birds, devotees of Julia Child, were into the gourmet dining circuit? And besides, they really only polished off maybe a dozen of his rares—*apiece!*

There remained but one more task ere the grand opening. Remove monkeys from travel box and place them in a much more spacious cage. I knew they'd be happy to get out. Yep, in the process of moving box to cage, it slipped from my hands onto the floor, the lid popped open and I had loose squirrel monkeys from Pomona all the way to Zanzibar. The joint went nuts!

Fortunately, most of them escaped into the walkway behind

the booth and, after two missed tackles and an interception, I finally rounded them all up...except for one. He climbed one of the light poles situated inside the building and opposite our booth, sat down and proceeded to swear at me. I tried bribery: peanuts, banana, popcorn and gumdrops—he ate the banana and then threw the peel at me. I hollered dire threats; all were disdainfully ignored.

"Listen guy," sez I. "You're forcing me to bring out the heavy artillery. I'll count to ten just once then...!" The bloody monkey promptly defecated on an elegant stetson worn by Marshal Dillon of the "Western Finery" booth.

MONKEY BUSINESS

Well, when the fox plays in the chicken coop, arm yourself with a mighty weapon and cold-cock him. I collected a long leash, a net, and a small collar. Carefully placing my deadly surprise upon the counter, I ducked below it and waited. Shazzam! Quicker than the farmer's daughter skinnying out her window and eloping with a crop duster, he was off the pole, waltzing up onto the counter and cozying up to *her*. I netted the little bum like I'd love to latch on to a big Chinook and put them both into their cage. *Ain't love grand!*

The Big Fair opened with the freeing of doves, the loosing of balloons and huzzahs! Why, they've all come to see! Just notice dearly beloved *customers* lining picturesque stalls' fronts; have they brought MONEY?

In a booth to our right a lady—nasal voiced—was hustling sachets. Small packets and pillows containing balsam pine. A revived cadaver, she narrated her spiel with all the fervor of a sphinx reading family epitaphs aloud.

"Balsam pine, it smells so fine."

Nothing as original as:

> *Ladies and gents, now don't you all look just fine,*
> *Can you spare a glimpse at a face such as mine?*
> *Not a wrinkle, not a blemish. And why not a line?*
> *'Cuz I pillows me head on this sweet smellin' pine.*

See what I mean? A spiel's gotta have *life*. It needs to sing, tantalize, mystify, bewitch, cajole, tempt, con, make you— wanna *buy*!

People flocked around our stall admiring the parrots, oohing and aahing at the macaws, chuckling at monkey antics and fingering our souvenirs. Sales? Look at it this way: Never have so few spent so little to support so many!

In the booth next door the old broad—a chanter from the dead—droned on: "Balsam pine, it smells so fine."

She outsold us thirty to one!

Each night at closing Clint took the birds and animals to El Monte, returning them early next morning. Now it chanced that he had two young African Grays at his place, Well's Bird Farm. One was a sweetheart bird, gentle and friendly, the other sat its

perch mean, and eager to bite. Withering on the vine of opportunity and trying to engender sales, Mom asked Clint to send us
the gentle parrot; you probably already know an African Gray
is rated the finest talking parrot in the world. They also don't
come cheap. Still, an avid collector might wander by and break
his arm trying to get his wallet out. Señor Cleent complied and
also sent along half a dozen pieces of pink and white—natural
colored—coral which a fast talker had conned him into buying.

"See and buy the best talking parrot in the world," sang Ma.
"They are quite rare and sell quickly. First come first served,"
she yodeled, holding one hand out of sight behind her back
from which was dripping, *blood!*

"Do those pretty birds bite?" asked a possible buyer.

"Not these little honeys," said Mom. "They are very sweet
and quite gentle. They have the gift of the gab and can out talk
a lawyer." The tab for an African Gray also totaled friendly,
four hundred and fifty Yankee dollars.

Her hidden hand continued to drip blood. Clint's rotten cow
of a manager had sent us the mean S.O.B.! It mattered not. The
customer had never seen four hundred and fifty clams, let alone
possessed them. He split.

Like a cat happily dipping whiskers in cream, we suddenly
began to sell. And what did we sell—exotics? Naw, we were
hustling that bloody coral! Amazingly, we couldn't keep up
with the demand and not only made expenses, we wandered
across the street into the black. If I live to be ninety, I never will
figure out what entices, and convinces, people to buy.

Closing day at the Pomona Fair. We'd sold one monkey, two
parrots, one cockatiel, ten parakeets and it seemed like—two
tons of coral. I wasn't sad to see it end. Selling's hard work.
Dusk having snuffed out the sun, but a single duty remained.
Time for our grand—hasta la vista folks—raffle.

"Hubba-hubba-hidey-ho, gather round folks for the really big
show. Hold out the lucky ticket one of you has surely got and take
home a parrot which you ain't bought. Hubba-hubba-ho-ho-ho!"

So the hustle left something to be desired. It didn't stop a
crowd from gathering. I spun the barrel, reached in and drew

out the winning ticket for our Amazon parrot—lucky winner to be present! Care to figure the odds?

Standing right there smack dab in front of me, have a gander at Mortimer Snerd! "I got that there lucky ticket mister, do he talk?"

"Not yet my man, he's too young. You'll have to teach him. Be careful of your choice of language though. Once a word is learned—polite or not—parrots won't forget it. Heartiest congratulations from Whispering Winds."

"Don't he come with no cage?"

"Son, he wasn't born in no cage and he don't come in no cage! I see two possible solutions. One: carry him home on your wrist, bearing in mind that they can and do fly. If he gets loose, it's by-by. Two: *buy* a cage and be sure he gets home safely. Your parrot is valued at eighty-five bucks. What shall be your ever loving pleasure?"

Groaning like he'd been mortally wounded, Mort hauled out a fat, moth-eaten wallet (I swear it had been pinned to his shorts) and bought one of the cheaper cages. Good sport that I was I hoped the parrot bit the living hell out of him!

Summation of life at the fair: One never, never knows what—other than food—will not only appeal to the public it persuades them to buy; who do you suppose socked away enough for a new Cadillac? Uh-huh, the ebullient Balsam Bertha! I know what you're thinking, how come I was down on the old broad? Although it shames me, it had to be envy. Still, if that lady had been an inventor and an apiarist, disdaining her Cadillac and desiring a Rolls, she'd have crossed a bumblebee with a doorbell and come up with a humdinger! And finally, determination is all, Goldy'd just unwound his 300th damn wing nut!

• • •

Two months later I flicked the bird business in. Because they had always been gracious and welcoming I went back to work for Lange and Runkel. It was November of 1956. In that one month, I returned to my old job, went in hock for a car and met my jewel, a cutie of the female persuasion.

Mollie-O and I met because of my working in the Chevrolet agency. Many public businesses pass slowly dying afternoons until—smack dab at closing—the dead crowd in for, "It's an emergency and I really have to have that part, that license, that leg of lamb, or that whatever."

The cutie was one of the dead. All the salesmen knew I was single, and so kept an eye peeled for likely prospects. I thought it was because they liked me but that wasn't it; the married firmly believe that the unharnessed and running free should also be roped and hogtied. Lest I escape, they kept a weather eye peeled; to be honest, I wasn't above keeping an eye out myself.

Scanning a parts catalog for a phone customer that day, I looked up and caught an eyeful of this cute little trick sporting

BUT IT ONLY NEEDS THE GLASS!

a ponytail. A salesman buddy had intercepted her breezing through the showroom door smack on the stroke of five, and steered her directly to me. The Parts manager was older and...married!

The little doll had side view mirror troubles on her 1956 Chevrolet convertible, the glass portion on the driver's side had fallen out. I walked her outside to view the patient. Dragging the examination out I informed her that mirror parts did not come separately; therefore, the whole shebang would have to be replaced. Deep-six the ailing old, install with healthy new.

"Why isn't it possible to divide a larger piece of glass and simply glue the smaller portion in place of that which has fallen out?" inquires the living doll.

I knew right away she was going to be trouble! By that time I'd already learned she was a native Californian, born in Highland Park, and taught school in Redlands which, of course, explained why she talked funny. No flies on me, slow is for folks in wheelchairs.

I further informed the little lady that General Motors was hip-deep into making money, and they could and would make ever so much more of it selling the whole contraption rather than an itty-bitty piece of glass.

I persuaded her to buy the whole mirror. Then I further persuaded her to date me. After awhile I also persuaded her to marry me. Now wouldn't you know, that flaming piece of mirror glass convinced her to continue to give me trouble. She's been doing it now for forty-four years. Not bad, huh?

While we were dating, I took Mollie-O out to meet the folks and show her Whispering Winds in all its glory. She had seen the sign on the boulevard, had been intrigued but, as she had a Sealpoint Siamese cat, buying a bird wasn't wise and she didn't feel right about just looking. It was a super Southern California fall day. Sitting in the garden, in Toodles vicinity after the tour, we chatted. I excused myself to go fetch us drinks and while I was gone she howdied my little guy. He took a good look, bared his vicious fangs, screeched, and charged her. Figuring it was scarring of body parts time, she still did not flinch but hung in there. An angry Toods bounded up, grabbed her hand and, throwing her his big, brown-eyed look, laid his cheek softly and gently on her wrist, then chirped. She'd been accepted. Tiny Toodles was truly a real love.

Ever notice how life is always yelling at you to make decisions? When you do, if they don't turn out to be a royal pain in the butt, they have a habit of coming back to taunt and haunt you?

Drastic changes were taking place. Mollie-O and I were going to marry. Her students had invited me to participate in a shower they were going to hold for her in their classroom. That unexpected invitation changed my life forever. I became totally enchanted with her wonderful kids—sixth graders. They were caring, mature and challenging. I couldn't get enough of them and used to run out on my lunch breaks to help out in the school cafeteria. I wanted to learn two things: Would a class of my own scare me? Did I have the gift for teaching? I knew years of college—if I qualified—were ahead. My Mollie-O offered encouragement and I decided to give it a try.

I would no longer be living on the farm. I had to work and save for at least another year to earn enough to pay school tuition. I also had to do something about Toodles. He could not be left alone all day in an apartment. Nor was it feasible for him to stay on at the farm. Clint located a young couple in the bird business who would give him a good home, and so I took my little buddy to them. I have agonized deeply over what I felt was truly an inescapable necessity for well over forty years, and no matter how I attempt to rationalize it, I continually come up short. I will always bitterly regret that decision; mea culpa little guy. Toods, I like to think you are up there with our beloved Megan. There just has to be a place for loving animals in Heaven.

• • •

The status of Whispering Winds Aviaries? Going down for the third time. The market for the backbone of our business—parakeets—due to an overabundance of backyard breeders, plus excessive breeding, flooded and then bottomed out. For the large aviarist it tolled the death bell. Exotics, bird and animal, appealed but didn't sell. They did continue to eat. Too much going out, too little coming in, spelled finis. It was time to move on.

Ten years had passed from my entrance into Air Force to my exit from the bird business. What had I accomplished? Damned if I knew. On the positive side I'd been many places and adventured where others hadn't. On the negative I hadn't made a flaming sou. Teetering here in the middle, attempting to make it balance, I've discovered one thing, I'd filled to overflowing a trunk full of laughs. Looking fondly back in retrospect today, that was payment enough.

• • •

I'm not too sure there is a fella named Fate circling about in each of our corrals. Nor, do I believe he can take the bit in his teeth and decide events for us with or without our consent. Still, some happenings are purely hard to explain, so perhaps a qualified "maybe" from me is acceptable.

Not long after Whispering Winds Aviaries had nose-thumped in the dust, Clint, seeking relief from his own dry-packed nasal passages, also called finis to "Fun with Feathers." He next ventured into selling Southern Cal real estate, a boomer at the time. Just shy of two years since enjoying Paco's surprise anniversary cake in Lima, while returning one afternoon from showing an estate, Clint stopped off in a bar for a drink and to watch the running of the Kentucky Derby on TV. I know damn well he'd have already placed a bet! A little tuckered from his sales pitch, he carefully laid his head down on the bar for a short rest before the start of the race. He never raised it again. A tired, worn-out heart had decided at that moment to call it quits. And so, without fuss, our partner had quietly left us. Wouldn't it be nice to know his horse had won.

I often think of Señor Cleent and our South American adventure. He was a man who'd enjoyed many different life styles while overcoming adversity. I'd truly been most fortunate to know him. Goodnight my friend.

• • •

So there I was, never having graduated from high school, at the ripe old age of thirty-one, setting off to take college entrance examinations. Was I nervous? How about scared spitless! The competition, youngsters of seventeen and eighteen, would leave me hunting for the starting line. Regardless, if I wanted to teach, the challenge had to be met. Pens in hand, I slunk through what they laughingly called the "welcome door" prepared to do battle.

Sweat-soaked, confident I'd passed most and done well in English, my best subject, I returned to hearth and home to await the results.

Some few days later, I opened the official letter and scanned the contents. Hot smash! I'd passed all my tests and been accepted.

"Look, Hon," I hollered to Mollie-O, "I passed and what's more got an "A" in English."

My wife, a veteran school teacher, quickly perused my scores, including Language, and promptly sputtered, "Why that means you're going to be in Bonehead English! You won't be starting out in the freshman class."

I had learned one or two things during my thirty plus years and one of them was how to stand up and fight for my rights. Besides, I knew damn well I'd passed that test. I jumped in my old jalopy and burned rubber straight to the registrar's office. Politely, but firmly, I asked them to trot out my test papers and show me the results. After some inner office rustling of papers, a little hemming, coughing, and hawing, a wheel came out to the counter and requested I go to a certain room where the professor was waiting.

Loaded for bear, I marched into his room prepared to go to war. He took one look at my angry face and said,

"It is all right (I argued with him about the spelling of that word later on in the course, hauled out the dictionary, and alright won!) Mr. Judge, a clerical error has inadvertently been made. You are certainly eligible for my class and I'll be happy to welcome you on Monday."

There's not a whole lot more to add. I enjoyed his class and performed rather well. Meeting him on the campus halfway through the semester, he apologized to me for the initial goof and stated he'd been dead wrong. It took a big man to admit to that.

At the end of my first two years, before heading on to San Jose State to complete my degree, I was asked to give the breakfast graduation speech. Sitting in the audience, during my presentation, Mollie-O was informed that I'd been wanted initially for valedictorian but, as most of the graduates were barely shaving or just beginning to use make-up, the powers that be felt it best to choose a younger student. I've never been asked for ID in a flaming bar either!

Not too shabby for a thirty-two year old high school dropout huh? See what reading books can do for you.

By now you've deduced that I passed the *bon vivant's* course, but I'm not really sure I got the "A" because I overwhelmed him with my story, or because I overloaded him with too much of the inner me! I wonder if he said a *novena* for the professor in my senior English class?

• • •

Oregon, summer of '63. Setting: eight acres in the middle of the Van Duzer Corridor bordering on Highway 18. In residence: Pop, Mom, Gran (Mom's mom), Mollie-O and me. Then add: Milly, Tilly and Buttercup (the goats), Mert and Bert (the sheep), Baron (the dog), Cuspid (a beaver busy damming the stream), and royal Katrinka, our cross-eyed, passive, Bluepoint Siamese.

I'd been out with the witcher attempting to identify the location for our desperately needed drilled well. I, too, am a witcher. You may ask which witcher did the witching? In the hands of the pro, the Y-shaped willow wand danced the Canebrake Stomp. In my hands the stick shyly curtsied. Natch, the pro located the drill site, I went indoors for a cup of java. Yo day's error!

"Dear, if you were to dig out your saw and hammer you could build some pens in the utility room for the Pekin Robins and Myna birds. Only take a smidge of time. Then—and you'll like this idea—you can remodel the funky chicken house, it's only twenty feet wide and forty long; that won't take much time or effort. True, it does need a new roof, glass windows, new sides, a proper door, and an oil stove installed for heat. You'll want to plumb it for water too, and build a *few shelves* to display geraniums and show off my African violets. I think it would look nice painted a fire house red. I know Mollie-O would love to paint the sign (she even nailed Molly). How about we name it the LI'L RED GREENHOUSE! Also, once that nice man drills our new well and you build a box to protect the pipes from the weather, we can grade and level the driveway for parking, and then we'll take a run into Portland to the wholesale flower market for some more geraniums, maybe even some mums, cyclamen, gloxinias and for sure, begonias; they're pretty and will sell. Don't forget we have to travel up to the airport in a few days when the birds come in. Oh, and we have to lay in a supply of mealworms for the Pekin Robins and lots of fruit for those Mynas."

"I know we have to install the new drain field for the septic tank and you have to finish the upstairs rooms and also repair the house roof, but those things won't take much time, will they? After all it's daylight saving time, still July, and you do have the rest of the summer before going back to teaching!"

"Oh, it's going to be such fun being in business again and just think, this time we'll really make *big m .... !*"

But that's another story.

• • •

Me old Sea-scout, I have to say it's been pleasant drifting and poling along here through my Bayou of Memory; I've truly enjoyed your company. But old Hooty Owl up there in that aged Cypress, sleepily blinking his eyes in the light of yon waning moon, watched you nearly fall out of the dugout during your last huge yawn! There's the dock, if you'll take the line and tie us up, we can call it a night and hit the sack. How'szat? Hooty can go prang his beak on a stump, you still have one last question for Señor Hootgay!

"Did I ever miss the beauty, excitement and yes—fear—of the jungle?"

Funny thing, at the time I was gearing up to say so long to Peru I asked that very same question of an ex-jungle dweller, then living in Lima. He said: "Oh, si, amigo, mebbe joos wan leedle bits, but joo know man I am theenkin' of thees bugs, muy malo water, thees mas grande esnakes, thees heat—mucho calor—an' mebbe I theenk, Jose, joo wan lucky fellow. Here een thees cool of thees Lima joo gots better of thees livin'. So mebbe I say to hell weeth thees beeg hots of thees jungle, thees mean of thees animales, an' thees rotten of thees bugs. I goin' stay right heres! Vaya con Dios, mi amigo, an' hasta luego, joo have wan muy bueno flights to jour casa."

As for my missing Lobonda's digs? Yes, maybe a tad. Nevertheless, you also have to know I settled down and gave up the dangerous life after Peru's "Green Hell." Excepting, of course, for raising of thees sheep, flying of thees airplanes, getting of thees married—and teaching of thees school!

• • •

Many thanks for joining me. May all *your* future endeavors be comforting, exciting, promising, fulfilling and—tax free.

Bayou of Memory

Another Time,

Another Place

published by
BookPartners, Inc.
Newberg, OR

Ordering information:

$14.95 U.S.
Shipping & Handling: $4.00

Visit our Web site: www.jackjudgeonline.com
FAX: 541-994-2479
Phone: 541-994-3472
E-mail: mojac@harborside.com